REVISE PEARSON EDEXCEL AS/A LEVEL
Economics
REVISION
GUIDE AND WORKBOOK

Series Consultant: Harry Smith

Authors: Keith Hirst, Andrew Redfern

Also available to support your revision:

Revise A Level Revision Planner 9781292191546

The **Revise A Level Revision Planner** helps you to plan and organise your time, step-by-step, throughout your A Level revision. Use this book and wall chart to mastermind your revision.

A small bit of small print
Pearson Edexcel publishes Sample Assessment Material and the Specification on its website. This is the official content and this book should be used in conjunction with it. The questions have been written to help you practise every topic in the book.

> **For the full range of Pearson revision titles across KS2, KS3, GCSE, Functional Skills, AS/A Level and BTEC visit:**
> www.pearsonschools.co.uk/revise

Contents

Published by Pearson Education Limited, 80 Strand, London, WC2R 0RL.

www.pearsonschoolsandfecolleges.co.uk

Copies of official specifications for all Pearson qualifications may be found on the website: qualifications.pearson.com

Text and illustrations © Pearson Education Limited 2019
Typeset and illustrated by PDQ Digital Media Solutions Ltd
Produced by Just Content Ltd
Cover illustration by Eoin Coveney
The rights of Keith Hirst and Andrew Redfern to be identified as authors of this work have been asserted by them in accordance with the Copyright, Designs and Patents Act 1988.

First published 2019

22 21 20 19
10 9 8 7 6 5 4 3 2 1

British Library Cataloguing in Publication Data
A catalogue record for this book is available from the British Library

ISBN 978 1 292 24642 0

Copyright notice
All rights reserved. No part of this publication may be reproduced in any form or by any means (including photocopying or storing it in any medium by electronic means and whether or not transiently or incidentally to some other use of this publication) without the written permission of the copyright owner, except in accordance with the provisions of the Copyright, Designs and Patents Act 1988 or under the terms of a licence issued by the Copyright Licensing Agency, 5th Floor, Shackleton House, Hay's Galleria, 4 Battle Bridge Lane, London, SE1 2HX (www.cla.co.uk). Applications for the copyright owner's written permission should be addressed to the publisher.

Printed in Slovakia by Neografia

Acknowledgements
The authors and publisher would like to thank the following individuals and organisations for permission to reproduce copyright material:

Text Credits:
p22: Toy prices in US, city average, all urban consumers, seasonally adjusted 1995-2018, https://www.bls.gov/regions/new-england/data/consumerpriceindex_us_table.htm [Accessed: 16/08/2018]. © 2019, U.S. Bureau of Labor Statistics; **p49:** Badstuber, Nicole, Detail from Fig 1: Revenue breakdown of congestion charge in London: net income and costs in 'London congestion charge has been a huge success. It's time to change it', Citymetric 12 March 2018 © 2018. Used with Permission; **p49:** Data from Transport for London Annual Report and Statement of Accounts 2017/18, © 2018, Powered by TfL Open Data. © Crown copyright and database rights 2016; **p49:** 'Rail Fares Index (January 2017) Statistical Release, 30 March 2017, http://orr.gov.uk/__data/assets/pdf_file/0020/24518-/rail-fares-index-january-2017.pdf. Accessed: 07/01/2019. Contains public sector information licensed under the Open Government Licence v3.0. © Crown Copyright / Office of Rail and Road; **p52:** Time series: Gross Domestic Product: chained volume measures: Seasonally adjusted £m. https://www.ons.gov.uk/economy/grossdomesticproductgdp/timeseries/abmi/pn2 (c) Crown/Office for National Statistics. 2018/ Contains public sector information licensed under the Open Government Licence v3.0. **p52:** Gross Domestic Product: chained volume measures: Seasonally adjusted £m. https://www.ons.gov.uk/economy/grossdomesticproductgdp/timeseries/abmi/pn2. © Crown/Office for National Statistics. 2018. Contains public sector information licensed under the Open Government Licence v3.0; **p52:** Office for National Statistics. GDP monthly estimate, UK: September 2018, 9 Nov 2018 Figure 1: Quarterly GDP grew at its fastest rate since Quarter 4 2016 UK GDP growth, Quarter 4 (Oct to Dec) 2016 to Quarter 3 (July to Sept) 2018 https://www.ons.gov.uk/economy/grossdomesticproductgdp/bulletins/gdpmonthlyestimateuk/september2018 [Accessed: 15/11/2018]. © Crown/Office for National Statistics. 2018/ Contains public sector information licensed under the Open Government Licence v3.0.; **p53:** Figure: Big Mac exchange rate: USA-China, The Big Mac Index. © 2018, The Economist Newspaper Limited. Used with Permission; www.economist.com/news/2019/01/10/the-big-mac-index Accessed: 24 April 2019. © 2018, The Economist Newspaper Limited. Used with Permission; **p53:** Figure: GDP Growth. World Bank Group. 2017. Global Economic Prospects, June 2017: A Fragile Recovery. Washington, DC: World Bank. Washington, DC: World Bank. doi: 10.1596/978-1-4648-1024-4. License: Creative Commons Attribution CC BY 3.0 IGO; **p55:** ONS, Statistical Bulletin: Consumer Price Indices, October 2012: Figure F RPI and CPI 12-month percentage change (UK). http://www.ons.gov.uk/ons/rel/cpi/consumer-priceindices/ october-2012/stb---consumer-price-indices---october-2012.html. Accessed 24/10/2018. © Crown/Office for National Statistics. 2012. Contains public sector information licensed under the Open Government Licence v3.0.; **p58:** ONS: Statistical Bulletin: UK Labour market: March 2018. Figure 13: UK economic inactivity rates (aged 16 to 64 years), seasonally adjusted January to March 1971 to November to January 2018. https://www.ons.gov.uk/employmentandlabourmarket/peopleinwork/employmentandemployeetypes/bulletins/uklabourmark et/march2018. © Crown/Office for National Statistics. 2012. Contains public sector information licensed under the Open Government Licence v3.0; **p62:** Data from Current account balance as per cent of GDP. © Crown/Office for National Statistics and Office for Budget Responsibility. Contains public sector information licensed under the Open Government Licence v3.0; **p64:** Figure adapted from Components of Aggregate Demand. © Crown/Office for National Statistics. Contains public sector information licensed under the Open Government Licence v3.0; **p67:** Gross fixed capital formation: Business investment: CVM NSA: £m (29 June 2018) https://www.ons.gov.uk/economy/grossdomesticproductgdp/ti meseries/npen [Accessed: 25/09/2018]. © Crown/Office for National Statistics. Contains public sector information licensed under the Open Government Licence v3.0; **p68:** Policy paper: Autumn Budget 2017, 22 November 2017. https://www.gov.uk/government/publications/autumn-budget-2017-documents/autumn-budget-2017. Accessed: 07/01/2018. © Crown/HM Treasury. Contains public sector information licensed under the Open Government Licence v3.0; **p68:** Paolo Mauro, Rafael Romeu, Ariel Binder and Asad Zaman, 2013, "A Modern History of Fiscal Prudence and Profligacy," IMF Working Paper No. 13/5, International Monetary Fund, Washington, DC; **p69:** UK trade: February 2018: Total value of UK imports and exports of goods together with indices of volume and price, including an early monthly estimate of the value of trade in services. https://www.ons.gov.uk/economy/nationalaccounts/balanceofpayments/bulletins/uktrade/february2018 [Accessed: 07/01/2018]. © Crown/Office for National Statistics. Contains public sector information licensed under the Open Government Licence v3.0.; **p87:** OECD (2018), Data, Income inequality – G20 countries, https://data.oecd.org/inequality/incomein equality.htm#indicator-chart. [Accessed 28/10/18), © OECD 2019; **p89:** Time Series: Public sector net borrowing, excluding public sector banks (£ million), https://www.ons.gov.uk/economy/governmentpublicsectorandtaxes/publicsectorfinance/timeseries/dzls/pusf [Accessed: 08/01/2019]. © Crown/Office for National Statistics, 2018. Contains public sector information licensed under the Open Government Licence v3.0.; **p100:** Adapted from G Jackson and C Giles., 'UK economic growth faltering according to new data', © 2018, The Financial Times. Used with Permission; **p145:** Public Sector Employment, UK: June 2018 https://www.ons.gov.uk/employmentandlabourmarket/peopleinwork/publicsectorpersonnel/bulletins/publicsectoremployment/june2018. [Accessed: 08/01/2019]. © Crown/Office for National Statistics. Contains public sector information licensed under the Open Government Licence v3.0; **p151:** Donald Trump's difficult decision on steel imports, © 2018, The Economist. Used with Permission; **p156:** House of Commons Environment, Food and Rural Affairs Committee Food waste in England Eighth Report of Session 2016–17. https://publications.parliament.uk/pa/cm201617/cmselect/cmenvfru/429/429.pdf [Accessed: 08/01/2019]. © Parliamentary Copyright, 2017. Contains Parliamentary information licensed under the Open Parliament Licence v3.0; **p156:** Butler, Sarah, Adapted from 'Wonky' fruit and veg sales put Morrisons on straight path to growth, © 2018, Guardian News and Media Limited. Used with Permission; **p163:** The UKs main trading partners; exports of goods and services to individual countries as a percentage of total exports, 2013 ONS.gov.uk https://www.ons.gov.uk/businessindustryandtrade/internationaltrade/bulletins/exportsandimportsstatisticsbycountryforuktradeinservices/quarter2aprtojun2017 [Accessed: 08/01/2019]. © Crown/Office for National Statistics. Contains public sector information licensed under the Open Government Licence v3.0; **p174:** Figure adapted from Global Poverty Headcount Ratio at International Poverty Line. Data Bank: Poverty and Equity http://povertydata.worldbank.org/poverty/home/ Accessed: 9 January 2019. © The World Bank, 2019. Data set available under Creative Commons Attribution 4.0 International License; **p176:** OECD Data: Income inequality https://data.oecd.org/inequality/income-inequality.htm Accessed: 9 January 2019, © OECD 2019; **p183:** What We Do, © 2019 The World Bank Group. Used with Permission; **p188:** Chart 1: Public sector spending 2018-19. Autumn Budget 2017, © 2017, Crown copyright. Contains public sector information licensed under the Open Government Licence v3.0; **p188:** Table 1.6 – Total managed expenditure (in £ billion, unless otherwise stated). Autumn Budget 2017, © 2017, Crown copyright. Contains public sector information licensed under the Open Government Licence v3.0; **p189:** Public Expenditure Statistical Analyses, © 2017, Crown copyright. Contains public sector information licensed under the Open Government Licence v3.0; **p191:** Data from Family Expenditure Survey 2005–06; Family Resources Survey 2006–07; HM Treasury, Pre-Budget Report 2008, November 2008. http://www.hm-treasury.gov.uk/prebud_pbr08_repindex.htm. © Crown copyright 2017. Contains public sector information licensed under the Open Government Licence v3.0.; **pp192,194:** Public sector net borrowing, % GDP. Government borrowing, debt and debt interest: Statistics, © 2019, House of Commons. Contains public sector information licensed under the Open Government Licence v3.0; **p193:** Data from Time Series PS: Net Debt (excluding public sector banks) as a % of GDP: NSA (19 October 2018). https://www.ons.gov.uk/economy/governmentpublicsectorandtaxes/publicsectorfinance/timeseries/hf6x/pusf. [Accessed: 09/01/2019]. © 2018, Crown/Office for National Statistics. Contains public sector information licensed under the Open Government Licence v3.0; **p196:** Consumer price inflation time series (MM23): CPIH Annual rate 00: ALL ITEMS 2015=100, https://www.ons.gov.uk/economy/inflationandpriceindices/timeseries/l55o/mm23/linechartimage. [Accessed: 05/11/2018]. © 2018, Crown/Office for National Statistics. Contains public sector information licensed under the Open Government Licence v3.0; **p197:** Jones, Rupert, Payday loan caps come into force, © 2015, Guardian News and Media Limited. Used with Permission; **p199:** Figure in Q1 adapted from CPI Annual rate 00: ALL ITEMS 2015=100 (MM23), https://www.ons.gov.uk/economy/inflationandpriceindices/timeseries/d7g7/mm23 [Accessed: 05/11/2018]. © 2018, Crown/Office for National Statistics. Contains public sector information licensed under the Open Government Licence v3.0; **p202:** Extract C: Data from ONS Time Series: Gross Domestic Product: Quarter on Quarter growth: CVM SA %, www.ons.gov.uk/economy/grossdomesticproductgdp/timeseries/ihyq [Accessed: 09/01/2019]. © 2019, Crown/Office for National Statistics. Contains public sector information licensed under the Open Government Licence v3.0; **p210:** Royal Mail fined £50m for breaking competition law, 14 August 2018. https://www.ofcom.org.uk/about-ofcom/latest/features-and-news/royal-mail-whistl-competition-law [Accessed: 09/01/2019]. © 2018, Ofcom. Contains public sector information licensed under the Open Government Licence v3.0; **p213:** W.Z., 'Do sin taxes work?' Aug 10th 2018. © 2018, The Economist Newspaper Limited. Used with Permission.

Pearson acknowledges use of the following extracts:
pp13,123: Anderton, Alain. Edexcel AS/A Level Economics, 6th edition © 2015, Pearson Education Ltd; **p146:** Bischoff, Victoria, Secret deal that lets greedy energy firms hide their obscene profits: Why NOW is the time to switch to a smaller supplier, © 2016, Daily Mail; **p151:** Data from Bank of America Merrill Lynch and Bloomberg, © 2018.

Photographs
(Key: t-top; b-bottom; c-centre; l-left; r-right)
Shutterstock: 77318 3tl, Michael D Brown 3tr, ppart 3bl, Titov Nikolai 3br, Amer Ghazzal 20, Shutterstock 26, StockphotoVideo 120, Baloncici 127, mypokcik 144, Thatmacroguy 166, Watch The World 168, Dean Drobot 186, **Alamy Stock Photo:** Geoff Moore 23, David J. Green 29, Richard Crease 32l, John James 32r, Harald Tittel/dpa 132, Alan Wilson 145, Trinity Mirror/Mirrorpix 160, Mark Boulton 182, **Royal Mail**: Stamp Design, featured with the kind permission of Royal Mail Group Ltd 33.

Websites
Pearson Education Limited is not responsible for the content of any external internet sites. It is essential for tutors to preview each website before using it in class so as to ensure that the URL is still accurate, relevant and appropriate. We suggest that tutors bookmark useful websites and consider enabling students to access them through the school/college intranet

Notes from the publisher
1. While the publishers have made every attempt to ensure that advice on the qualification and its assessment is accurate, the official specification and associated assessment guidance materials are the only authoritative source of information and should always be referred to for definitive guidance.

   Pearson examiners have not contributed to any sections in this resource relevant to examination papers for which they have responsibility.

2. Pearson has robust editorial processes, including answer and fact checks, to ensure the accuracy of the content in this publication, and every effort is made to ensure this publication is free of errors. We are, however, only human, and occasionally errors do occur. Pearson is not liable for any misunderstandings that arise as a result of errors in this publication, but it is our priority to ensure that the content is accurate. If you spot an error, please do contact us at resourcescorrections@pearson.com so we can make sure it is corrected.

Economics as a social science

Economics is the study of how people satisfy unlimited wants with scarce resources. It is a **social science**; the scientific study of human society and social relationships. Other social sciences include sociology, psychology and politics.

The scientific method

The scientific method involves a scientist putting forward a theory that can be proved or refuted through observations, experimentation and evidence. When theories are universally accepted, they become known as laws, for example, the law of gravity. It is difficult to use the scientific method in economics because too many variables are involved. Control groups cannot be set up and variables cannot be isolated.

Models

The real world is very complex, with multiple variables and factors influencing people and the environment. A model, whether physical or conceptual (based on an idea), is a simplification of real life. Models help economists explain concepts and test ideas.

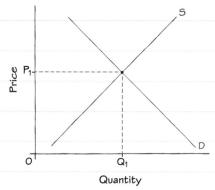

Most economic models use graphs to represent the relationship between economic variables.

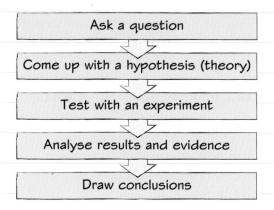

The scientific method process

Economic models

Economic models also simplify the complex reality of the interactions within an economy. Because there are too many interconnected variables to deal with, economic models make certain assumptions in order to explain economic concepts and model how reality works. Examples of economic models include:

- production possibility frontiers (see pages 4–5)
- supply and demand diagrams (see pages 11–12 and 17)
- the circular flow of income (see pages 74–75).

Ceteris paribus

Ceteris paribus is a Latin phrase that means 'other things being equal'. The term is used in economics when applying economic models. It is used when economists want to explain a situation cause and effect, but do not want to examine all of the factors in a situation at once; rather, they want to focus on how the change in one independent variable will affect another dependent variable when all the other factors in the situation stay the same.

Ceteris paribus means focusing on the relationship between two variables and no other external factors.

1 What is an economic model?
2 Why is it difficult to use the scientific method in economics?

Positive and normative economic statements

Certain aspects of economics can be proven. **Positive economic statements** are objective and testable. Other areas of economics are harder to prove and are subject to **value judgements** and people's opinions. These are **normative economic statements**.

Positive economic statements

Positive economics involves **objective** explanation including proving and rejecting theories. Examples of positive economic statements include:

- A fall in incomes will lead to a rise in demand for inferior goods.
- Higher interest rates will reduce spending on white goods.
- A rise in taxation will reduce inflation.

Normative economic statements

A normative economic statement is based on opinion and is difficult to prove through evidence. Examples of normative statements are:

- Poverty is the most serious economic problem.
- Interest rates should fall to improve economic growth.
- The government should ban diesel cars.

Value judgements

When governments are making decisions about economic policy, there are often multiple options and choices. The degree to which a decision is taken is also a value judgement. For example, a decision to invest more in social housing is a value judgement, as is the amount that could be invested.

The UK government should introduce a car scrappage scheme for vehicles over 10 years old in order to reduce emissions pollution.

The government should ensure all housing developments include at least 5% socially affordable housing in order to fix the housing crisis.

Corporation tax should rise by 1% for firms generating a net profit margin greater than 15%.

Examples of political value judgements

Farming subsidies should be abolished in order to lower food prices and increase productivity.

£5 million aid should be made available to support refugees in war-torn Libya.

The UK government should spend £1 billion on labour market reform.

Now try this

1 What is positive economics?

2 What is a normative economic statement?

3 Why do political decisions involve value judgements?

The economic problem

The study of economics is about the efficient allocation of resources – the choices that are made by economic agents (consumers, producers, government) who have unlimited wants from a limited or finite number of resources. This is the **economic problem** which leads to **opportunity cost**. Resources can be renewable or non-renewable.

Scarcity and choice

The world's resources are **finite**. Food, water, oil, land and labour are all limited. Resources that are scarce are called **economic goods**. However, people have **infinite** wants – food, shelter, clothing and warmth as well as emotional needs such as self-esteem and excitement. There is always something that someone wants more of – this is the basic **economic problem**.

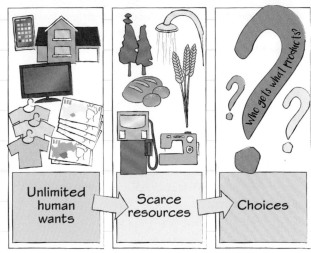

Wants, resources and choices

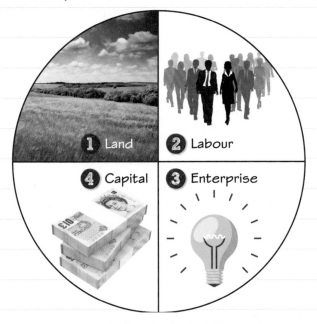

There are four finite **factors of production** that are used to create goods and services to satisfy our wants and needs

Renewable and non-renewable resources

The factors of production can be classified as renewable and non-renewable resources. Coal, gold and copper (land) are non-renewable resources. Renewable resources include fish stocks, wheat, electricity and water. We can replace renewable resources.

Opportunity cost

The economic problem leads to opportunity cost – the benefits forgone of the 'next best' alternative. When an economic agent makes a choice, such as purchasing a good, building a new school or allocating resources in production, all the other possible choices (and the benefits gained) are forgone.

Making the best choice

The study of economics is about making the choices that bring the greatest benefits to the economic agent making the decision.

Now try this

1 What are the factors of production?
2 Why is scarcity a problem in economics?
3 Give one example of opportunity cost for a car manufacturer.

Production possibility frontiers 1

An economy cannot produce everything that people want, which means there has to be a trade-off between the production of one good and another. A **production possibility frontier (PPF)**, or production possibility curve, can be used to explore the opportunity cost of production decisions in an economy.

Production possibility frontier curves

The curve in the diagram represents the combination of goods which can be produced if all resources in an economy (factors of production) are fully and efficiently employed. The PPF curve compares the production of combinations of different economic goods in an economy.

PPF opportunity cost

PPFs can be used to show the **maximum productive potential of an economy**. In the PPF above:

A	All resources employed producing non-manufactured goods
B	45 units non-manufactured goods, 15 units manufactured goods
C	30 units non-manufactured goods, 30 units manufactured goods
F	Production is below the economy's maximum potential output of either good
G	Production is not yet attainable

Production cannot take place to the right of the curve (G) because the PPF shows the maximum output of an economy. This would be unobtainable production.

Marginal analysis

The PPF **above** clearly demonstrates **opportunity cost** (what has to be given up because of the choice being made). This can be expressed in the concept of the **margin**. The margin is a point of possible change, for example, the move from C to D. The marginal cost of 5 more manufactured goods is 10 non-manufactured goods.

Economic growth and decline

The PPF can move to the left (economic decline) or the right (economic growth). Economic growth is an increase in the productive potential of an economy, whereas economic decline refers to the decline of productive potential, perhaps through depreciation of capital stocks. Economic growth could come about from:

- an increase in resources
- improved education
- investment in capital goods (goods that enable production).

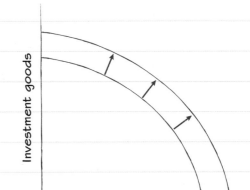

A shift to the right of a PPF demonstrates economic growth. All points within the PPF curve are possible points of production of consumer goods (those bought by consumers) and capital goods.

Now try this

1 What does a production possibility frontier show?
2 What is the margin?

Production possibility frontiers 2

A PPF can be used to distinguish between **consumer goods** and **capital goods**. There is an opportunity cost when choosing between consuming now and investment for the future. There may also be efficient or inefficient allocation of resources.

Consumer goods and capital goods

- **Consumer goods** – these are goods and services that are used by people to satisfy their needs and wants, for example, restaurant meals, clothing, concert tickets.
- **Capital goods** – these are goods that are used in the production of other goods and services, such as roads, machines and equipment. Spending on capital goods is classed as investment.

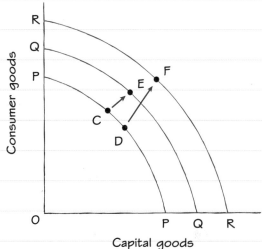

Devoting more resources to the production of capital goods now could lead to a greater economic growth in the future. The choice of production at D might lead to long-term growth and the PPF shifting to RR instead of QQ if more had been invested in consumer goods.

Efficiency

Any point along the PPF shows the maximum allocation of a country's resources where resources are fully and efficiently employed. All points along the curve show **productive efficiency**. However, not all points demonstrate **allocative efficiency**, the point where a country's social welfare is maximised. The combination of goods at this point is of most benefit to society. It may only be one point on the curve.

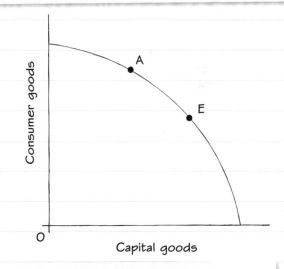

Both points A and E show productive efficiency (lowest cost of production) but only E may be the point of allocative efficiency.

Limitations of PPF

The PPF gives no indication of which combination of goods will be produced in an economy. It only shows the possible choices.

Only considers two variables

A simplified model of reality — **Limitations** — Does not identify the point at which maximum social welfare is achieved

Now try this

1 What is a capital good?
2 What is productive efficiency?
3 What is allocative efficiency?

Specialisation and division of labour

In *An Inquiry into the Nature and Causes of the Wealth of Nations* (1776), Adam Smith explored the productive efficiencies of a pin factory through workers focusing and specialising on a specific aspect of the production process. From this, the economic concepts of **specialisation** and **division of labour** developed. They have brought benefits but also have disadvantages.

Specialisation

Specialisation involves the production of a single or narrow range of goods by an individual, a business or a nation. When a range of individuals, businesses or nations specialise, they are able to produce a greater quantity of goods more efficiently than if one tried to produce a variety of goods. Specialisation by individuals is called the **division of labour**.

Greater productivity

Specialisation and the division of labour lead to **greater productivity**:

- No need for workers to waste time transferring between the production of different goods.
- Workers can be provided with specialist tools, which can be shared.
- Workers acquire skills in a narrow range of tasks.
- The speed of production is increased as workers' skills improve and specialist machinery is applied.

Advantages and disadvantages of specialisation and division of labour

👍 Specialisation enables a greater number of products and services to be produced.

👍 Lower costs of production for economic goods.

👍 Encourages trade and partnerships between nations.

👍 Leads to mass production and more people's wants being satisfied.

👎 Where jobs are too narrow, work can become repetitive and monotonous.

👎 Specialisation can lead to over-reliance on a certain industry.

👎 Division of labour can lead to interdependence (if one industry or group of workers goes on strike, the whole production chain falters).

Sectors of the economy

Specialisation is supported through sectors of the economy working together to produce goods. Many goods pass through the industries that make up these sectors, each sector specialising in an aspect of production. There are three main sectors:

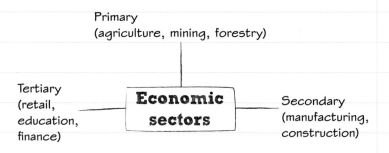

Primary
(agriculture, mining, forestry)

Tertiary
(retail, education, finance)

Economic sectors

Secondary
(manufacturing, construction)

Markets

The benefits of specialisation are realised through markets. A market is any system where buyers and sellers come together to exchange goods and services. Markets (often) lead to economic prosperity through the efficient trade of goods.

Now try this

What are the benefits of division of labour?

The functions of money

Modern economies have developed and people's standard of living has increased through the function of money. To work, money must have five functions.

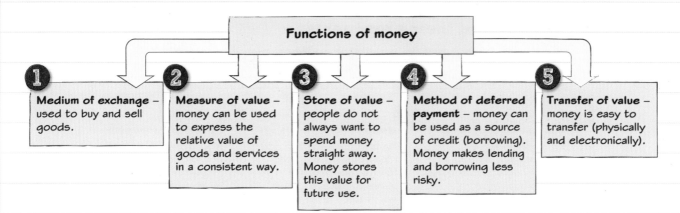

Functions of money

1 Medium of exchange – used to buy and sell goods.

2 Measure of value – money can be used to express the relative value of goods and services in a consistent way.

3 Store of value – people do not always want to spend money straight away. Money stores this value for future use.

4 Method of deferred payment – money can be used as a source of credit (borrowing). Money makes lending and borrowing less risky.

5 Transfer of value – money is easy to transfer (physically and electronically).

Capital

Money is the most liquid asset among all assets. You can easily convert money into any type of asset according to your needs. For example, if you own a hotel and it is failing, selling the hotel creates money which can easily be exchanged for a retail store.

The future value of money

Inflation diminishes the future value of money. Money in the future is worth less than it is now.

Equalising marginal utility

Marginal utility is the additional satisfaction a consumer gains from consuming one more unit of a good. Money equalises marginal utility because the value of each extra pound does not diminish in value in terms of the benefits it can buy. This helps people decide whether spending an extra pound on a good or service is worthwhile, or whether they should spend it on something else. (To revise marginal utility, see page 12.)

Forms of money in an economy

Money in current accounts – allowing cash to be withdrawn and money to be transferred between accounts (using e-commerce, debit cards and cheque books).

Forms of money

Money substitutes, e.g. credit cards.

Near monies, e.g. savings accounts.

Non-money financial assets, e.g. shares and stocks.

Now try this

1 How does money act as a measure of value?

2 Give three examples of forms of money that can be found in an economy.

Types of economy

The function of an economy is to resolve the basic economic problem. In doing so, an economic system should decide what is to be produced, how it is to be produced and for whom it is to be produced. There are three main economic systems: **free market economies**, **mixed economies** and **command economies**.

Types of economy and their proponents

Type of economy

① Free market economies

The majority of resources are allocated through markets rather than government.

Examples: USA, Hong Kong

Propronent: **Friedrich Hayek**, *The Road to Serfdom* (1944)

- Total market freedom.
- Unregulated markets are the most efficient.
- Promoted the liberty of the individual.
- Central planning imposes the will of a small minority on the whole.

② Mixed economies

Typically, 40–60% of resources are allocated through government planning in areas such as education, state benefits, transport.

Example: government planning of healthcare in the UK

Proponent: **Adam Smith**, *An Inquiry into the Nature and Causes of the Wealth of Nations* (1776)

- Invisible hand of the market.
- Pursuit of profit will maximise the benefits of all.
- Limit protectionism.
- Laissez-faire government.
- Governments provide framework for markets to operate in.
- People need protecting against firms distorting markets and fixing prices.

③ Command economies

Also known as planned economies. Most resources are allocated by the state. Free markets only form a small part of the allocation of resources.

Examples: Cuba, North Korea

Propronent: **Karl Marx**, *Das Capital* (1867)

- Capitalist systems are unequal, benefiting only owners and managers.
- Collective ownership through the state.
- Closely linked to communism.

The market mechanism

The market mechanism allocates resources by bringing together buyers and sellers. The market mechanism works because suppliers (sellers) will produce goods and services to meet the needs of consumers (buyers) providing they can do so profitably.

Planning

The alternative to the market mechanism is to plan the allocation of resources through administrative decisions. This may happen at a household or family level, or at government level, for example, the allocation of resources to the National Health Service.

Now try this

1 What is the market mechanism?

2 How are the theories of Adam Smith different from those of Karl Marx?

3 How are resources allocated in a command economy?

Economic systems

The type of economic system influences the factors that determine the characteristics of an economy. Free market economies and command economies have their advantages and disadvantages.

Characteristics of an economy influenced by economic systems

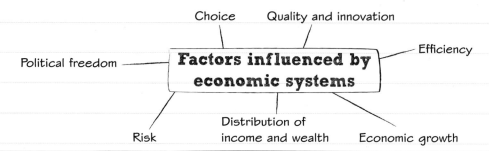

Choice   Quality and innovation

Political freedom ——— **Factors influenced by economic systems** ——— Efficiency

Risk   Distribution of income and wealth   Economic growth

Free market economies

👍 More choice – competition encourages multiple versions and varieties of goods.

👍 Incentive for firms to innovate and produce high quality goods in order to compete.

👍 Competition leads to greater efficiency of industries.

👍 Dynamic markets are a catalyst for economic growth.

👍 Associated with political freedom.

👎 Choice can become privilege of the wealthy.

👎 Most successful firms can manipulate and dominate the market.

👎 Higher levels of inequality and distribution of wealth.

👎 Greater risk to citizens – more exposure to unemployment, poverty and ill health.

Command economies

👍 No one firm is able to dominate and exploit consumers by fixing high prices.

👍 Wealth distributed more fairly through government planning.

👍 Social welfare is the main concern of the state.

👎 Central planning imposes the will of a small minority on the whole.

👎 Less choice – planning produces uniform goods.

👎 No incentive to innovate due to lack of competition.

👎 Little incentive to work efficiently – high job security with no profit incentive.

👎 Slower growth than efficient free/mixed market economies.

👎 Political control (totalitarianism).

Comparisons

Command economies have not been as successful at delivering wealth and prosperity to their citizens in comparison with the success of free market economies and mixed economies.

Mixed economies

Mixed economies generally offer a balance of advantages and disadvantages relative to the two extremes. Economic growth in mixed economies has matched that of free market economies.

Now try this

1 How is wealth and income distributed in a free market economy?

2 What factors might result in free market economies being more efficient than command economies?

Rational decision making

Neo-classical economic theory assumes that economic agents (consumers, firms, governments) make decisions in a rational way: that by evaluating the benefits of a range of options, economic agents will make choices to maximise their net benefits. This is also known as maximising utility from consuming goods.

Maximising benefits

On the basis of rational decision making, economic agents may make choices that maximise their **economic welfare**.

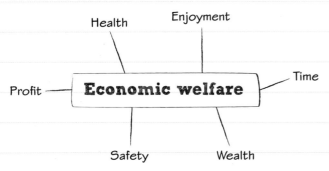

Consumers

As resources are limited and there are a wide variety of choices available to consumers, they will spend their time, money and energy in a way that maximises their welfare and enjoyment. This is known as **maximising utility** from consuming goods. For example, consumers will evaluate spending £120 on an expensive pair of trainers or £80 on a cheaper pair with the benefit of spending the remaining £40 on a concert ticket.

Firms

On the basis of rational decision making, firms will make choices that **maximise profitability**. However, decisions made by firms may be subjective and depend on a short-term versus a long-term perspective.

Workers

Workers within a firm may seek to maximise their income through a high wage or bonuses. However, some workers may choose the benefits of job security, low stress environments and social interactions over income.

Government

The role of government is to maximise the benefits to society. This includes decisions that will maximise economic growth, reduce unemployment, reduce social problems and improve the standard of living. It is difficult for governments to achieve these objectives for all people all of the time.

Complications with rational decision making

Rational decision making is not always easy to predict. These assumptions can be simplistic. For example, consumers may make a decision that benefits them in the short term, but could have a long-term negative impact on their welfare, such as choosing to smoke. Managers within a firm may also make decisions that benefit themselves, rather than maximising profitability, and corrupt governments may make decisions that benefit their supporters, rather than all citizens.

Now try this

1 Why might someone choose to buy one good even though it is more expensive than another?

2 Explain one factor an individual may consider when attempting to maximise their economic welfare at work.

Demand

Demand is defined as the quantity of goods or services that consumers are willing and able to buy at any given price over a period of time. A **demand curve** is used to show the quantity demanded at any given price. There may be movements along the demand curve. The demand curve may also shift to the right or the left.

Demand curve

As prices rise then, *ceteris paribus* (all other things being equal), the quantity of a good demanded will fall. For example, as the average price of computers falls from £650 to £550 there may be an increase of 200,000 computers bought in the UK that year. This can be seen in the example of a demand curve (right).

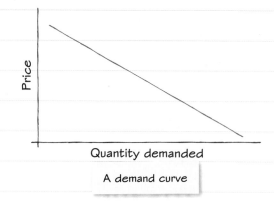

A demand curve

Movements along the curve

The demand curve is, almost always, downwards sloping. When the price (or average price) changes, there is said to be a movement along the demand curve (see diagram below).

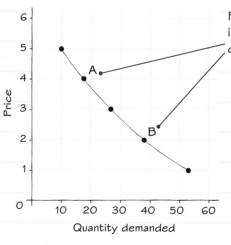

From Point A to Point B, the movement to the right indicates a rise in demand from 18 units to 38 units due to the price falling from £4 to £2.

Extension and contraction

An extension occurs where **demand rises** as a result of a fall in price (A to B). A contraction occurs where **demand falls** as a result of a rise in prices (B to A). In almost all cases a rise in price leads to a fall in the quantity demanded and vice versa.

Shifts in the demand curve

There are many other factors, other than price, that can cause demand to change. These other factors will cause a shift in demand. A shift in demand will rise (shift to the right) or fall (a shift to the left) for any given price.

D_1 to D_2 represents a **fall in demand (shift to the left)** and D_1 to D_3 represents a **rise in demand (shift to the right)**. A number of conditions will cause a shift in demand.

Now try this

1 What causes a movement along the demand curve?

2 What does a shift to the left in the demand curve represent?

The conditions of demand

There are numerous factors that can determine the shape of the demand curve. These factors – **conditions of demand** – go beyond price and include income, social factors and the relative demand for other goods and services. The shape of the demand curve may also be influenced by the **concept of diminishing marginal utility**.

Factors causing a shift in a demand curve

Any change in the following factors will lead to a shift to the left (decrease) or right (increase) in demand.

Legislation. The government can influence markets and buying behaviour through legislation. For example, introducing compulsory use of bicycle helmets would significantly shift the demand curve to the right.

Real income. As real incomes rise, so will demand for normal goods. At any given price more will be demanded at the new higher level of income, and vice versa.

The price of other goods. Demand for a good may increase or decrease depending on the price of other related goods such as complementary goods or substitutes. For example, rice may be considered a substitute for bread.

Conditions of demand

Advertising. This is closely linked to fashion, but the degree to which a good or brand is advertised can directly influence demand.

Fashion. Social trends such as fashion and fads also influence demand for items.

Population changes. At a local and national level, population changes will influence the conditions of demand.

Diminishing marginal utility

The more buyers are offered, the less value they put on the last one bought. This fact is known as the concept of diminishing marginal utility. The marginal utility of a good or service falls as more units are consumed over a given period of time.

 Real world **Chocolate Easter Eggs**

At Easter, children will often receive chocolate Easter eggs. The satisfaction from eating the first Easter egg is high, as may be the second. The satisfaction from consuming the third and then the fourth Easter egg diminishes. This concept demonstrates the law of diminishing marginal utility. At some point the nth Easter egg will provide zero satisfaction and may even make the child sick. This is known as negative marginal utility. With marginal utility one more may, or may not, be better.

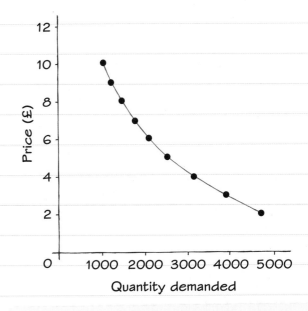

The utility of the 4000th unit has less value to the consumer (around £3.50) than the 2000th unit (£6)

Now try this

1 How can real income affect demand?

2 How might a fall in the price of train fares affect the demand for petrol?

3 What is the law of diminishing utility?

Price elasticity of demand

The quantity demanded of a good is affected by the changes in the price of that good. The extent of the change is known as its **price elasticity**. Elasticity is a measure of how responsive demand is to a change in some other factor – price, income and the price of other goods.

Calculating price elasticity of demand (PED)

The extent to which a change in price will affect the quantity demanded for a good or service depends on a number of factors. For economists, understanding the responsiveness of quantity demanded to a change in price is very important. Price elasticity of demand (PED) is calculated by the formula shown on the right.

PED formula

PED = percentage change in quantity demanded ÷ percentage change in price

or

$$\frac{\Delta QD}{\Delta P}$$

(See page 14 for worked examples of PED calculations.)

Calculating percentage changes

The following formulae should be used where the percentage change is not given:

$$\text{Percentage change} = \frac{\text{new value} - \text{original value}}{\text{original value}} \times 100$$

or

$$\frac{\Delta Q}{Q} \text{ and } \frac{\Delta P}{P}$$

Technical points about elasticities

 A downward sloping demand curve will always have negative elasticity because a rise in one variable is always matched by a fall in the other. However, when calculating elasticities negative values are usually omitted. For example, −0.2 becomes 0.2.

2 Elasticities over the same price range can also differ. For example, the elasticity for a price change of £5 to £10 will be different from a price fall from £10 to £5.

From perfectly inelastic to perfectly elastic demand

Type of demand	What it means	Numerical measure of elasticity using PED formula
Perfectly inelastic	Quantity demanded does not change as price changes	Zero
Inelastic	Quantity demanded changes by a smaller percentage than price changes	Between 0 and 1
Unitary elasticity	Quantity demanded changes by the same percentage as a change in price	1
Elastic	Quantity demanded changes by a larger percentage than a change in price	Between 1 and infinity ∞
Perfectly elastic	Buyers will purchase all they can at a given price but none at a higher price	Infinity ∞

Now try this

1 What is meant by elasticity in economics?

2 What is the formula for the price elasticity of demand?

3 What does it mean when a good has inelastic demand?

Graphical representations of PED

Different elasticities can be expressed graphically. The shape of the demand curve is influenced by its elasticity.

Points on the demand curve

The elasticity of demand along the points of a demand curve are not constant. At the top end of all demand curves demand is elastic, whilst at the bottom end demand is inelastic, no matter what gradient the lines are. The gradient of a demand curve will represent its elasticity.

A shallow demand curve represents elastic demand whilst a steep demand curve represents inelastic demand.

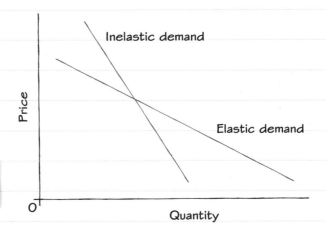

Demand curves representing different PED

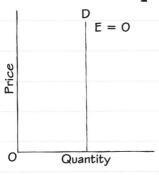

a Perfectly elastic demand

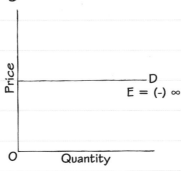

b Perfectly inelastic demand

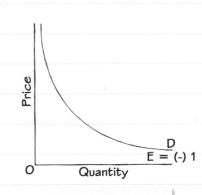

c Unitary elasticity

PED = K where K equals a constant value

The determinants of PED

Availability of substitutes

The greater number and quality of substitutes a product has the higher the elasticity of demand. Specific food products, such as wine gums, have many substitutes and demand for them is relatively less price elastic. However, chocolate in general has fewer substitutes and is relatively less elastic.

Time

Time has a considerable impact on elasticity of demand. If the price of petrol rose sharply, there would be relatively little impact on demand (petrol is an inelastic good). However, over time, people would find alternative means of travel and demand would fall.

Now try this

1 If demand is price inelastic then what effect would a price change have on quantity demanded?

2 What is meant by the term perfectly inelastic demand?

3 How might a fall in the number of substitutes for a good affect its price elasticity of demand?

Income and cross elasticities

Other factors that influence the elasticity of demand are people's incomes and the price of related goods and services. These are referred to as **income elasticity of demand** and **cross elasticity of demand**. Goods are of different types.

Income elasticity of demand (YED)

As people's incomes rise they tend to purchase proportionately more of most normal goods. These goods have income elastic demand. For other goods, there is relatively little percentage change in the quantity demanded as incomes change. For example, bleach tends to have low income elasticity of demand whereas sirloin steak has a relatively high income elasticity of demand.

Cross elasticity of demand (CED)

This measures the proportionate response of the quantity demanded of one good (X) to the proportionate change in price of another (Y). Cross elasticity is an important factor affecting demand where products are related. For example, a fall in the price of garden furniture will increase demand, but it may also increase demand for garden water features – a complementary product.

Complement – a good that is typically bought alongside another/used together. Two goods which are complements have a negative CED. An increase in the price of one will result in a fall in demand for the other, e.g. cereals and milk.

Normal goods – consumers tend to increase their demand as their incomes rise and vice versa. The demand for normal goods is represented by D_1 in the diagram to the right.

Types of goods

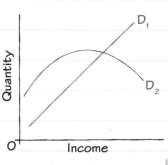

Normal and inferior goods

Substitute – a good which can be replaced by another good. Two goods which are substitutes will have a positive cross-elasticity. An increase in the rise of one leads to an increase in the demand for another, e.g. similar holiday destinations.

Luxuries – have elasticity YED of greater than +1. The income elasticity of most luxury goods falls as incomes rise.

Necessities – in theory, people will buy these even when prices rise or their incomes fall because they need them.

Inferior goods – consumers tend to buy less of these as their incomes rise. This is generally true when incomes are high. In the diagram above, D_2 represents a product such as bread that people will buy more of as their incomes rise from a low point, but will buy less of at a high level of income because they switch to better quality foods such as meat.

 Calculating YED and CED

$$YED = \frac{\text{percentage change in quantity demanded}}{\text{percentage change in income}}$$

or

$$\frac{\%\Delta Q}{\%\Delta Y}$$

$$CED = \frac{\text{percentage change in quantity demanded of good X}}{\text{percentage change in price of good Y}}$$

Now try this

1 Give an example of a complementary good for a smartphone.
2 Why do necessities have an income elasticity of demand between 0 and +1?

Elasticities of demand and revenue

Firms and government will use information on elasticities of demand to make important decisions about pricing and policies. For example, the imposition of a government subsidy may have little impact in markets where PED is inelastic.

The impact of different PED

The graph (right) shows that PED varies from infinity at a high price/zero demand through to minus one at the midpoint to an elasticity of zero at zero price/high quantity demanded.

Firms can use this information to maximise sales. **Total revenue is maximised when PED equals +/−1**. The nearer a firm sets its prices to this midpoint of the demand curve, the higher its total revenue will be. Similarly, governments can use PED to help set the tax level to maximise income.

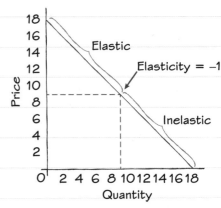

Maximising revenue

The table below represents total revenue generated at points on the diagram (right). Revenue is maximised at point C where PED is unitary elastic.

Revenue = selling price × quantity

	Price	Quantity	Total revenue
Point A	£80	10	£500
Point B	£60	20	£1000
Point C	£55	25	£1375
Point D	£20	40	£500

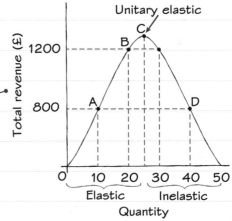

Total revenue of a firm across different price points. Revenue is maximised where PED has unitary elasticity.

Summary of PED impact on revenue

PED	Prices rise	Prices fall
Inelastic	Total revenue rises	Total revenue falls
Unitary elastic	Total revenue unchanged	Total revenue unchanged
Elastic	Total revenue falls	Total revenue rises

Maths skills — Unit elasticity

Remember, unit elasticity is where

%ΔQ is equal to %ΔP

Using knowledge of elasticities

👍 Information about YED can be used in sales forecasting – if the YED of a product and likely changes in real income are known, then sales levels can be predicted.

👍 If YED is known for various products, a firm may choose to sell different products depending on the economic climate; for example, a product with a high YED during a boom.

👍 Understanding CEDs will help a firm monitor the price changes in substitutes and complements in order to adjust their own prices accordingly. For example, if the price of a substitute product with a CED of 1.8 falls, then the firm may have to respond quickly to reduce its own prices.

Now try this

1 At what PED would a firm's revenue be maximised?

2 How might a government use information on CED?

Supply

Supply is defined as the quantity of goods that sellers are prepared to sell to buyers at any given price over a period of time. A **supply curve** is used to show the quantity supplied at any given price. There may be movements along the supply curve. The supply curve may also shift to the right or the left. Apart from price, various factors may change supply in a market.

Supply and price

As the price of a good rises, assuming no other factors have changed, supply will increase through a movement along the supply curve – an expansion in supply from point A to B (see diagram right). Supply will rise as sellers move to supply more of the good through the incentive to maximise profits at the higher price. Conversely, as prices fall, there will be a contraction in quantity supplied as some suppliers cut back on potentially unprofitable production.

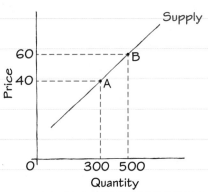

A supply curve. An upward sloping supply curve assumes that suppliers are motivated by profit.

Shifts in supply

Apart from price, there are other factors that change supply in a market: the **conditions of supply**. These conditions will create a shift in supply. For example, a rise in the cost of production will cause a shift to the left (S_1 to S_3). If suppliers cannot pass these costs on to customers through a higher price, they will make less profit and supply less of that good (supply will fall from Q_1 to Q_3). If costs of production fall, supply will shift to the right (S_2) as suppliers will be attracted by the higher profit margins due to the lower costs of production.

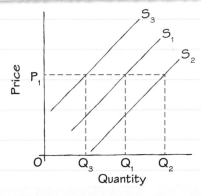

A shift to the **left** ← means a **fall** ↓ in supply. A shift to the **right** → means a **rise** in supply ↑

Costs of production. See example above.

Technology. New technology often leads to greater efficiency in the production process and a fall in production costs.

The existence of indirect taxes or subsidies (see pages 25–26).

Conditions of supply

Anticipating future events. If firms anticipate prices to fall or demand to rise in the future, they may choose to stockpile goods.

Legislation. New legislation often forces firms to make changes. These changes will incur costs and increase the overall cost of production. Legislation, such as import barriers, may also make it harder to supply a good.

The price of other goods, including substitutes. Suppliers may switch production to more profitable products, for example, producing wheat-based products instead of rice when the price of wheat rises.

Now try this

1 What is a contraction in supply?
2 Identify three conditions of supply.

Price elasticity of supply

The quantity of a good supplied is affected by the changes in the price of that good. The extent of the change is known as its price elasticity. **Elasticity of supply** is a measure of how responsive supply is to a change in price.

Price elasticity of supply

The extent to which a change in price will affect the supply of a good or service depends on a number of factors. For economists, understanding the responsiveness of quantity supplied to a change in price for a good or service is very important. Price elasticity of supply (PES) is calculated by the formula shown in the box.

(See page 13 for calculating percentage changes.)

 Maths skills

$$PES = \frac{\text{percentage change in quantity supplied}}{\text{percentage change in price}}$$

or $\dfrac{\%\Delta Qs}{\%\Delta P}$

(See page 48 for an example of a PES calculation question. The answer is on page 215.)

Numerical values of elasticities of supply

Remember, negative values are ignored when interpreting price elasticity, for example: -0.8 is read as 0.8 and is inelastic'.

Numerical value:
0–1
PES range:
Inelastic
Sensitivity:
There is a less than proportionate response in quantity supplied to a change in price, e.g. price falls by 10% leading to supply falling by 6%
($\frac{6}{10}$ = 0.6)

Numerical value:
1–∞
PES range:
Elastic
Sensitivity:
There is a more than proportionate response in quantity supplied to a change in price e.g. a price rise of 3% leads to supply increasing by 9%
($\frac{9}{3}$ = 3)

0   1   ∞

Numerical value:
0
PES range:
Perfectly inelastic
Sensitivity:
There is no response in quantity supplied to a change in price.

Numerical value:
1
PES range:
Unitary
Sensitivity:
The percentage change in quantity supplied equals the percentage change in price, e.g. 5% fall in price leads to a 5% fall in quantity supplied
($\frac{5}{5}$ = 1)

Numerical value:
∞
PES range:
Perfectly elastic
Sensitivity:
If producers are prepared to supply any amount at a given price

Now try this

1 What is the formula for calculating price elasticity of supply?

2 What is represented by a PES value of 1.2?

Determinants of elasticity of supply

There are several factors that will determine the PES for a good or service. The gradient of the supply curve is influenced by its elasticity. In microeconomics, economists refer to time as the **short run** and the **long run**.

Gradient of supply

As with demand, the gradient of the supply curve represents its elasticity. In diagram 1, a percentage change in price will have a smaller percentage change in quantity supplied. The opposite is true in diagram 2.

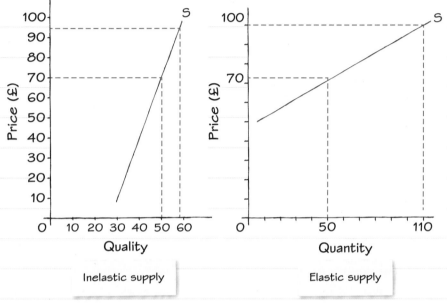

Inelastic supply

Elastic supply

Determinants of elasticity of supply

1 **Nature of the good.** For example, perishable goods such as fresh fruit and flowers tend to have inelastic supply as they cannot be stored for very long.

2 **Capacity.** In the short term, it may be difficult for a producer to increase supply in the face of rising prices. For example, their warehouse may be full or their workforce working to capacity.

3 **Stockpiling.** Some goods can easily be stockpiled and then released when prices rise. However, some products that are perishable or that go out of fashion quickly are less suitable for stockpiling.

The short run and the long run

A key factor in the elasticity of supply (and elasticity of demand) is **time**. In microeconomics, this is referred to as the short run and the long run. The **short run** is defined as a period where at least one factor of production is **fixed** (labour, capital, availability of resources). In the short run, the supply of most goods is inelastic because suppliers cannot adapt quickly to a change in price. Theoretically, in the **long run**, all factors of production are variable and can be **changed** – suppliers can adapt.

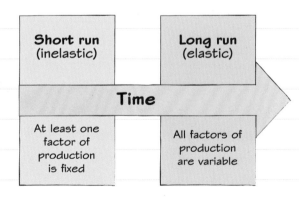

Now try this

1 How can the production capacity of producers influence the price elasticity of supply?

2 What is meant by the long run?

Price determination

The **market price** refers to the price agreed for the sale of goods and services between buyers and sellers. The market price may not always be the **equilibrium price**.

Equilibrium price

The equilibrium price, also known as the **market clearing price**, is the price at which supply meets demand. This means that all of the products supplied to the market are bought and no buyers are left disappointed in their desire to buy those products. The equilibrium price can be demonstrated on a supply and demand diagram as the point at which the demand curve and the supply curve intersect (see below).

Equilibrium

1 At a price of £6, £6 million units will be supplied and bought. £6 is the equilibrium price

2 At a price of £2, consumers will demand 12 million units. This is because the price is low and more consumers are willing and able to buy. However, at £2 profits will be small and few suppliers will be willing to supply at this price. Only £2 million units will be supplied. Excess demand is 10 million units.

3 At a price of £8, more firms will be attracted to supply as profits will be high. However, fewer consumers will be willing to pay this price and only 3 million units will be sold. Excess supply is 5 million units.

Excess demand and excess supply

The market price is not always at equilibrium and the quantity demanded does not always equal the quantity supplied.

- Where the quantity demanded is greater than supply, there is excess demand in the market.
- Where the quantity supplied is greater than the quantity demanded, there is excess supply.

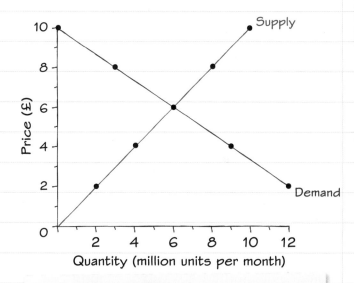

In both **2** and **3**, the price will either rise or fall in order for the market to clear.

 Real world ## Market clearing price

During the last few hours of the Chelsea Flower Show, prices of plants, flowers and garden accessories fall sharply to ensure sellers are not left with excess stock that they have to take away.

Now try this

1 Draw and label a simple demand and supply diagram.

2 What is meant by the market clearing price?

3 What is excess supply?

Changes in supply and demand

Where demand and supply intersect, equilibrium is achieved at the market clearing price. If the price is above the equilibrium point, supply is greater than demand and there is excess supply. If the price is below the equilibrium price, demand is greater than supply, causing excess demand. A shift in either demand or supply can increase or eliminate excess demand or excess supply.

Eliminating excess demand and excess supply

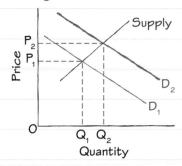

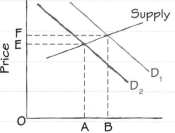

1 A shift in demand from D_1 to D_2 may come from an increase in average incomes. Consumers are willing and able to purchase more at any given price point. The equilibrium market price will rise from P_1 to P_2 and the quantity supplied from Q_1 to Q_2. For example, a national salary increase of 2% for all public sector workers, such as teachers and nurses, may have the impact of shifting demand to the right in demand for camping equipment.

2 A shift to the left in demand from D_1 to D_2 has been caused by a rise in the price of a complementary good. There is now excess supply in the market. Prices will eventually fall (a contraction in supply) from price F to E in order for the market to clear. For example, a sharp rise in the price of ink (ink cartridges) would shift demand for desktop printers to the left.

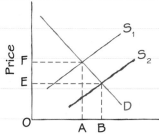

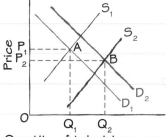

3 An increase in supply, represented by a shift from S_1 to S_2, comes from a fall in the price of a key commodity used to produce the good. At any given price suppliers are willing to supply more. At price F there is excess supply in the market. Prices will eventually fall to E in order for the market to clear. There will be an expansion along the demand curve. For example, a fall in the price of mango wood increases the supply of mango wood furniture, shifting the supply curve to the right.

4 The introduction of more efficient technology leads to an increase in supply from S_1 to S_2. There is also an increase in demand from D_1 to D_2 due to the product becoming more popular on the back of a successful advertising campaign. There is a fall in price from P_1 to P_2. An increase in both supply and demand could lead to a fall in price, an increase in price or no change at all. For example, LED lighting technology has lowered the costs of lighting products such as camping lanterns and made them more efficient.

Now try this

1 What effect would a shift to the right in the demand curve have on supply?

2 What effect would a shift to the left in the supply curve have on demand?

3 In theory, why should the market price always achieve equilibrium?

The price mechanism

The price mechanism of a market exists to allocate resources between conflicting uses. Price changes send important signals and give incentive for economic agents, such as consumers and firms, to act. The price mechanism is the reason why markets will adjust to an equilibrium price through the functions of rationing, signalling and incentives.

Rationing

The rationing function occurs when there is a shortage of a product. Prices will rise and deter some consumers from buying the product. For example, land available for developing houses that overlooks the sea is very desirable but not plentiful. The rise in the price of coastal land has a rationing effect as only wealthy people who are able and willing to pay the high price can afford to buy the land or the properties built on it. The price strips out those consumers who are unable to afford the higher price.

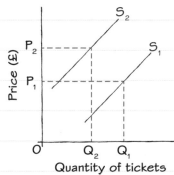

The diagram shows an inward shift in supply for popular gig tickets. The resulting increase in prices from P_1 to P_2 rations the tickets so the quantity demanded falls.

Signalling

Prices rise and fall to:

- demonstrate where resources are required
- reflect **scarcity** and **surpluses**.

A rise in price may indicate that demand is rising. This will signal to producers that they need to expand production. Similarly, a fall in prices may indicate that there is a surplus in the market, signalling to producers that they need to cut back production.

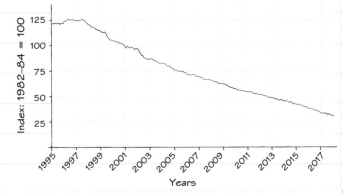

Toy prices in the US have been falling since the late 1990s. The price fall is a signal to manufacturers to allocate resources elsewhere as toy production may no longer be profitable.

Incentives

A change in price is an incentive for both producers and consumers. Higher prices allow firms to produce more goods/services and encourage increased production. As prices fall, the incentive for consumers is the value for money they may gain from buying a good or service at a price lower than what they are usually willing to pay or are unlikely to pay at a future time.

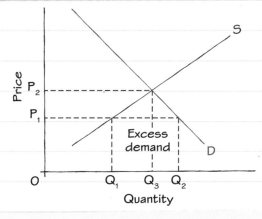

Where there is excess demand, a rise in price creates an incentive for suppliers to produce more and has a rationing effect on demand. The market always tends towards equilibrium (Q_3).

Now try this

1 How does the price mechanism ration a scarce resource?

2 How does the price mechanism create an incentive for suppliers?

Price mechanism in real markets

There are a number of key local, national and international markets that have some unique characteristics that you need to be familiar with.

Agricultural market

The agricultural market consists of a number of markets, such as a range of crops. Key features of the agricultural market are:

- agricultural products such as wheat are a commodity
- supply of agricultural products is heavily affected by the weather, therefore supply is very unpredictable
- the agricultural market is linked to seasonal unemployment – workers are only required when crops are harvested
- the long run price of agricultural products is falling due to advances in technology
- buffer stocks are used to affect the price of agricultural products. (See page 181 for a more detailed explanation of buffer stock schemes.)

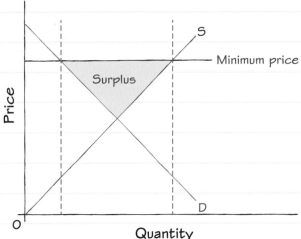

The government may use a buffer stock scheme to buy up excess supply in order to keep prices high and protect producers. It may then release buffer stocks onto the market when supply falls.

Oil market

Oil is a commodity and one of the most important resources in the world because it is used in the production of many goods and transportation.

- Demand for oil is closely linked to the business cycle and the consumption of goods.
- Speculators can affect the demand for oil when hoping to make a profit from a rise in price.
- Supply side shocks, such as war in oil producing countries, can significantly affect the price of oil.
- The long run supply of oil is affected by the world oil reserves and the cost of extracting oil. For example, some oil reserves are more difficult to reach.

The Organization of Petroleum Exporting Countries (OPEC)

OPEC members include several of the oil exporting nations such as Saudi Arabia, Iran and Libya. They have a significant influence on oil prices. OPEC nations may work closely to increase production and therefore lower the price of oil.

Housing market

The housing market has a significant impact on the whole UK economy.

- Houses are seen as an investment. The appreciation of house prices creates wealth and can boost consumer confidence, leading to greater consumption.
- A rise in demand for houses will also create demand in complementary goods such as furniture and home improvements.

- Supply of new houses is affected by the price of labour, building materials, and legal and planning costs.
- There are no close substitutes for housing. The price elasticity of demand is inelastic.
- There is a shortage of affordable housing in the UK.
- A fall in house prices can result in negative equity. This is where the value of a house is lower than the value of the mortgage being paid by the owner. This is bad for home owners.

Now try this

1 Identify one factor that may influence the supply of oil.
2 Identify one factor that may affect the demand for housing.

Consumer and producer surplus

In economic terms, a surplus refers to the benefits (also known as welfare or utility) that either a consumer or a producer receives from purchasing or selling goods and services. A rise in supply or demand will lead to a consumer or a producer surplus.

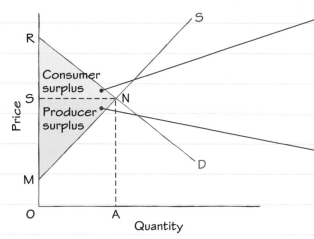

Consumer surplus is the difference between the total amount that consumers are willing to pay for a good or service and the total amount they actually pay (JGH on the diagram) – the area under the demand curve and above the market clearing price.

Producer surplus is the difference between the price a producer receives for a good or service and the minimum amount the producer is willing to accept for that good or service (FGJ on the diagram) – the area above the supply curve and below the market clearing price.

Rise in demand

A rise in demand (D_1 to D_2) increases consumer surplus (SNR to WTV) and producer surplus (MNS to MTW).

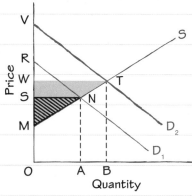

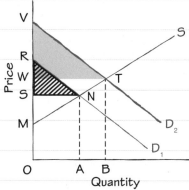

The greater the consumer surplus, the greater the utility for consumers.

Rise in supply

A rise in supply (S_1 to S_2) increases consumer surplus (RTV to WNV) and producer surplus (STR to MNW).

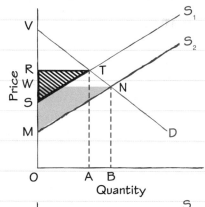

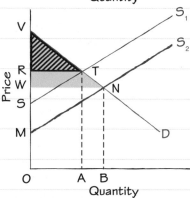

The greater the producer surplus, the greater the potential for producers to increase their profitability (as the difference between cost per unit and price increases).

Now try this

1 What will happen to consumer surplus as a result of the demand curve shifting to the left?

2 What will happen to producer surplus as a result of the supply curve shifting to the right?

Indirect taxes

An indirect tax is a tax on **expenditure**. There are two types – *ad valorem* and *specific*. Indirect taxes have impacts on producers and consumers.

Ad valorem tax and specific tax

- An *ad valorem* **tax** increases in proportion to the value of the tax. For example, VAT – 20% VAT is paid on most goods and services in the UK.

- A **specific** or **unit tax** does not change with the value of the goods, but instead with the amount or volume. For example, excise duties – such as 41.5p per pint of beer.

Imposing an indirect tax

The imposition or increase in the rate of an indirect tax will have the effect of shifting the supply curve upwards and to the left. The imposition of a tax refers to the **cost** of a tax.

Impact of indirect taxes

- **Consumers:** as an indirect tax raises the price of goods and services, consumers will pay a proportion of the higher price – the tax burden. The proportion depends on the elasticities of demand. An indirect tax may have a regressive effect on lower income groups.

- **Governments:** impose indirect taxes to raise income, for example for investment in an industry, social services or to cover negative externalities caused by an industry or good, such as lung disease through smoking cigarettes. In the unit tax example above:
  £1 unit tax × 40 million units = £40 million tax revenue

- **Producers:** As an indirect tax rises, so will the cost of production for producers, and supply will shift to the left. Producers will try to pass on the incidence of the tax but are likely to pay a proportion, which will depend on the elasticities of demand. An indirect tax could lead to a loss of jobs and lower competitiveness of some firms.

(To revise the effects of elasticities on taxes, see page 27.)

Incidence of tax

Price theory can be used to analyse the incidence of tax. This involves measuring the burden of the tax imposed by a government on taxpayers – consumers and producers.

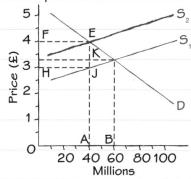

The diagram represents the incidence of a specific tax of £1. The equilibrium price rises from £3.30 to £4 and demand falls to 40 million units. Consumers pay the incidence of 70p per unit (GF). Producers will pay the incidence of 30p per unit (HG).

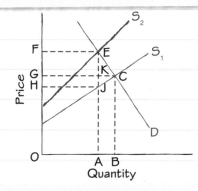

The incidence of an *ad valorem* tax. The same principle of rising prices applies to an *ad valorem* tax; however, the value of the tax will increase as a percentage of the price rise.

🖩 Maths skills   Useful formulae

Value of tax (at any given quantity) = difference between the old and new supply curves

Incidence on consumers = difference between the old and new equilibrium prices

Incidence on producers = value of tax – incidence on consumers

Now try this

1 What is an *ad valorem* tax?

2 What is the incidence of a tax?

The impact of subsidies

A subsidy is a grant given by the government to encourage the production or consumption of a particular good or service. Subsidies have an effect on consumers, producers and the government.

Subsidies

A subsidy on a good will lead to an increase in supply – a shift downwards and to the right. At any given quantity supplied, the price will be lower because the price charged by suppliers will be higher than the price paid by consumers. As with an indirect tax, not all of the subsidy will be passed on to the consumer.

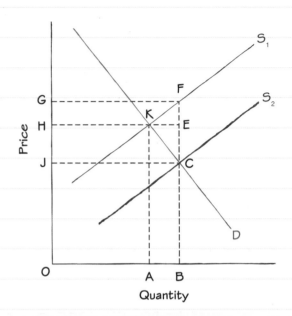

 Apprenticeship Schemes

An Apprenticeship Scheme is an example of an **input** subsidy used to reduce the cost of the inputs used in production – the cost of labour.

The diagram represents the introduction of a subsidy. The equilibrium price falls from OH to OC and quantity demanded rises from OA to OB. Total subsidy received by consumers is JCEH, whilst that received by producers is HEFG. The total cost of the subsidy given by the government is JCFG.

Impact of subsidies on consumers, producers and government

(To revise the effects of elasticities on subsidies, see page 27.)

The impact of a subsidy

Consumers

The introduction of a subsidy will have the effect of lowering the price consumers pay for goods and services, therefore increasing the utility of each unit consumed. The proportion of the subsidy that consumers receive (through lower prices) depends on the elasticity of demand.

Government

A subsidy is a cost to the government. However, the benefit will be the increased consumption of a desirable good or service and greater welfare to society, for example more people being able to afford homes. In the example above quantity demanded increased from A to B. A subsidy may also improve the competitiveness of an industry and protect jobs.

Producers

The introduction of a subsidy will lower the cost of production for producers and supply will shift downwards and to the right. Producers will try to retain the subsidy in order to maximise profitability. The proportion of the subsidy retained by producers depends on the elasticity of demand. Subsidies help firms increase output, increase profitability and grow.

Now try this

1 What is a subsidy?

2 Why might a government offer a subsidy to the fishing industry?

3 What impact will a subsidy have on supply?

The effect of elasticities

The elasticity of both demand and supply for a given good will determine the extent to which the tax incidence or benefit of a subsidy falls on consumers rather than producers.

The impact of price elasticity of demand (PED)

The diagrams below represent the incidence of the same tax on two different goods. Good A has a co-efficient of price elasticity of demand >1 (elastic). In this case, the majority of the incidence of the tax is paid (absorbed) by the producer. Good B has a co-efficient of price elasticity of demand <1 (inelastic). In this case, the majority of the incidence of tax is paid (absorbed) by the consumer.

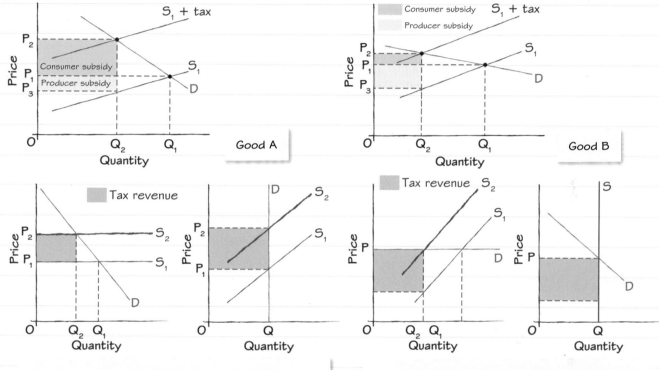

Consumers will pay the full incidence of a tax if supply is perfectly elastic or demand is perfectly inelastic.

Producers will pay the full incidence of tax if supply is perfectly inelastic or demand is perfectly elastic.

Summary of impact of elasticity

As with a tax, the same principles of elasticity applies to subsidies.

	Tax		Subsidy	
	Demand	Supply	Demand	Supply
Inelastic	Most paid by consumers	Most paid by producers	Most benefit passed on to consumers (fall in price)	Little benefit passed on to consumers (little price change)
Elastic	Most paid by producers	Most paid by consumers	Little benefit passed on to consumers (little price change)	Most benefit passed on to consumers (fall in price)
Perfectly elastic	Wholly paid by producers	Wholly paid by consumers	No benefit passed on to consumers	Whole benefit passed on to consumers (fall in price)
Perfectly inelastic	Wholly paid by consumers	Wholly paid by producers	Whole benefit passed on to consumers (fall in price)	No benefit passed on to consumers

Now try this

In what circumstance might the majority of a tax be paid for by a producer?

Alternative views of consumer behaviour

Neo-classical economics assumes that consumers are rational decision-makers. However, some economists would argue that economic agents, such as consumers, do not always act rationally with the intention of maximising utility and welfare.

 Other people's behaviour. When making decisions, individuals are often influenced by others through social norms in different contexts. These social behaviours sometimes skew rational decision making. This will occur when consumers make decisions based on peer pressure or to fit in with a social group, even if the choice (the good or service they consume) does not give them the greatest satisfaction or benefits. For example:

> Going to a movie not of your choice with friends so as not to 'miss out'.

Consumer behaviour

 Habitual behaviour. Habits act as a short cut to decision making. This also includes generalisations and making predictions based on past experiences. Sometimes habits will override the rational decision-making process. Examples include:

- Choosing a product based on past experience of a brand without considering value for money.
- Shopping in the same places due to familiarity.
- Addiction to goods and services that will not maximise benefits, e.g. gambling and alcohol.
- Choosing goods and services based on image alone.

 Consumer weakness at computation. Some individuals are unable to process all the necessary information to enable them to make the decision that will lead to the greatest utility. Examples include:

- Unwilling to find out the price of an alternative good or service.
- False information provided by firms.
- Inability to calculate the value/price per unit.
- Lack of understanding of the product (not actually knowing the features or what they need).

Now try this

1 Why might a consumer purchase a product from a particular supplier even though they know they can buy it cheaper elsewhere?

2 How can social norms influence rational decision making?

Market failure

Markets sometimes do not work as effectively as they appear to do in economic theory. Markets can – and do – fail. Market failure occurs when the allocation of goods and services is not efficient. The price mechanism sometimes fails to allocate scarce resource efficiently. There are different types of market failure.

Reasons for market failure

👎 **Externalities.** Profits and prices often do not represent the true price (cost) of economic activities. There are often **costs and benefits** that affect the wider society. These costs and benefits are known as externalities and they should be accounted for in economic transactions. (You can revise externalities in more detail in on page 30.)

👎 **Under-provision of public goods.** Markets sometimes fail to provide certain goods. One example is public goods. A public good is a good or service provided without profit to all members of society. Examples include defence, policing and street lighting. Public goods may be underprovided by a free market because there is no incentive to pay for them. (You can revise public goods in more detail on page 33.)

👎 **Information gaps.** These occur where a buyer does not have all of the necessary information to make an informed (and rational) decision. When buying milk, most people have all the information they need: they know which variety best suits their needs and how much they should expect to pay. When buying unfamiliar goods or those purchased infrequently, all the information needed to make an informed decision is not available – lack of information may lead to a decision that does not **maximise utility**. (You can revise information gaps in more detail on page 34.)

Misallocation of resources

When markets fail there is a **misallocation of resources** and the market may under-supply or over-supply a good or service. Here there may be excess supply or excess demand.

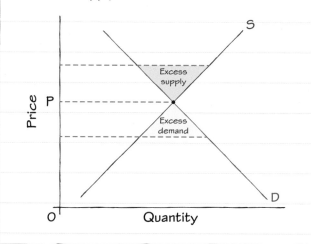

🌐 Real world Street lighting as a public good

The household next to the streetlight pays for access to the street light. However, the household on the other side of the road chooses not to pay their council tax. The other household still benefits from the light, despite not paying (although the council will take legal action). Markets work best when the price reflects the utility received by the consumer.

Now try this

1 Why are externalities an example of market failure?

2 Give one example of an 'information gap'.

Externalities

Externalities are created when social costs and benefits differ from private costs and benefits. The greater the externality, the greater the likelihood of market failure. Externalities are also known as **spillover effects** because they have an impact on the wider society.

Types of externalities

Externalities can be both positive and negative. As the costs and benefits of free markets are not the same for individuals and the wider society, we need to distinguish between the private costs/benefits and the social costs/benefits.

Externalities

Negative (external costs)

Positive (external benefits)

Private costs – the costs to an individual economic agent

Social costs – the cost to individuals and society

Private benefits – the benefit to an individual economic agent

Social benefits – the benefit to individuals and society

Summary of terms

MSC = marginal social cost

MPC = marginal private cost

MSB = marginal social benefit

MPB = marginal private benefit

Social costs/benefits

Social costs and benefits are the sum of both private costs/benefits and the external costs/benefits.

Private cost + external cost = social cost   Private benefit + external benefit = social benefit

Production and consumption externalities

Externalities arise from the production of goods and services and the consumption of goods and services. These are referred to as **production externalities** and **consumption externalities**.

Negative production externalities	Negative consumption externalities
👎 Damage to the environment from production in factories, farming or construction	👎 Damage to the environment from consumption, such as fly-tipping and household waste
👎 Noise pollution from the airline industry	👎 Passive smoking
👎 Over-fishing of the seas	👎 Anti-social behaviour from a sporting event

Positive production externalities	Positive consumption externalities
👍 Redevelopment of an industrial site for retail	👍 'Flu vaccinations
👍 Subsidised construction of social housing a large local employer	👍 Children receiving a high-quality education

Marginal costs and benefits

The difference between social costs and social benefits changes at different levels of output. In the diagram OA, OB is the optimum output and price where private benefits meet private costs – **the market equilibrium**. At any point beyond OA, the greater cost of production would be greater than the extra benefit from consumption.

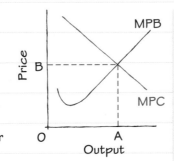

Maths skills MPB = MSB = demand

MPB curve slopes upward because marginal costs (every extra unit) increases as output rises

MPC curve slopes downward because the utility falls for each additional unit consumed

Now try this

What is the difference between social costs and external costs?

Externality diagrams

Social costs and benefits can be analysed using economic diagrams through marginal analysis. On this page, you will revise how to draw the diagrams that represent a welfare loss (negative externality) and a welfare gain (positive externality).

External costs of production

From the diagram below, you can see that the marginal social cost (MSC) curve lies above the marginal private cost (MPC) curve. The difference between the two curves is the additional external cost. In this example, the MSC pivots away from MPC because the external cost grows proportionately with output (imagine how the cost of pollution in the ocean grows the more there is!).

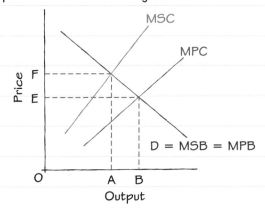

Identifying welfare gains

Welfare gains (see right) occur where the consumption of a good or service benefits the wider community, for example, healthcare and fitness services (gym memberships) and goods (low-fat food).

Over-production/over-consumption

Free markets will often over-produce/over-consume where there are negative externalities.

Solving negative externalities	Solving positive externalities
Where there are negative externalities, the social optimum level of output will be below the free market equilibrium (lower production/consumption at a higher price).	Where there are positive externalities, the social optimum level of output will be above the free market equilibrium (higher production/consumption at a higher price).

Identifying welfare loss

Welfare loss is where the consumption of a good or service creates a negative externality for the wider community.

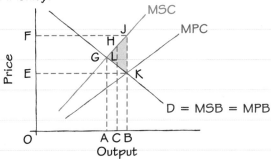

At OB, the market is not taking into account the additional external cost and the market will fail. For this to happen, consumption must fall to OA and the price rise from OE to OG – the **social optimum level of output**. GJK represents the **welfare loss area** – the allocative inefficiency or external cost of consumption between A and B.

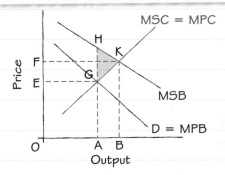

As with MSC, the MSB curve sits above the MPB because MPB does not take into account the external benefits. At output OA, MPC equals MPB. However, GJK of social welfare could be achieved if production was to increase to OB where MSC = MSB (MPC = MPB).

Equilibrium point and socially optimal point

The **equilibrium point** may be different to the **socially optimal point**.

Equilibrium occurs when MPC = MPB

The socially optimal level of output is where MSC = MSB

Now try this

1 What is the socially optimal level of output?

2 What is the welfare loss area?

Impact of externalities and government intervention

Externalities can have both positive and negative effects on economic agents. Where governments intervene to correct market failure, this will impact on consumers and producers.

Impact of externalities on economic agents

Benefits

👍 Sustainable production – 'green' business and recycling

👍 Attractive and desirable places to live – architecture and art

👍 Improved health of the nation

👍 A happy society – positive and confident consumers

External costs and benefits

Costs

👎 Damage to the natural environment – global warming and resource depletion

👎 Damage to the health of the nation – consumption of de-merit goods and addiction

👎 Social problems – antisocial behaviour, loss of community and civic duty and local culture

👎 Closure of small businesses – loss of jobs

An art installation may provide enjoyment for the local community.

International competition may lead to the closure of small local businesses.

Impact of government intervention on economic agents

1 **Subsidies** – reduce cost of production to incentivise certain types of goods that may benefit society or protect an industry. A proportion of the subsidy is usually passed on to the consumer.

Forms of government intervention in markets

2 **Taxation** – (indirect) to disincentivise production and consumption of certain goods, such as those that produce negative externalities, and to cover the external costs of consumption.

3 **Regulating markets** – adopting legislation to minimise misallocation of resources and prevent market failure.

(For more on government intervention to correct market failure, see pages 35–37.)

Now try this

1 How might negative externalities lead to social problems?

2 Why might a government increase regulation of a market?

Public goods

Unlike private goods, public goods are provided without profit to all citizens in a society. Everyone has the right to benefit from public goods at no financial cost to themselves. Because of the nature of public goods, they may be underprovided which gives rise to the free rider problem.

Private goods

Most goods are private goods, such as anything you might buy from a shop. Private goods have specific characteristics that mean the market function can work.

 Rivalrous – the consumption of the good by one person results in the good not being available for consumption by another.

 Excludable – once provided it is possible to prevent others from using it.

A postage stamp bought from the Post Office is a private good because it can only be used once by one person. The Post Office is a public sector organisation.

Don't confuse!

Private goods are not the same thing as goods produced by the private sector.

Public goods

A public good is a commodity or service that is provided without profit to everyone in society. It is impossible to prevent people from receiving the benefits of the good once it has been provided. For this reason, the free market will often not provide these goods and governments have to intervene.

Public goods have the opposite characteristics to private goods.

 Non-rivalry – the consumption of the good by one person does not reduce the amount available for consumption by another person.

 Non-excludability – once provided, no person can be excluded from benefiting. Similarly, no person can opt out of receiving the good (non-rejectability).

Water sanitation

Public service broadcasting

Policing

Examples of public goods

Online knowledge

Flood defence systems

Street lighting

The free rider problem

Consumers may benefit from consuming public goods at no financial cost to themselves. As a result, public goods will be underprovided because only a few individuals, if any, would be willing to pay. This is because there is no incentive for people to pay for consumption due to non-rivalry and non-excludability. Economists call this the **free rider problem**.

Providing public goods

In most cases the market will not efficiently provide public goods and this leads to market failure. In examples such as local and national defence, it is better for the good to be provided by the state and paid for through taxation. However, there are some other ways the government can enforce payment of public goods. These include:

- toll roads
- subscriptions
- paying to use public toilets.

Now try this

1 What are the two characteristics of a public good?

2 Why are public goods underprovided by free markets?

Information gaps

Markets are most efficient when buyers and sellers have access to the same information. This is known as **symmetric information** and should lead to efficient allocation of resources in a market. In some markets, however, there will be an information gap which may lead to a misallocation of resources.

Asymmetric information

When buyers and sellers are unable to find the necessary information to maximise their welfare there is an **information gap**. Sometimes the buyer or seller will have more information than the other and this is a situation of **asymmetric information**. Here there is the opportunity for the buyer or seller to exploit the situation for their own benefit. Information gaps lead to buyers overestimating the benefits of a product and sellers overstating the benefits.

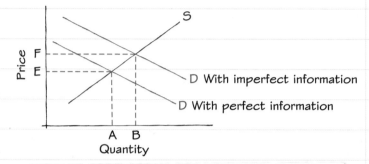

Here the buyer does not have all the information and so overestimates the benefits of the product. Demand is higher and the buyer pays a higher price.

Information required to make rational economic decisions

Where consumers and sellers have all the necessary information, they are able to make decisions to maximise their economic welfare. This leads to the efficient allocation of resources.

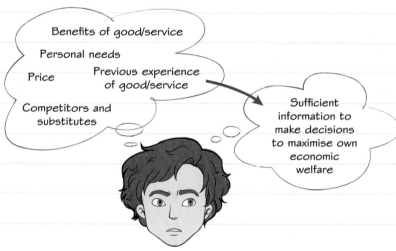

Markets with information gaps

The following markets are common examples where asymmetric information exists.

- **Second-hand car market** – it is difficult for customers to understand the real quality of a second-hand car and any potential defects.
- **Substance abuse** (drugs, tobacco and alcohol) – many consumers do not appreciate the long-term effect of consumption.
- **Healthcare** – a patient visiting the dentist is unlikely to know if they actually need treatment if they are not in pain, so generally trust the advice of their dentist.

The impact of advertising

Consumers use adverts to provide them with information they need to make informed purchases. However, although a lot of information is shared through advertising (such as prices, benefits and features), they are primarily designed to **persuade** consumers. Advertising has a natural bias that can lead to asymmetric information. This is why the advertising industry is regulated by the Advertising Standards Authority (ASA).

Now try this

1 How might a seller exploit a buyer where there is asymmetric information?

2 Why might some young people not invest in a pension scheme?

Government intervention 1

Governments can intervene in markets in a number of different ways to correct market failure. Total welfare will be increased where the cost of intervention is less than the benefits gained from intervention. One type of intervention involves imposing indirect taxes (*ad valorem* and specific).

(To revise indirect taxes, see page 25.)

Effects of government intervention

In both the examples below, an indirect tax can have the benefit of achieving two government objectives:

 Reduce output to minimise the impact of a negative externality.

 Raise revenue to support the market/industry or contribute towards other government policies.

Effects of imposing an *ad valorem* tax

The diagram shows the imposition of an *ad valorem* tax. At output OB, the tax per unit is EG.

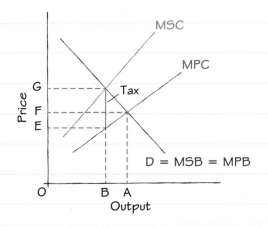

With an *ad valorem* tax, the value increases with the level of output as the tax is a percentage of the price. This might be appropriate where negative externalities exist as the impact of the externality (such as pollution) will also rise with output.

Effects of imposing a specific tax

In the example of imposing a specific tax below, the MSC and MPC lines are parallel. The rate of the marginal social cost does not increase with output. Here, a specific (unit) tax would be more appropriate than an *ad valorem* tax.

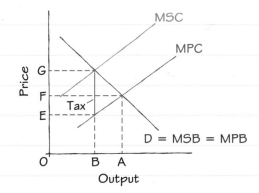

In this example, an increase in excise duties on tobacco of EG per unit would reduce consumption from A to B and maximise welfare.

Negatives of indirect taxation

Imposing an indirect tax does not always work.

👎 Setting the right level of taxation – a tax may be too large or too small. This may be due to information failure on the part of the government.

👎 Reduce market failure or raise revenue – a tax can achieve both objectives, but there may be conflict when the objective is not clear.

👎 An indirect tax may not reduce demand to the socially optimal level if PED is inelastic.

👎 Taxes are unpopular – governments have to think carefully about imposing taxes. Taxes are never welcomed by producers or consumers.

Now try this

1 Why might a government choose to introduce an indirect tax?

2 What is a limitation of increasing the rate of an indirect tax?

Government intervention 2

Governments can also intervene by introducing subsidies and setting controls on pricing.

Subsidies

The introduction of a subsidy can provide an incentive for producers to increase supply and, in many cases, reduce the price consumers pay. The result is an increase in consumption of certain goods.

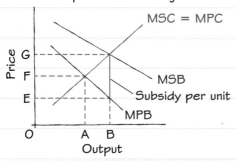

The introduction of a subsidy (EG) will increase consumption from OA to OB and maximise social welfare. MPB will equal MSB.

Pros and cons of subsidies

👍 Increase consumption of goods that benefit society

👍 Support local industries that are vulnerable to competition

👎 Government policy objectives – how should the subsidy be paid? Where should the money come from and what will be the trade-off (what else could the money be spent on)?

👎 Targeting the subsidy – what level of subsidy should be set to correct market failure? Will some groups benefit who may not necessarily need support from a subsidy?

Setting prices

One reason that markets fail is that the price mechanism rations goods that are socially desirable and provides incentives for goods that are not. One strategy that a government can use is to legislate to impose a **maximum price** or a **minimum price**.

Black markets

Where a government uses maximum and minimum prices there is the tendency for black markets to surface. For example, a minimum price imposed on alcohol could cause cheap 'bootleg' varieties to be produced and sold illegally.

Maximum prices

It is important that some goods are affordable to most consumers for the social welfare of the nation, for example, food and housing. In this case, a government might introduce a maximum price for a good.

In the diagram below, F is set as the maximum price for the good. This is below the market equilibrium price of G. Here demand (consumption) of the good will increase from B to C – more people can afford the good.

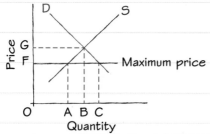

Using maximum prices can create excess demand. Above, at price F the market is willing to supply A but the quantity demanded is C (excess demand of AC).

Minimum prices

A government might set a minimum price for certain goods that have negative externalities in consumption, such as cigarettes and alcohol. Setting a minimum price above the market equilibrium will reduce consumption. It should also attempt to align MSB with MSC and reduce the external costs of consumption.

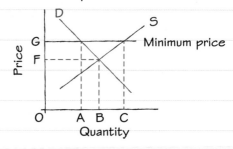

Using a minimum price can create excess supply. Above, at price G the market will supply C and buyers will demand A (excess supply of AC).

Now try this

How might the introduction of a subsidy correct market failure?

Government intervention 3

Apart from setting controls on pricing, there are other methods that governments can use to correct market failure. Examples include regulating a market or using direct provision of the good or service.

Regulation

Regulation is a common intervention used by governments to correct market failure. Regulation is often enforced through legislation. It is also relatively cheap, but enforcing regulation can be expensive if independent inspectors and regulators need to be set up. Governments have to be careful to ensure the level of regulation in a market is appropriate. The appropriate level of regulation will depend on the market. If regulation is too tight, suppliers will leave the market. Too loose and market failure will not be corrected.

Closing information gaps – forcing producers to disclose information such as ingredients on packaging.

Setting maximum pollution levels, such as setting the standards for emission levels.

Creating trade pollution permits – permits issued to firms up to the limit of the government's cap (target), such as the EU Emissions Trading Scheme covering a variety of industries that create carbon emissions.

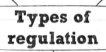

Types of regulation

Grading the standard of service providers, such as Ofsted grading education providers.

Setting quality standards for manufacturing – such as the British Standards Institution (BSI).

State provision of public goods

Where goods or services have the characteristic of non-rivalry and non-excludability (e.g. public goods, such as street lighting) then the state may decide to directly provide these goods and pay for them via taxes instead of leaving provision to markets. However, direct provision of goods and services can be inefficient.

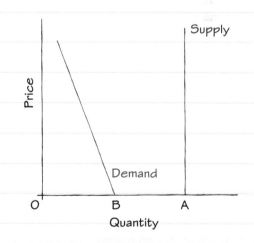

Here the government supplies A to the market, but maximum demand in the free market is B (price O). The resources could have been used more efficiently elsewhere.

Now try this

Why might a government choose to launch a campaign to inform the public about the health risks associated with excessive sugar consumption by children?

Government failure

Just as markets fail, so too can government intervention. Failure occurs where government intervention leads to a **net loss of economic welfare** rather than a gain. Sometimes government intervention can lead to unintended outcomes that were not anticipated.

The law of unintended consequences

The **law of unintended consequences** is that the actions of people – and especially of governments – always have effects that are unanticipated or **unintended**. For example, a government may respond to excessive rents by imposing a maximum price on rent for accommodation. But a maximum price which lowers the price could lead to less incentive for landlords to supply accommodation. Therefore, there is less supply and more people struggle to find accommodation.

Distortion of price signals

When governments distort prices through imposing maximum or minimum prices, taxation or subsidies, false price signals can lead to problems such as inflated prices, inefficient allocation of resources and uncompetitive industries being supported. For example, increasing the minimum wage could lead to firms making redundant some of the lowest-paid workers to cut back on labour costs.

Excessive administrative costs

Government intervention is not free. Indeed, one reason why governments support free markets is that they can run with little cost to the government. However, where intervention is necessary, governments will pay for administrative costs. One example is the cost of funding a regulatory body. For example, the administrative costs necessary to pay out social benefits to the nation is a huge cost, even before anyone receives any money.

Information gaps

Information gaps (see page 33) can lead to consumers making decisions that do not maximise their welfare or that give firms an advantage and opportunity to distort prices. An example is the risk and true cost to consumers of using payday loans with exorbitant interest rates.

Influences on government decision making

There are many other factors that influence government decision making beyond simply maximising social welfare. Even when government objectives are clear, it is not always obvious which policy is likely to lead to the greatest gains. The illustration (right) outlines factors that may influence political decisions leading to a policy or course of action.

Party political loyalties

Information gaps

Self-interest   Interests of constitutents

Short-sighted decision making   Policy decisions

Factors influencing decision making

Now try this

1 Why might a government not act in the best interests of society?

2 Give an example of an information gap that could lead to government failure.

Government failure in various markets

Below are several examples where government policy has failed to maximise welfare.

👎 **Common Agricultural Policy (CAP)** – with the aim of securing reasonable and stable incomes for farmers in the European Union, CAP introduced a number of measures to correct market failure, for example by guaranteeing minimum prices for agricultural products. This resulted in the oversupply of some agricultural goods. Governments then sold the excess supply outside the EU at low prices, impacting on the incomes of non-EU farmers.

👎 **Housing market** – introducing maximum prices on rental accommodation with the aim of ensuring affordable accommodation. However, this limits the profit incentive and landlords may decide to invest in other areas. The existence of maximum pricing may also lead to the development of a black market for accommodation. Examples include multiple families living in cramped housing.

> **Examples of government failure**

👎 **Public transport** – the government may choose to provide a subsidy for public transport such as local bus services to help reduce bus fares. However, many people see public transport as an inferior good, preferring the privacy, convenience and comfort of driving a car. These subsidies then become a misallocation of resources as the number of car journeys fails to fall and congestion and emissions issues remain.

👎 **Fishing industry** – fishing quotas were introduced in the EU to help ensure stocks of fish remained stable by preventing the overfishing of the oceans. However, fish stocks have continued to fall, suggesting that the quotas have been set too high. Furthermore, fishing boats often discard excess fish from their catch to ensure their quota is not breached. Dumping dead fish back into the ocean is wasteful and makes it difficult to monitor the quota.

Market vs government failure

There are numerous examples of free market failure and many examples where governments have failed to maximise economic welfare. Evidence would suggest that there needs to be a balance between the two extremes. For example, the government's Work Programme introduced in 2011 aimed to get long-term unemployed people into work through partnerships between a range of public and private sector organisations. The Department for Work and Pensions estimated that the scheme would cost £3–5 billion, but there was considerable debate over its effectiveness.

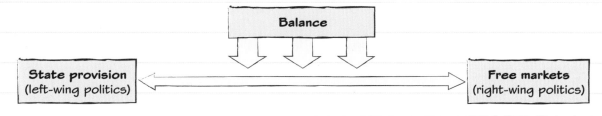

Balance

State provision (left-wing politics) ⟷ **Free markets** (right-wing politics)

There needs to be a balance between state provision and free markets in order to maximise welfare.

Now try this

1 Why might a quota imposed on a market not work?

2 Why might the introduction of a maximum price fail to ensure consumers can afford the related good or service?

Exam skills 1: Section A

Section A of **AS Paper 1** and **A level Paper 1** consists of multiple-choice and short-answer questions. There are five questions in Section A, often with stimulus material. These assess your knowledge and understanding of economic concepts and your ability to interpret economic data. You can use the data (such as tables, diagrams or graphs) to support your answers, where relevant. Below are some exam-style multiple-choice questions with exemplar answers.

AS Paper 1 covers **Theme 1**. A level Paper 1 covers **Theme 1 and Theme 3**. Make sure you know which paper you are taking, and the themes they cover.

Worked example

AS/AL

1 The diagram shows a production possibility frontier (PPF) for a firm producing electrical goods which is initially operating at point X.

Quantity of televisions (vertical axis)

Quantity of games consoles (horizontal axis)

The decision to increase the output of security cameras from 0M to 0N gives rise to an opportunity cost to the firm equivalent to:

A NZ ☐
B LK ☑
C KJ ☐
D 0M ☐

(1 mark)

Links To revise production possibility frontiers, see pages 4 and 5.

Read the question and the options carefully. In this PPF diagram, increasing one variable will cause a fall in the other. Look for how this is represented through the guide lines on the diagram. Look for any option that you can rule out easily and think about the remaining options.

If the firm increases production of security cameras from 0M to 0N, it will have to reduce the output of hard drives by LK. This is the opportunity cost, the difference between point X and point Y.

Worked example

AS/AL

2 Market failure arises when:

A the market is unable to provide essential goods for the population. ☑
B positive externalities exist in consumption. ☐
C firms make zero profits. ☐
D costs increase as firms expand production. ☐ **(1 mark)**

Links See page 29 for more on market failure.

Make sure you are familiar with the definitions of the main economic concepts.

Options B–D are not consequences of market failure. Firms may fail to make a profit in any market but this may lead to a more efficient allocation of resources. 'A' suggests that the market is under-providing a good. This is a feature of market failure. Remember that free markets will only produce goods and services where it is profitable to do so.

Exam skills 2: Section A

Below are some exam-style short-answer questions with exemplar answers. Use the data provided where relevant.

Worked example (AS)

3 Illustrate a contraction in supply using the diagram below.

(1 mark)

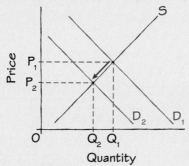

Links For the questions on this page revise page 17 and page 23

Illustrate

'Illustrate' questions require you to demonstrate a change in some economic variable using an appropriate diagram. No explanation is required, but you must ensure your diagrams are clear and fully labelled. These questions test AO1 knowledge.

Worked example (AS)

4 As a result of competition between large gym and fitness companies, the average price of a monthly gym membership in 2018 fell by 10%. Explain how the price of gym memberships acts as a signal to producers and consumers. **(3 marks)**

The price of gym memberships performs a signalling function in that they adjust to demonstrate where resources are required and where they are not. If the prices of gym membership are falling, perhaps because of an increase in competition, then this sends a signal to producers to cut supply – some gyms may no longer be profitable. Large fitness companies may also decide not to expand and open new branches. Alternatively, If the price of gym membership is rising, perhaps because of a supply shock (e.g. a significant increase in insurance for fitness companies), then this sends a signal to consumers to contract their demand.

The signalling mechanism of price has been fully explained and applied to the context of a fall in the price of gym membership.

Worked example (AL)

5 The diagram shows a production possibility frontier (PPF) for a country's production of cars and computers.

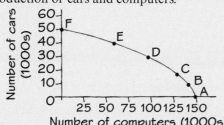

PPF curves can be used to illustrate opportunity cost. The shift from C to D represents an increase in output of cars. Production of 30 000 computers is forgone.

Calculate the opportunity cost of a nation moving production from point C to point D. Show your workings. **(2 marks)**

30 000 – 20 000 = 10 000 extra cars

130 000 – 100 000 = 30 000 less computers

Moving C to D means that a nation can produce 10 000 more cars. However, it has to give up 30 000 computers as a result and this is the opportunity cost.

 Maths skills To calculate the opportunity cost, find the difference between what is gained (extra cars) and what is forgone (fewer computers).

Exam Skills 3: Section B

Section B of **AS Paper 1** and **A level Paper 1** consists of a case study based on a real-world topic. Always read the data carefully before you begin answering the questions.

Extract A: Norway's sugar tax

In January 2018, the Norwegian government raised the tax on high-sugar food, such as chocolate, by up to 83%. On chocolate the tax was raised to around £1.50 per 450g.

However, it is argued that the higher prices could send even more Norwegians to Sweden to make their purchases, which already benefits from cross-border trade.

 Links   Revise the conditions of supply on page 17.

Worked example

 AS/AL

6 Assess the likely impact of a rise in sugar tax in Norway on the market for sugar-free soft drinks.   **(10 marks)**

A rise in the sugar tax will increase the price of sugary drinks in Norway. As a result, fewer consumers will want to purchase sugary drinks as they now take up a greater proportion of their disposable income. Some consumers will look to switch their spending to complementary goods such as sugar-free soft drinks. The resulting increase in demand will cause the price of sugar-free drinks to increase from P_1 to P_2 and the quantity traded will increase from Q_1 to Q_2. <u>As a consequence of producing and selling more sugar-free drinks</u>, manufacturers may be able to benefit more from economies of scale. They may be able to bulk buy ingredients and packaging which will lead to a reduction in average costs of production.

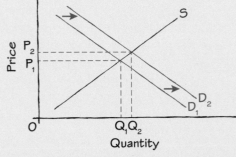

However, the increase in demand for sugar-free soft drinks depends on the strength of the relationship between these substitutes. If they are strong substitutes, with a CED more than 1, then an increase in the price of sugary drinks will lead to a more than proportionate increase in demand for sugar-free drinks. In reality it is likely that they may be weak substitutes as many soft drinks containing sugar have very strong brand images and many loyal customers.

Overall, the impact of the sugar tax is likely to have a minimal impact on the sugar-free soft drink sector. As the demand for sugary drinks is likely to be inelastic and sugar-free drinks are weak substitutes, there is unlikely to be a significant increase in demand for sugar-free drinks.

Assess

You need to apply theories and concepts in context by explaining the impact of economic concepts and theories on economic agents through a chain of reasoning. 'Assess' questions test all four assessment objectives.

 Look at both sides of the debate. Here, the student has discussed how the sugar tax may benefit other related markets.

 Using a diagram can help you to apply the concept and identify the impact on economic agents, e.g. the impact of a shift in demand.

 Explaining a limiting factor provides balance – the impact on sugar-free drinks may depend on the cross elasticity of demand.

 A clear evaluation. The arguments are justified by stating that demand for sugary drinks may be relatively price inelastic. A good evaluation may identify factors that determine the **extent** of the impact.

Exam skills 4: Section B

Below is an example of exam-style extract followed by an 'explain' question and an exemplar answer.

Extract B: UK tourist industry

Over the six years from 2012, UK tourism saw a healthy rise with an estimated record number of visits of almost 37.5m in 2018, a gradual increase year on year from 31m in 2012. Research suggests that for the majority of European holidaymakers, Brexit does not 5 affect their decision to travel to Britain and most see Britain as a friendly destination. The exchange rate also means that, for Europeans, it is now a good time to visit.

Nevertheless, the impact of Brexit remains uncertain. 10 It is not known how the transition period could impact on travel and regulations.

Highlight key figures and note whether they have increased or decreased.

Explain

You need to apply your knowledge to a particular context and make a point (or points) to demonstrate your knowledge.

Worked example   AS

7 Explain **two** likely impacts on hotels in the UK of increased regulation on the UK tourist industry brought about by Brexit (Extract B).   **(6 marks)**

Increased regulation on the UK tourism industry may lead to an increase in costs for businesses. For example, stricter immigration rules may make it harder to employ EU nationals in hotels. This may make it harder for hotels to fill vacancies so they may have to increase wages to attract more UK nationals to fill these vacancies. If they cannot pass these increased costs on to consumers, their profits will fall.

Any regulations which make it more difficult to travel to the UK, such as visa requirements or longer queues at airports, will make the UK a less attractive destination for foreign visitors. This will cause a fall in demand for UK tourist attractions and hotels and as a result they may have to lower prices.

Some 'explain' questions require you to develop two points of explanation. Make sure you highlight what is required in your answer by underlining key words in the question. If two impacts are required, 'two' will always be in bold.

Make reference to the extract to support your points. The student has applied their answer to the tourist industry by referencing 'immigration' and 'airports' in their explanation.

Exam skills 5: Section B

Below are examples of 'explain' and 'calculate' questions and exemplar answers.

Extract C: Chinese steel

In 2018, the USA announced that it will introduce 25% tariffs on imported steel and 10% tariffs on aluminium. The USA is the world's biggest steel importer, receiving shipments from over 85 countries. Historically, China has been accused of dumping cheap steel on global markets. China consumes 85% of the steel it produces domestically but has been reducing overcapacity in its steel sector with a reduction of 50 million tonnes in 2017. By comparison, China exported 1 million tonnes (2% of its total steel production) to the US in 2017. In fact, a number of other countries export more to the US than China does, including Canada and South Korea.

5

Worked example   AS

8 Explain why the plans to 'introduce 25% tariffs on imported steel' (Extract C, line 1) would reduce demand for Chinese steel in the USA. Use a supply and demand diagram in your answer.   **(5 marks)**

Some 'explain' questions require an appropriate diagram to be used in your answer.

A tariff is a tax placed by the government on imports. It has the effect of increasing the cost of importing steel, which reduces the supply of imported Chinese steel into the USA because domestically produced steel will be more competitive. This inward shift in the supply curve causes an increase in price from P to P_1 and as a result there is a contraction in demand which reduces the quantity traded from Q to Q_1.

The impact of the tariff is the fall from Q to Q_1. The student has also given a reason for the fall in supply by stating that domestically produced steel (steel made in the USA) will be more competitive – cheaper in comparison with the Chinese steel with a tax imposed.

Worked example   AL

9 China produced 831m tonnes of steel in 2017. Calculate the number of tonnes of steel China consumed domestically in 2017 and the percentage by which China reduced steel output in 2017. You are advised to show your working.   **(4 marks)**

Number of tonnes of steel consumed

85% of 831m tonnes =

831 × 0.85 = 706m tonnes consumed domestically

Reduction in steel

831m tonnes + 50m tonnes = 881m tonnes
(steel output in 2016)

50 ÷ 881 × 100 = 5.7

 Maths skills As 85% of China's steel is consumed domestically, the student needed to calculate 85% of 831m tonnes. A quick way to find a percentage of a value is to multiply the value by the percentage as a decimal. In this case 85% is 0.85.

 Maths skills Again, a percentage is required. This time the student should have calculated a percentage fall from 2016 to 2017.

Exam skills 6: Section B

Below is an example of an exam-style 'discuss' question and exemplar answer. The question is based on Extract C on page 44.

Worked example (AL)

> 10 With reference to Extract C, discuss the likely impact of China dumping cheap steel on the UK steel market. Include an appropriate diagram in your answer.   **(12 marks)**
>
> If China dumps cheap steel in the UK steel market, this will increase the supply of steel products. The resulting outward shift in the supply curve to S_2 will cause a fall in the price of steel (P_1 to P_2) and an increase in quantity traded (Q_1 to Q_2). This will have a negative impact on steel producers as it will reduce the price they are able to charge. It may mean that they are no longer able to sell steel at a price which generates a profit and as a result some businesses may become insolvent. This is particularly likely to be the case if Chinese steel is being dumped at below cost price, making it virtually impossible for UK firms to compete.
>
>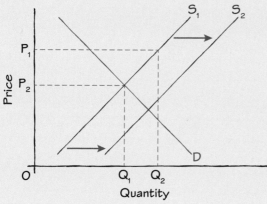
>
> UK firms may have to look at other ways in which they can cut costs to compete more effectively. They may look to cut back on unnecessary expenditure and limit cost increases such as wage increases for staff. However, this is unlikely to be effective given that China has significantly lower wage and energy costs than the UK so can produce their steel much more cheaply that the UK can.
>
> However, the impact on UK firms may depend on the type of steel China is dumping in the UK. If most Chinese steel is low quality and most producers of UK steel make high quality goods, then they will not be in direct competition so the impact on UK businesses may be minimal.
>
> Overall it is likely that the impact on the UK steel industry will be overwhelmingly negative. UK firms will find it difficult to compete with Chinese steel on cost alone. However, those firms which produce higher quality more specialised steel may be insulated from these cheaper imports to a degree.

 Links To revise price determination see page 20.

Discuss

'Discuss' questions may be worth between 12–15 marks and may ask you to include a diagram.

 A 'discuss' question requires you to carefully choose relevant economic concepts to provide a balanced argument, in this case price theory and factors determining the competitiveness of firms. You should also show you have evaluated the different points of view.

In your answer, you should refer to your diagram and analyse the impact (in this example, the impact of an outward shift in supply).

 A good response should offer various options/ solutions and identify any limiting factors, as here.

 Good evaluations may include 'it depends'. This allows you to include additional factors in your response that may influence the outcome. Here, the response identifies the quality of the steel as a determining factor.

Exam skills 7: Sections B and C

Section B of **AS Paper 1** and Section C of **A level Paper 1** contain a choice of two extended open-response questions – you must answer **one** question only. The skills required are the same at both AS and A level. Below is an example of a Section B **AS exam-style** 20-mark question which appears as the final part question in Section B and relates to the case study, and an exemplar answer.

You will find a practice Section C **A level** exam-style 25-mark open-response question on page 51.

Worked example

(AS)

11 Evaluate whether governments should assume that consumers are rational decision makers when making decisions about economic policy.

(20 marks)

Economic theory has generally assumed that all consumers are rational decision makers and make their choices based on a desire to maximise their utility. For example, when consumers make choices about how to spend their limited incomes they will choose combinations of goods and services which maximise their satisfaction from consumption. They do this by weighing up the costs and benefits of decisions and make decisions which maximise their net benefit.

Government policy decisions often assume that consumers will react rationally to any policy changes. For example, the government may decide to implement regulation on food labelling so businesses have to make the sugar and fat content clearer with a standard, easy to understand traffic light system adopted by all businesses. This would provide consumers with easy to understand information which would allow them to easily compare the relative merits of consuming similar products. Acting rationally would mean that consumers may now be less willing to consume products with very high levels of sugar and fat and may instead switch to foods lower in sugar and fat as this will have a positive impact on their health...

> Next you would need to show balance by discussing at least one reason why consumers do not always make rational decisions that maximise their utility, for example, time, consideration of short-term rather than long-term consequences and so on. Aim to show both cause and consequence.

...Overall, it is clear that governments have to make assumptions when making economic policy decisions. However, humans are complex beings and it is highly unlikely that individuals have the capacity to consistently make rational decisions. For government policy to be effective it must take into account that consumers do make irrational decisions and if governments can appreciate when this is most likely to happen and how it happens then policy is more likely to achieve its aims.

Evaluate

'Evaluate' questions require you to weigh up a scenario before offering some evaluation. They test all four assessment objectives. There are no right or wrong answers – it is up to you to present your arguments.

At AS, you may be asked to use an appropriate diagram in your answer. Think carefully about how you could support your response with clear diagrams.

The answer starts well with an explanation of the concept of 'rational decision makers'.

Use examples to illustrate the point you are making and help develop your answer further. Draw examples from your understanding of different markets and economies and economic policies that you have learnt about.

The response includes a clear evaluation. It is important to question the validity of the evidence and the validity of underlying assumptions. Remember that marks are awarded for the quality of your evaluation.

Exam-style practice: Section A

Section A of **AS Paper 1** and **A level Paper 1** consists of multiple-choice and short-answer questions. You can use the stimulus material (tables, diagrams, graphs etc) to support your answers, where relevant. Below are some exam-style multiple-choice and short-answer questions for you to practise. There are answers on page 215.

AS Paper 1 covers **Theme 1**. A level Paper 1 covers **Theme 1 and Theme 3**. Make sure you know which paper you are taking, and the themes they cover.

1 The Lerwick Port Authority has confirmed plans to construct a new fish market on the Shetland Islands to be built by 2020. The new fish market is budgeted to cost £7.6m.

AS/AL

A shift to the right in the supply curve represents an increase in supply at any given price level.

What impact will the new fish market have on supply and/or demand for the Shetland fishing market? **(1 mark)**

A A shift to the left in the supply curve. ☐

B A shift to the right in the supply curve. ☐

C A shift to the left in the demand curve. ☐

D A contraction along the demand curve. ☐

2 Long term under-investment in industries like the fishing industry in Shetland could contribute to negative economic growth. Illustrate negative economic growth using the diagram below. **(1 mark)**

AS

A PPF curve shows the possible production capacity of an economy comparing two types of good.

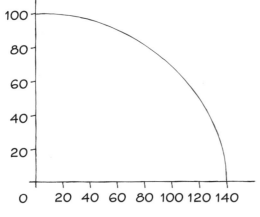

Always ensure any points or lines on diagrams are clearly labelled. Use a ruler.

3 The Scottish fishing industry has seen a period of robust growth in the last year with the stock of fish being caught rising by almost 8% in the first quarter of 2018. Concerns had been raised that fish stocks will need to be managed to prevent overfishing.

AS

Consider the different approaches a government can take to prevent market failure.

Explain one policy the government could use to prevent the negative externalities associated with overfishing in Scotland.

(3 marks)

Exam-style practice: Section A

4 The table below shows benefits and costs of a new airport.

Private benefits	£130 million	Private costs	£110 million
External benefits	£20 million	External costs	£30 million

From the table it can be concluded that:

A the social costs are £80 million. ☐

B the social costs are less than the private costs. ☐

C the social costs are less than the social benefits. ☐

D social benefits are £20 million. ☐   **(1 mark)**

> **Links** The question refers to positive and negative externalities. Remind yourself of externalities on page 30.

5 Figures for the three months to March 2018 showed the volume of landed white fish in Shetland was up 7.8%. Its value had also increased by 13% with the same period in 2017.

Explain the impact on the Scottish fishing industry of a rise in the value of white fish. **(3 marks)**

> Consider the impact on both supply and demand.

6 The supply and demand diagram below relates to the market for a merit good.

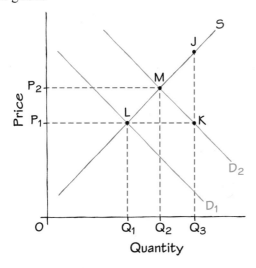

> A government can use maximum and minimum prices, taxation and subsidies to influence the supply and demand in a market.

The demand curve for the merit good shifts from D_1 to D_2, raising the market price from P_1 to P_2. To reduce the price back to P_1, the government could introduce a:

A minimum price of OP1 per unit. ☐

B subsidy of KM per unit. ☐

C subsidy of JK per unit. ☐

D subsidy of LM per unit. ☐   **(1 mark)**

> **Links** To revise price elasticity of supply see page 18.

7 The average price of 1kg of plaice (a popular fresh fish) has increased from £6 to £7.50 in the last six months. In the same period the Scottish fishing industry's supply of plaice has increased by 22%. Calculate the price elasticity of supply for plaice. **(4 marks)**

> **Maths skills** Start by writing out the formula for PES.
>
> $$\frac{\Delta Qs}{\Delta P}$$

Exam-style practice: Section B data

On this page, you will find exam-style extracts for Section B of **AS Paper 1** and **A level Paper 1**.

Before you practise answering the exam-style questions that follow on page 50, make sure you read this stimulus material carefully, highlighting any key terms and annotating useful points.

Transport

Extract A: Congestion in the capital

London's congestion charge was launched in 2003 to try to reduce congestion, improve bus services and make journey times more reliable for drivers and distributors. Reports by Transport for London (TfL) in 2006 showed that the charge had reduced traffic by 15% and congestion by 30%. Traffic volumes in the congestion zone are now nearly 25% lower than ten years ago. However, between 2015 and 2016 taxi and private hire vehicle journeys rose by almost 10% – and have increased by nearly 30% since 2000.

5

Source: Transport for London

Figure 1: Revenue breakdown of congestion charge in London – net income and costs

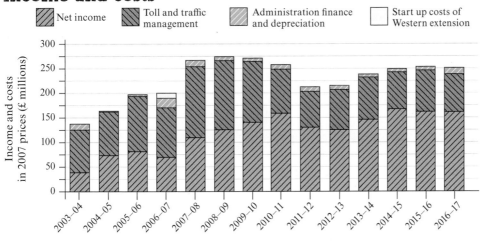

Source: City Metric

Extract B: On the buses

The percentage of all public transport journeys taken by bus has fallen from around 85% in the 1960s to 59% in 2017.
The decline has been influenced by the proportion of commuters travelling further to a place of work via train and by road congestion in busy urban areas. The consequence has been a cut in the number of bus routes in the UK and rising fares. The reduction in bus services has made it difficult for some rural communities to access jobs, public services and education.

Source: Transport for London

Extract C: Funding the railway

The government supports the rail industry through grants and subsidies to Network Rail and private train operators. In 2016–17 support totalled £4.1 billion. In real terms, this was up £32 million on the previous year and the highest it has been since 2008–09. Network Rail uses this money to maintain, renew and improve the network.

Rail ticket prices have continued to rise in recent years. The Rail Fares Index increased by an average of 121.3% between 1995 and 2017, with Long Distance fares (150.9%) increasing at a faster rate than the other sectors.

5

Source: Office of Rail and Road (ORR)

Exam-style practice: Section B

On this page are exam-style questions for Section B of **AS Paper 1** and **A level Paper 1**. Make sure you read the stimulus material on page 49 carefully. There are answers on page 215.

8 Explain how the introduction of a congestion charge in London can help reduce the dead welfare loss. Use an appropriate diagram in your answer. **(5 marks)**

(AS/AL)

Some 'explain' questions require the use of economic diagrams. Marks are awarded for application of the source data and accurate impact being identified on your diagram.

Your answer could also relate to pollution, infrastructure or the impact on drivers in London.

9 Assess the impact of falling income from the London Congestion Charge for the government. **(10 marks)**

(AS/AL)

An 'assess' question has 4 marks for evaluation. Here, this involves determining how significant the fall in government income from the congestion charge is.

10 With reference to Figure 1, calculate:

(a) the percentage change in government income between 2008–09 and 2016–17 **(2 marks)**

(b) the value of administration, finance and depreciation as a percentage of total costs and income in 2016–17. **(2 marks)**

(AS)

Maths skills (a) Requires you to calculate a percentage increase and (b) requires you to calculate a value as a percentage of a total.

11 With reference to Extracts A and B, examine **two** reasons why the demand for public transport on buses could be influenced by factors other than the price of a bus ticket. **(8 marks)**

(AL)

You could examine how public transport might be affected by cross-elasticities of demand, joint supply or substitute products. For more on how to answer 'examine' questions, look at page 99.

12 With reference to Extract C, discuss the likely impact of a rise in the subsidy paid to Network Rail and private train operators on the price of rail tickets. Use an appropriate diagram in your answer. **(12 marks)**

(AS/AL)

Use an appropriate diagram to illustrate the impact of a government subsidy on price. Use the extract to discuss other factors that may counteract any fall in price for consumers.

13 With reference to Extract A, discuss the impact on tourism in London of an increase of 9.8% in trips by taxi and private vehicle hire in the capital. **(15 marks)**

(AS/AL)

Consider factors that may limit the impact of the price rise. For example, what if the value of the pound fell? Or perhaps the introduction of new tourist attractions?

Exam-style practice: Section C

On this page, you will find an exam-style extended open-response question to practise for Section B of **AS Paper 1** and one for Section C of **A level Paper 1**. There are answers on pages 215–216.

14 Evaluate the likely microeconomic impact of a maximum **(AS)** price on rail tickets. **(20 marks)**

Intro and definitions	Start by defining the concepts in the question.
On the one hand...	Develop an analysis of the **first point of view**. This might include the positive impact of a maximum price. You may develop one or two relevant points. • Use developed **chains of reasoning** and apply your answer to the context. • Use a diagram if it helps explain your point – this could be a diagram to show the demand for rail tickets with a maximum price imposed. • Use real examples if you can. • Use evaluative statements.
On the other hand...	Develop an analysis of the **opposite point of view**. This might include a discussion of how a maximum price may have a **limited impact**. • Use developed **chains of reasoning** and apply your answer to the context. • Use real examples if you can. • Use a diagram if it helps explain your point. • Use evaluative statements.
Judgement	• Explicitly answer the question. • Justify your decision using evidence wherever possible and weigh up the importance of the points you made. • **Show balance** by showing an appreciation of other factors. 'Yes I agree... so long as...' • Consider the short-run and long-run consequences/issues.

Remember: in the AS paper the extended response question is based on the sources given in Section B.

Use the sample essay plan to draw up your own plan for answering questions 14 and 15.

15 Governments should always ensure there is state **(AL)** provision of healthcare for everyone.

To what extent do you agree with this statement? **(25 marks)**

Remember: the A level Section C questions stand alone and are **not connected** to the Section B extracts, but the same skills are used.

Economic growth

Economic growth is the long-term expansion of productive potential. In the short term, growth is measured by the annual percentage change in real national output. The standard measure of national output used to compare the economic performance of countries is **gross domestic product** (GDP). Another national income measure is **gross national income** (GNI).

GDP vs GDP per capita

- **GDP** is a measure of the total output for a country. It is the value of all newly produced final goods and services produced in an economy within a given time period. GDP (and its variations) are a key indicator of the standard of living in an economy.
- **GDP per capita** (per head or per person) is the total output divided by the estimated total population.

Currency used to measure GDP

GDP is usually measured in a common currency – normally the US dollar.

UK GDP

During the 2008 financial crisis that led to a world economic recession, UK real GDP fell between 2008 and 2010 to the national output that had been achieved in 2006. In took until 2013 for real GDP to reach the levels achieved before the world economic recession. The % growth rate of real GDP in the UK has averaged 0.4% over the past five years.

Gross national income

Not all income for the UK is earned within its geographical boundaries. A considerable proportion of the UK's income comes from overseas investments and remittances (transfer of money to a foreign country by a worker). Where the measure of GDP takes into account these additional incomes it is called **gross national income** (GNI). This includes interest from foreign investments, profits and dividends. It also includes transfers of money back to the UK from UK nationals working abroad.

Formula for GNI

GNI = GDP + net property income from abroad (NPIA)

Real GDP vs nominal GDP

- **Real GDP** measures the value of an economy's output in a particular year adjusted for changes in the price level from a base year.
- **Nominal GDP** is the measure of an economy's output produced in a year. It is expressed in the value of the prices charged for that year: Q × P where Q = output (volume) and P = value. Nominal GDP does not take into account price changes due to inflation. (See pages 55–57 for more on inflation.)

Volume = adding up the quantity of goods produced in one year.
Value = calculating the value (£billions) of all the goods and services produced in one year.

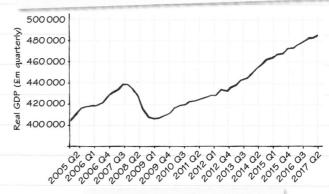

UK GDP over time, 2005–2017.

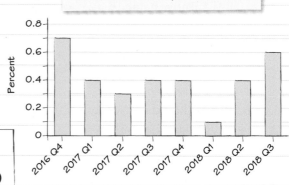

UK GDP growth rate, October 2016–September 2018.

Now try this

1 What is GDP per capita?

2 What is the difference between GDP and GNI?

Comparing economic growth

Comparing the economic performance of different countries can be difficult. One problem is market exchange rate fluctuations (the changing value of world currencies). **Purchasing power parity (PPP)** can be used to provide an accurate comparison.

Purchasing power parity

Purchasing power parity (PPP) allows comparison between different countries' currencies through a 'basket of goods' approach. According to this concept, two currencies are in equilibrium or at par when a basket of goods (taking into account the exchange rate) is priced the same in both countries. PPP is the exchange rate needed to buy the same 'basket of goods' in each country.

Why is PPP necessary?

1 Exchange rates can be very volatile and fluctuations may suggest that the standard of living has fallen when output may actually be rising.

2 Exchange rates are more relevant for some goods and not others. The price of internationally traded goods may relate to an exchange rate but domestically traded goods, such as haircuts and window cleaning, can fluctuate greatly across nations.

The Big Mac index

The Big Mac index is a light-hearted, but widely referenced, test of PPP between nations. It uses the price of a McDonald's Big Mac across nations to test exchange rates and measure the PPP between countries. This index replaces a basket of goods with the price of a McDonald's Big Mac in different countries.

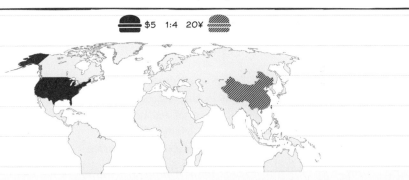

🍔 $5   1:4   20¥ 🍔

Big Mac exchange rate: USA–China. The US dollar is used as the base currency.

Comparing economic growth of the top world economies

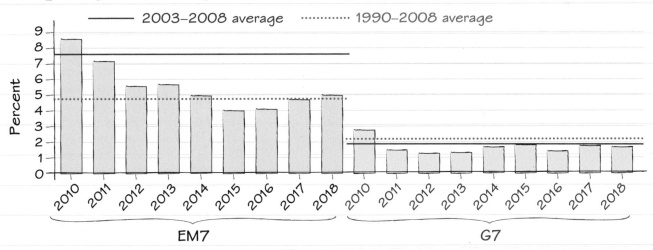

The graph compares the nominal GDP of the Emerging Market 7 (the EM7, seven developing economies with the highest growth rates) and the G7 (the seven countries with the most advanced economies). Growth rates in the world's leading emerging markets have doubled that of the G7.

Now try this

1 Regarding purchasing power parity (PPP), what is meant by the 'basket of goods'?

2 The UK is part of the G7. What does this indicate about the UK economy?

53

Limitations of measuring economic growth

GDP is the main basis for comparing economic growth and success across different countries. However, both GDP and PPP have their own limitations and there may be other ways of measuring economic success or the standard of living.

Limitations of GDP	Limitations of PPP
👎 Does not take into account the quality of goods, only their value.	👎 Does not take into account the relative quality of goods across nations.
👎 Does not take into account the 'underground economy' – transactions or goods and services in cash that are not registered.	👎 The decision about what should go into the 'basket of goods' is disputed.
👎 Non-market production – goods that are produced but not traded, e.g. home-grown food, are not recorded as contributing to GDP.	👎 Basket needs to be updated each year.
	👎 The quality of economic data and systems for collecting the data varies considerably across countries.

National happiness

Many people would argue that economic output and income are not the best indicators of economic success or the standard of living. Many people believe that well-being should be measured in terms of health, friends and family, and job satisfaction. The world's first happiness report was published in 2012. The annual World Happiness Report considers traditional evaluations of economic growth alongside subjective indicators.

Some of the indicators that are taken into account when calculating a nation's happiness

Real incomes and subjective happiness

At lower levels of income, increasing income is generally agreed to increase happiness. This is because rising incomes allow people to buy basic goods and services essential for life. At lower levels of income, traditional economic theory about the link between income and utility is strong.

However, some evidence suggests that at a certain level of income there is rapid diminishing marginal utility (see page 12). Rising real incomes have less of an effect on happiness (utility).

UK national well-being

In the World Happiness Report (2018), the UK is ranked 19th in the world in terms of its happiness ranking with a score of 6.8. The report ranks Finland (7.6) as the nation with the highest well-being. The report considers factors such as GDP per capita, social support, healthy life expectancy and freedom to make life choices.

Now try this

1 What are two limitations of comparing economic growth between nations?

2 Why is income not always a good indicator of economic well-being and utility?

Inflation and its measurement

Inflation is the general and sustained **rise** in the price level in an economy. Deflation is the opposite of inflation, the general and sustained **fall** in the price level in an economy. Disinflation refers to the slowing down of the rate of inflation. Inflation may be measured in different ways.

Inflation, deflation and disinflation

Inflation and deflation are measured as a percentage change in prices. Prices generally rise over time so deflation is less common and can have a more detrimental effect on an economy.

Inflation may slow down or speed up. The process of the rate of inflation slowing down is known as **disinflation**.

	Trend		
Inflation	2%	2%	3%
Deflation	2%	−0.5%	−2%
Disinflation	3%	2%	1%

Don't confuse

Disinflation is not the same as prices falling.

Measuring inflation – CPI

The consumer price index (CPI) measures changes in the price level of a basket of consumer goods and services. The goods and services within the CPI basket are weighted based on the proportion of a household's income that is spent on each category. Categories included are food and beverages, clothing and footwear, transport, furniture and household goods.

Measuring inflation – RPI

As with CPI, the retail price index (RPI) measures the change in average prices based on a theoretical basket of goods. However, this basket is different to CPI in a number of ways:

1 RPI takes into account council tax.

2 RPI takes into account mortgage payments.

RPI uses a different formula and weightings to calculate the average price for a basket of goods.

Indices

Inflation can be expressed as a percentage or indices. An index number is an economic data figure that reflects prices compared with a standard or base value. The base year is set at 100. Therefore, an index of 102 will show a 2% increase in price from the base year.

Calculating a price index is complicated as it uses the principle of a theoretical basket of goods. The accuracy of measuring inflation using the basket of goods is problematic. For example, the contents of the basket change from year to year and different households purchase different proportions of the goods in the basket, so households will experience different rates of inflation.

Limitations of CPI

CPI is the main measure of inflation and is used as the government's target for inflation.

👎 As a measure of inflation, CPI does not take into account all production and consumption in the economy.

👎 CPI does not take into account substitutes – consumers will often switch to alternative products as prices rise.

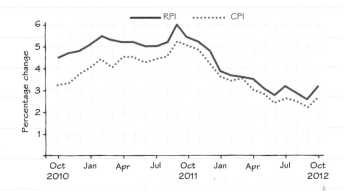

RPI calculates a higher rate of inflation than CPI.

Now try this

1 What is disinflation?

2 What is an index number?

3 What is one difference between CPI and RPI?

Causes of inflation

There are three main causes of inflation: cost-push, demand-pull and growth of the money supply.

Cost-push inflation

Cost-push inflation occurs because of rising costs (changes in the supply side of the economy).

The key factors leading to rising costs are:

1 **Wages** – an increase in wages is the most significant factor leading to an increase in costs of production.

2 **Imports** – including the rising price of commodities brought into the UK.

3 **Profits** – firms may raise prices to boost profits. The more price inelastic demand is, the more feasible it is for firms to raise prices.

4 **Taxes and subsidies** – government policy can influence prices.

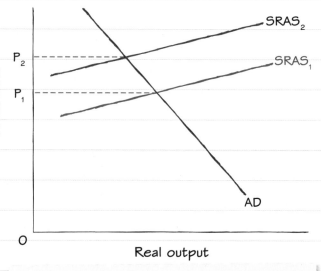

Cost-push inflation leads to a shift to the left in aggregate supply, causing a price rise from P_1 to P_2.

Demand-pull inflation

Demand-pull inflation occurs where there is excess demand in the economy. Where excess demand occurs, producers are unable to raise supply quickly enough and prices rise. Demand-pull inflation may occur because of:

1 sharp rises in **consumer spending**

2 substantial increase in **investment and spending by firms**

3 governments substantially increasing **spending or cutting taxes**

4 a sharp rise in demand for UK **exports**.

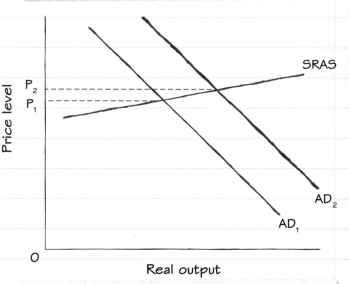

Demand-pull inflation leads to a shift to the right in aggregate demand, causing a price rise from P_1 to P_2.

Growth of the money supply

The money supply refers to the stock of currency (including cash, coins and balances in bank accounts and savings accounts) circulating in an economy. An increase in the money supply:

- lowers interest rates and makes money more available for spending and investment
- will lead to an increase in the rate of inflation because increased spending can create demand-pull inflation.

Now try this

1 Give two examples of cost-push inflation.
2 Give two possible causes of demand-pull inflation.

Impact of inflation

Controlling inflation is a key macroeconomic objective of the government. Achieving a rate of inflation of 2% is seen to be desirable. A high rate of inflation can have a significant impact on consumers, firms, workers and the government.

Effects of inflation

A rate of inflation of 2% allows an economy to avoid the problems associated with deflation and high inflation. Price rises are steady and consumers and producers can keep up with price rises. The real value of borrowing falls gradually, making borrowing easier. The table below shows the effects of a **high rate** of inflation (5%).

Firms and workers	Makes it difficult for firms to plan expenditure. As firms cannot plan, they are less likely to take risks and may stop investing. This can lead to an unstable macroeconomic climate and job losses.
Government	May affect the country's balance of payments if prices are rising faster than in other countries. Exports become less competitive.
Consumers	Leads to uncertainty and 'shoe leather costs'. Consumers are less able to understand what a reasonable price for a good or service is and will tend to shop around to find the best prices.
	With high inflation there is also a psychological cost for consumers as they will feel worse off, further lowering consumer confidence to spend.

Inflation and the value of money

Inflation can affect consumers by devaluing the value of their savings. The example on the right shows the value of £1500 with an inflation rate of 2% in 10 and 20 years time.

The value of savings over time (2% inflation rate)

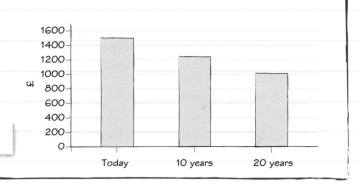

The impact of deflation

 Falling prices lead to low consumer confidence and the knock-on effect of low business confidence.

 The real cost of borrowing rises (although interest rates will be low).

 Savers suffer as the value of assets fall.

 Deflation can lead to a depression in the economy.

🌐 Real world   Hyperinflation in Zimbabwe

In 2007 inflation in Zimbabwe spiralled out of control leading to hyperinflation. This was caused by political turbulence and the seizure and redistribution of agricultural land, which led to foreign capital being withdrawn from the economy. That year, Zimbabwe also faced a terrible drought. The government attempted to solve the problems by printing more money. The economy collapsed with hyperinflation reaching 79 billion % at its peak.

Now try this

Why would an inflation rate of 6% be undesirable?

Employment and unemployment

The claimant count and the Labour Force Survey are different measures of unemployment. Unemployment and under-employment are not the same. You need to understand why changes in the rates of employment, unemployment and inactivity may be significant.

 Key terms

Employed People in paid work – includes people that work for someone else or a firm and a minority that work for themselves (self-employed).

Unemployed People not in work but actively seeking employment.

Full-time Working the hours and days associated with a particular job.

Part-time Working a proportion of the hours of a full-time job.

Active population The labour force of working age 16–65.

Inactive population People not seeking work – students, children, the retired, stay at home carers.

Under-employment The proportion of part-time employees who would prefer to work longer hours/full-time or those working in jobs below their skill level.

Claimant count

The **claimant count** records those claiming unemployment benefit and who can prove they are actively looking for work. The claimant count may not reflect the true level of unemployment in the UK economy, given that not all the unemployed will claim benefits.

Changes in UK unemployment rates and inactivity

Over the past 35 years more women have taken up employment. More men are classed as inactive as more stay in education and the proportion of the population at retirement age increases. A reduction in the inactivity rate benefits an economy as fewer people are dependent on benefits. Between 2017 and 2018 the number of additional jobs in the UK increased at a greater rate than the increase in the proportion of people actively seeking work. The consequence is greater economic output.

The UK Labour Force Survey and the ILO

The **UK Labour Force Survey** is a study conducted by the Office for National Statistics which provides official measures of employment and unemployment. Approximately 40,000 households and 80,000 individuals are interviewed for the survey, and the results are scaled up to represent the unemployment situation for the whole of the UK. The ONS uses the **International Labour Organization's (ILO)** definition of unemployment for the survey: all people aged 16 and over can be classified as in employment, unemployed or economically inactive.

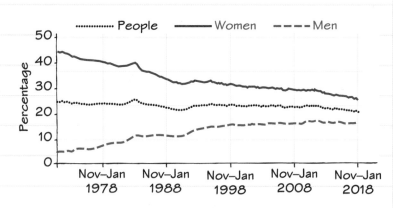

Labour Force Survey, UK inactivity rates (aged 16–64 years), 1971–2018.

Now try this

1 What is the difference between unemployment and the inactive population?

2 How is unemployment measured in the UK?

Causes and types of unemployment

The causes of unemployment are linked to a lack of aggregate demand and supply-side factors. Cyclical unemployment is caused by a **lack of demand** in the economy. Frictional, seasonal, structural and real wage unemployment are caused by **supply-side factors**. Some forms of unemployment are more serious than others.

Causes of unemployment

Frictional	Short-term unemployment as workers move between jobs. In a free market economy frictional unemployment is common as labour is distributed where there is greatest demand. The rate that people move into new jobs will depend on the availability of information (opportunities for employment), the level of unemployment benefits and redundancy pay. Frictional unemployment is less of a concern than other types of unemployment.
Seasonal	In different industries, demand for labour varies throughout the year. For example, tourism jobs peak in the summer months and part-time retail work increases leading up to Christmas. Most industries have their own pattern of employment, which is unavoidable.
Structural	A more serious cause of unemployment that is created where demand for labour is less than supply. It may have an impact on a region of the country where there is a lack of mobility. Structural unemployment may be caused by a decline in a particular industry (such as shipbuilding in the North East) or the advancement of technology replacing skilled workers.
Cyclical (demand deficient)	Results from a fall in aggregate demand in the economy as a result of business cycles (shifts from boom to recession over time). Fewer jobs are available when the economy is in recession, but these jobs return as the economy returns to growth.
Real wage inflexibility	Unemployment may also exist where real wage rates are stuck at a level above that needed to reduce unemployment. Workers and firms may be willing to accept a lower wage/pay less, but factors such as the minimum wage prevent the price of labour falling.

Cyclical unemployment in diagrams

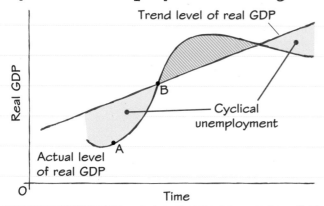

There is cyclical unemployment when the actual level of real GDP is below the long-run trend level. It can create an output gap where there is demand deficiency.

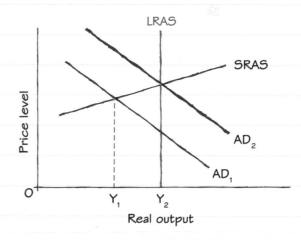

LRAS is the productive potential of the economy. Cyclical unemployment can be eliminated by shifting the aggregate demand curve from AD_1 to AD_2. (See pages 71 and 73 for more on SRAS and LRAS.)

Now try this

1 What is the difference between frictional unemployment and structural unemployment?

2 What is the cause of cyclical unemployment?

The impact of unemployment

The changing profile of migration and skills in an economy can have both significant positive and negative effects on employment and unemployment. Unemployment can impact on consumers, firms, workers, government and society.

The significance of migration and skills

Positive impact	Negative impact
👍 Migrants are less likely to claim benefits.	👎 Increased migration increases the supply of labour and reduces the equilibrium price – wage rates rise slower than inflation.
👍 Migrants are usually of working age and increase employment figures, not unemployment figures.	👎 The level of skills required by the economy gradually increases over time. If skills in the labour force do not also rise, this will lead to structural unemployment.
👍 Migrants represent good value for money for UK firms.	👎 If firms do not invest in developing employees, the labour market will fail and the government will have to intervene.
👍 Migrants close skills shortages in the UK economy, e.g. in healthcare.	

The effect on economic agents

The impact of unemployment

Cost to unemployed and their dependents
- Stigma of being unemployed
- Loss of earnings (offset by any benefits)
- Increased chance of stress, depression and family breakdown
- Long-term costs of deskilling and less likely to find a new job
- Short-term costs less severe if redundancy is paid

Cost to local communities
- Increased crime rates
- Run-down housing
- Closure of local businesses
- Degrading of the local environment

Cost to the government
- Increased benefit payments
- Loss of income tax and national insurance
- Burden to retrain workers
- Subsidies for employers to encourage people back into work

Cost to firms
- Loss of demand for goods and services
- Long-term unemployment can lead to a shortage of skills, making it harder to find high-quality workers

Two-fold impact on the economy

① Loss of output and consumption, leading to a slowdown or fall in economic growth.

② A rise in social problems such as violence, crime and ill-health.

Now try this

1 What social problems are caused by unemployment?
2 What impact does migration have on unemployment in the UK?

Balance of payments

A key macroeconomic objective of the government is to balance payments with other nations through international trade. This involves balancing the flow of money into and out of the economy. The main record of these transactions is the **balance of payments** account. This is a record of all financial dealings over a period of time between economic agents in the UK and all other countries. Economies are interconnected through international trade.

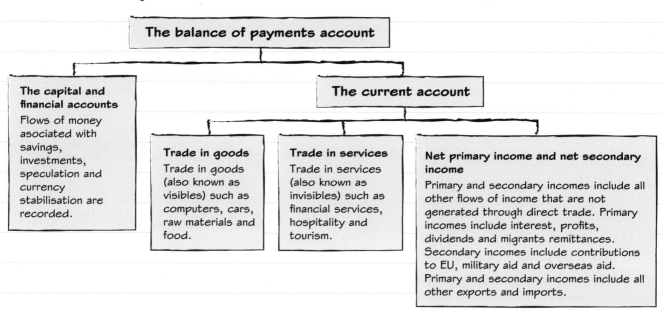

The current account (deficit and surpluses)

- The current account is the UK's main indicator of the country's external trade performance. The first two components of the current account – **trade in goods** and **trade in services** – are the most significant because they account for the largest proportion of cash inflows and cash outflows. A current account deficit refers to a situation where there is a negative balance of trade in goods and services.

- A current account surplus is the opposite and will lead to an increase in aggregate demand (see page 63).

Interconnectedness through international trade

In theory, the sum of all countries' trade balances will be zero. Economic growth in one country will often lead to greater demand for imports from other trade partners.

Balance of trade in goods and services

The balance of trade refers to the difference between a country's value of exports minus its imports (the difference between what goods a country produces and how many goods it buys from abroad). It is the difference between a country's output and its domestic demand.

Countries want a positive trade balance (the value of exports greater than the value of imports) because this creates a positive flow of cash into the economy.

🖩 Maths skills Net trade formula

Net trade balance = value of exports in goods and services – value of imports in goods and services

Now try this

1 What factors make up the UK's balance of payments account?

2 Why is a net balance of trade deficit undesirable?

The current account imbalances

The balancing of the current account is a key macroeconomic objective for the government. However, achieving a current account surplus can create a **trade-off** with other macroeconomic objectives.

The current account and other macroeconomic objectives

Economic growth – as economies become wealthier and standards of living rise, consumers will naturally import more goods and services, leading to a current account deficit.

Protectionism – protectionism may help to curb imports, but this can lead to foreign countries counteracting this with their own policies, thus leading to reduced international trade and economic prosperity.

A current account deficit reduces the money supply, and the fall in domestic demand can put downward pressure on prices.

> **Impact of current account balances**

A current account deficit could lead to job losses in the UK as export industries underperform.

A lack of foreign direct investment (flow of money into the UK) will lead to a fall in capital investment and the long-term productive potential of the economy.

A current account deficit represents a trade deficit. This leads to a fall in aggregate demand and consequently economic growth.

The UK current account over time

Since 2011, the UK's current account balance has fallen into greater deficit and reached −5% of UK GDP. The UK government has reduced this deficit over the past few years and the trend is forecast to continue into 2022 (see diagram below). Governments will want to avoid a large, long-term deficit as this could cause other economic problems such as job losses and uncompetitive industries.

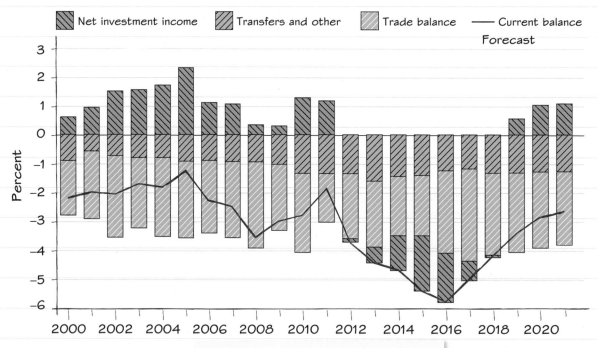

Current account balance as a share of GDP.

Now try this

1 Why is a large, long-term trade deficit bad for the UK?

2 Explain how the current account balance is linked to one other macroeconomic objective.

Aggregate demand

In economics, aggregate means total. **Aggregate demand (AD)** is the total demand in an economy. A number of factors contribute to aggregate demand: **consumption (C)**, **investment (I)**, **government spending (G)** and **exports (X) minus imports (M)**. The aggregate demand curve is downward sloping.

Consumption (C)

Consumption refers to the spending of households on goods and services. Consumption is influenced by interest rates. As interest rates rise, households spend less, particularly on goods that are traditionally bought on credit, such as cars. Price rises also lead to a consumer's real wealth being lower. This too will lead to a fall in consumption and aggregate demand.

Investment (I)

Investment refers to the spending by firms on investment goods, for example, a firm opening a new factory or a new product line. Price levels have a similar impact on investment as they do on consumption. Investment spending is similarly linked to interest rates. Firms will cut back on investments when interest rates rise as these investments will be less profitable.

Government spending (G)

Government spending includes the costs of running government agencies such as local councils and the wages of civil servants. It also includes spending on areas such as healthcare, education, transport and infrastructure such as new roads. With aggregate demand, government spending is independent of other economic variables such as interest rates, exchanges rates and inflation.

Exports and imports (X – M)

Exported goods and services contribute to national income (consumption of UK goods and services from other economies). Imports include goods and services purchased from abroad, for example, UK consumers spending on holidays abroad. As imports lead to a flow of money out of the economy, they become a negative in the AD calculation (X – M). The quality of UK goods, UK interest rates and the value of the pound all influence imports and exports (see page 69).

🔢 Maths skills — Formula for AD

Aggregate demand can be expressed by the formula: $AD = C + I + G + (X - M)$.

The aggregate demand curve

The aggregate demand curve shows the relationship between the price level and the level of real expenditure in the economy. The price level refers to the average price level in the economy. This can be measured in a number of ways, including CPI (see page 55). Changes in the price level are represented by inflation. Aggregate demand falls as the price level increases. As a result, fewer goods and services will be consumed.

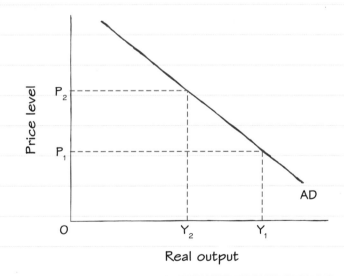

Now try this

1 All other things remaining constant, what will be the effect on consumption of a fall in interest rates?

2 What impact will an increase in imports have on aggregate demand?

Movements along and shifts of the AD curve

You need to know the distinction between movements along and shifts in the aggregate demand (AD) curve.

Movements along the AD curve

The AD curve demonstrates how the equilibrium price level relates to the equilibrium level of real income and output. A **change** in the average price level will lead to a **movement** along the AD curve:

- A **fall** will lead to an **expansion** along the AD curve (P to P₁).

- A **rise** in the average price level, due to inflation, will lead to a **contraction** along the AD curve (P to P₂).

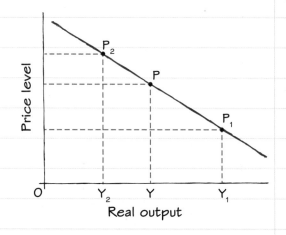

Shifts in the AD curve

A shift in the AD curve will be caused by a change in any other factor (C, I, G, X or M – see page 64) that is not linked to a change in the price level. These changes can be monetary variables, for example, a decrease in interest rates will lead to consumption rising and the AD curve shifting to the right (AD₁ to AD₂).

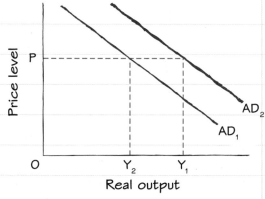

Largest component of AD

The largest component of AD is consumption – spending by households in the economy.

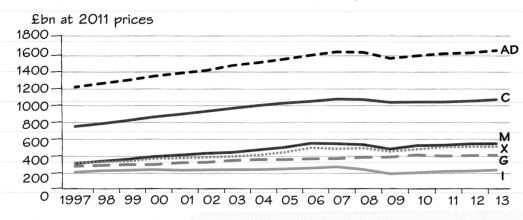

£bn at 2011 prices

Consumer spending is the largest component of aggregate demand, followed by net trade. The most significant way to influence aggregate demand is to encourage and stimulate consumer spending in the economy through monetary and fiscal policy (see pages 88–90 on demand-side policies).

Now try this

1 What will be the effect on aggregate demand of an increase in the average price level of 3%?

2 Explain one factor that could lead to a shift to the left in the AD curve.

Consumption

Consumption is the spending of households on consumer goods and services such as home electronics, clothing, visits to the cinema and eating out. There is a relationship between people's savings and household consumption. Other factors may also affect consumption.

Income and consumption

Money for consumption comes from household income. Income comes from salaries/wages, benefits, and interest on investments or savings. However, not all income is spent. A proportion of a person's income is sometimes saved, increasing a stock of cash or money in the bank.

The proportion of a household's income that is spent is referred to as **disposable income**. The most important factor that influences consumption is disposable income.

Average propensity to consume

The **average propensity to consume** (APC) measures the average proportion of income that is spent on consumption across an economy. It is calculated by:

Maths skills

$$APC = \frac{\text{consumption}}{\text{income}} \quad \text{or} \quad \frac{C}{Y}$$

Keynesian economists believe that as incomes rise the average propensity to consume will decline – people save more as they become wealthier. Higher income households consume less as a proportion of their income compared with poorer households.

The consumption function

As household incomes rise, so will consumption. How much it will rise is measured by the **marginal propensity to consume** (MPC):

 Maths skills

$$MPC = \frac{\text{change in consumption}}{\text{change in income}} \quad \frac{\Delta C}{\Delta Y}$$

For example, if income rises by £200 and consumption rises by £150, then the MPC would be 0.75 (£150 ÷ £200)

Average propensity to save

Just as the propensity to consume can be calculated, economists also calculate the **average propensity to save** (APS) by substituting consumption with savings in each of the calculations on this page. As well as the level of income, household saving is also influenced by:

- inflation
- consumer expectations
- interest rates
- the age profile of the population.

Saving

Remember, savings is the part of disposable income not consumed. Young people and the elderly spend a greater proportion of their income than middle-aged people because their incomes are generally lower and they have a lower propensity to save.

Other influences on consumer spending

Interest rates – households often borrow money to consume big ticket durables such as cars, home improvements and furniture. An increase in interest rates will increase the monthly repayments on these goods which in turn absorbs a larger proportion of a household's income and may mean they are inclined to spend less.

Other factors

Consumer confidence – when consumers are more confident in the performance of the economy or their future earning potential they are likely to spend a greater proportion of income on consumption.

Wealth effect – a household's wealth is made up of **physical wealth** (property, cars and physical assets) and **monetary wealth** (money in the bank, stocks and cash). As wealth increases in the short term, such as property values rising or the value of stocks and shares, so will the household's consumption.

Now try this

1 What is disposable income?

2 What factors may lead to households cutting back on consumption?

Investment

In economics, investment is the addition to the capital stock of the economy. This involves spending which increases the capability to produce other goods and services. Investment can be made in **physical capital** (machinery and factories) and **human capital** (investment in people such as education and training). You need to understand the difference between gross investment and net investment. Investment may be affected by various factors.

Gross investment and net investment

The value of capital stock decreases over time. For example, the value (and effectiveness) of a machine bought ten years ago will be a fraction of what it cost when it was purchased. This is known as **depreciation**.

- **Gross investment** measures investment before depreciation.
- **Net investment** deducts the value of depreciation from spending on investment.

The distinction between gross and net investment is made because some investment is intended to replace capital stocks (the replacement level), not actually to enable a business to grow and expand.

Factors affecting investment

- Interest rates (page 67)
- Keynes and 'animal spirits' (page 67)
- The influence of government and regulations (page 67)
- Access to credit (page 67)
- Demand for exports
- The rate of economic growth
- Business expectations and confidence

Business expectations and confidence

Up to 70 per cent of industrial and commercial investment in the UK is financed through retained profit (profit reinvested back into a business and not returned to its owners). Therefore, firms will invest more when they are profitable. Similarly, as business costs rise, profitability falls and firms are less able to retain profit for investment. Any factors increasing costs for firms, such as inflation, will also reduce their ability to invest.

The rate of economic growth

Where there is no growth in the economy as measured by GDP, firms will not increase investment and may only spend to replace depreciated capital stocks. Where the economy is shrinking, such as during a recession, firms may choose to cut back on spending altogether in order to reduce excess capacity. In times of real economic growth, firms will increase new investment (or net investment) in order to increase their productive capabilities.

Demand for exports

Domestic investment by firms is also closely linked to performance of the world economy. When the world economy is booming, demand for UK goods and services rises, leading to an increase in exports. To meet this demand from abroad, UK firms that export or supply exporters will increase new investment.

A world economic recession would have the reverse impact and dampen new investment as UK exporters see a fall in demand from foreign buyers for their goods and services.

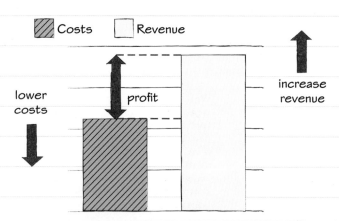

To increase profits, and therefore retained profit, a firm can either increase revenue through higher prices (whilst maintaining demand) or higher sales volume. It can also find ways to increase efficiency by reducing its costs (whilst maintaining value for customers).

Now try this

1 How does depreciation affect investment?

2 How is investment in the UK linked to the world economy?

Further influences on investment

There are many influences on investment, including those discussed on the previous page. Others include the influence of government, interest rates, access to credit and what Keynes described as 'animal spirits'.

The influence of government and regulations

Taxation – decreasing the taxation on business profits (corporation tax) will reduce business costs and increase retained profits.

Examples of government policies linked to the level of investment

Grants – governments can offer grants to businesses investing in social, environmental or ethical causes.

Guaranteeing loans – government can act as a guarantor for a business loan used for investment. A government guarantee increases access to credit (30% of investment comes from loans).

Regulation – regulation translates into costs for businesses. Therefore, highly regulated industries are expensive for firms to operate in. Fewer regulations can lead to greater profits.

Access to credit

Many firms use credit to finance investment. Apart from the rate of interest, access to credit is another factor. Following the financial crisis in 2008, UK banks were far more risk averse and this led to more firms' loan applications being turned down. As a result, investment also fell as retained profit and owner capital alone were not sufficient. The amount of credit will often vary dependent on the economic conditions and the monetary policy adopted by the government (see page 88 for more on monetary policy). Access to credit is closely linked to business expectations and confidence.

Interest rates

When firms borrow money to finance investment, part of the cost is the interest repaid on the loan. Where interest rates are high, firms will pay a larger percentage and this will reduce the profitability of the investment. Where interest rates are low, more firms are encouraged to borrow money to finance investment because it is less costly.

'Animal spirits'

John Maynard Keynes used the phrase '**animal spirits**', referring to the mood and attitude of managers when making decisions about investment.

👍 An optimistic outlook for the future and anticipated demand leading to increased sales will encourage firms to invest for growth.

👎 A pessimistic outlook will curb any ambition and risk-taking to invest for the future.

'Animal spirits' is a key factor in the level of investment in an economy, but the mood of firms is very difficult to measure. However, in a modern society, greater access to economic information through government statistics and industry reports can certainly influence the level of optimism shown by firms and consumers.

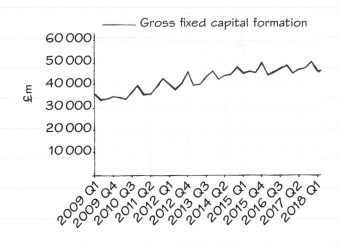

——— Gross fixed capital formation

Since 2010, UK investment has been rising as the confidence of UK firms has returned in anticipation of economic growth. Nevertheless, from 2016, the uncertainty around Brexit dampened confidence.

Now try this

1 How might a government encourage firms to invest?

2 In Keynesian economics, what does 'animal spirits' refer to?

3 What impact will a fall in the base rate of interest have on investment?

Government expenditure

Much of government spending on areas such as public services, education and defence are fixed from year to year, but governments can make decisions on **fiscal policy** to affect economic variables such as unemployment and inflation. Through spending and taxation, governments can directly increase or decrease AD. AD can be tracked using the trade cycle.

The trade cycle

The trade cycle represents the cyclical nature of economic growth in an economy. During periods of economic boom, real output will rise and the economy may grow. During a boom, governments may look to increase national infrastructure and invest the higher taxes collected from consumers and firms. However, in an economic recession, governments may strategically spend in order to provide a stimulus for economic growth. Increased government spending to reduce unemployment would increase demand in the economy. Government spending may also rise during a recession, because increased unemployment will lead to an increased need for unemployment and welfare benefits.

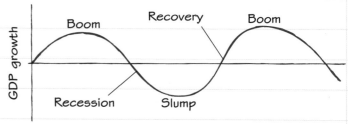

The trade cycle. Government's tax revenue will fall during a recession and place pressure on a budget deficit. Raising taxes to counteract this will only lower consumption and aggregate demand further.

Fiscal policy

Fiscal policy relates to government policies on taxation and spending. Taxation can influence consumption (C) and investment (I). How governments choose to spend will depend on economic conditions and government priorities. Examples of specific spending strategies include:

- increased spending on education in order to invest in human capital

- increased spending on housing to create more affordable housing

- increased spending on transport to increase labour mobility and support regeneration of towns in the North.

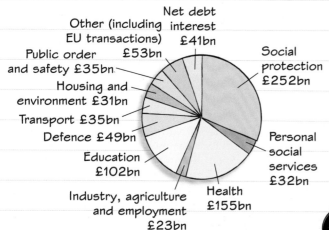

Budget deficits and surpluses

Government spending can be used to boost overall spending and aggregate demand in the economy, even if tax revenue does not meet government spending. Governments may run:

- a budget **surplus**, where tax revenue is greater than spending, or

- a budget **deficit**, where spending is greater than tax revenue. Where governments run a budget deficit, they will need to borrow the money.

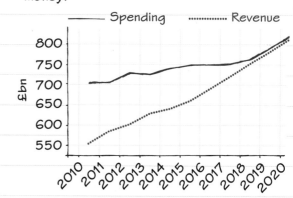

Total UK government spending and tax revenue. The rate of borrowing has been falling since 2010, but the UK government still runs a budget deficit.

Now try this

1 What is fiscal policy?

2 Why might a government set a budget deficit?

3 Why might a government cut back on spending?

Net trade

The net trade balance is exports minus imports (X – M). Exports contribute towards aggregate demand, whilst imports deduct from it. Several factors influence the net trade balance.

Real incomes

- As real incomes (income after taking into account the effects of inflation and purchasing power) in the UK rise, consumers will increase their consumption of UK goods and services. For example, UK consumers will tend to purchase holidays abroad instead of staying in the UK. This contributes towards an increase in imports. Consumers will also demand more goods and services from abroad, which will be brought into the UK through imports. These imports lead to a flow of money out of the economy and a negative contribution to AD.

- As real incomes fall, consumers cut back on spending and net imports will fall.

Current account balance of goods and services

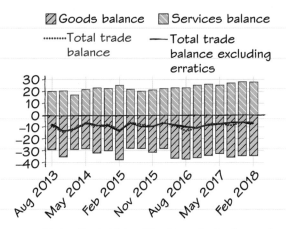

The UK has a trade surplus in services but a trade deficit in goods. Overall, the UK currently has a net trade deficit.

State of the world economy

During a world economic recession, UK exports will fall, as was seen in 2008. The EU is currently the UK's largest export market followed by the USA. As these markets experience economic growth, UK firms will benefit by seeing a rise in exports. However, UK goods and services must be competitive in order to compete with similar goods and services from other parts of the world.

Exchange rates

An exchange rate is the price at which one currency is sold for another. The value of the pound has a significant impact on imports and exports.

	Strong pound (e.g. £1 = US$2)	Weak pound (e.g. £1 = US$1.2)
Imports	UK consumers have greater spending power when buying from abroad so imports rise.	The pound buys less abroad. Consumers and firms will buy less or switch to domestic goods.
Exports	UK goods are less competitive (more expensive) abroad, therefore demand for UK exports falls.	UK goods are more competitive (cheaper) abroad, therefore demand for UK exports rises.

Non-price factors

Imports and exports are not only affected by incomes and relative prices. Some countries have a reputation for certain products or services, which helps to protect exports. For example:

- the UK has strong exports of financial services, partly due to the expertise the UK has in this industry and the concentration of financial services in the City of London

- champagne produced in the Champagne region of France.

The geography of different nations and political relationships also makes it easier for some countries to trade with others and this too protects or inhibits trade.

Degree of protectionism

All countries will seek a positive balance of trade. To do this, they may protect domestic firms by limiting the quantity of goods and services that are imported. Governments do this by using a range of protectionist strategies such as **tariffs** (a tax on imports) and **quotas** (a limit on a certain good). Some regions of the world have agreements to minimise protectionism, such as the EU single market and other trading blocs such as the North American Free Trade Agreement (NAFTA). Changes to UK and foreign protectionism will influence imports and exports.

Now try this

Why might a nation impose a tariff on the imports of certain goods?

Aggregate supply

Just as the supply curve in microeconomics shows the relationships between price and the quantity producers are willing to supply in a given market, the aggregate supply (AS) curve represents the sum of all industry supply curves in the economy, represented as real GDP. You need to know the distinction between movements along and shifts in the aggregate supply (AS) curve. There is a relationship between short-run AS and long-run AS.

Short-run aggregate supply

The short-run aggregate supply (SRAS) curve is upward sloping. This is because as average prices level rises, the economy will tend to produce more in the short run. Reasons for this may include:

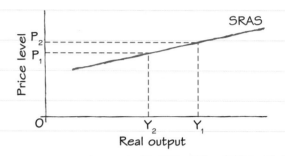

- some parts of the economy (certain producers in certain industries) will see the rise in average prices as a profit incentive for their market and will increase supply accordingly

- firms' costs (such as wages or costs of raw materials) will not respond quickly to the average price rise (they are 'sticky') so in the short run firms will benefit from the higher prices and produce more whilst it is profitable.

The SRAS curve is relatively elastic because an increase in output (Y_1 to Y_2) in the economy will have a relatively little impact on prices in the short run (P_1 to P_2). Wages are fixed in the short term, as are other costs of production, because firms will have fixed contracts with suppliers. Over time, these adapt.

Movements in SRAS

A change in real output will result in a movement along the SRAS curve. Although wage rates and some production costs are fixed in the short run, firms will experience some additional costs, such as overtime payments to meet demand for increased output.

Shifts in SRAS

As with the microeconomic supply curve, several factors can cause a shift in the SRAS curve. These factors will cause a shock to the economy and result in the average price level rising (a shift to the left of SRAS) or falling (a shift to the right of SRAS) at any given level of output. These factors do not just affect one market but instead have an impact on the whole economy. (See page 71 for more on these factors.)

Short-run and long-run aggregate supply

In the short run, SRAS is linked to the price level. However, the classical view of economics suggests that in the long run real GDP does not depend on the price level. Regardless of the price level, real GDP will remain the same unless the productive capacity of the economy changes, such as an increase in the population. For this reason, in the long run the aggregate supply curve is vertical. All other things being equal, an economy's ability to produce does not change with fluctuations in the price level but will shift over time as the population, education, technology and infrastructure change. (See page 72 for the difference between the classical AS curve and the Keynesian AS curve.)

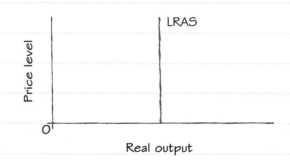

A vertical LRAS curve represents an economy's productive capability in the long run and is similar to the model of the production possibility frontier on pages 4–5.

Now try this

1 What is SRAS?

2 Why is the classical long-run aggregate supply curve vertical?

Factors affecting SRAS

Various factors can affect the costs of production in an economy and lead to a shift in SRAS. Factors may include changes in tax rates, exchange rates and costs of raw materials and energy. Some of these can be influenced by government policy (internal factors), while others are linked to the state of the world economy (external factors).

Short-run aggregate supply

The SRAS suggests that there will be some change to output in the economy as a result of a change in the average price level. As in the microeconomic model (but for different reasons), there are a number of factors that can create a shift in aggregate supply. Where there is a shift in aggregate supply, there will be changes in the costs of production.

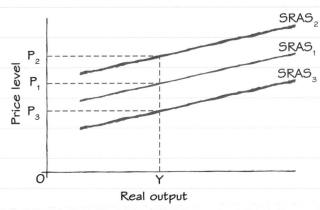

A shift in the SRAS curve results in average prices being higher (a shift upwards and to the left – $SRAS_2$) or lower (a shift downwards and to the right – $SRAS_3$).

Internal and external factors influencing SRAS

- Internal factors are those that may be influenced by government policy and linked to the UK economy.
- External factors are those that create an external shock, often linked to factors in the world economy. These factors can be indirectly influenced by the UK government, such as subsidising an industry that is hit heavily by rising commodity prices.

Internal factors (changes in cost of production)	External factors (external shocks)
• **Wage costs** – a change in wage costs will shift aggregate supply, due to a rise in production costs. For example, the introduction of a new higher minimum national wage will push production costs up for many firms and shift SRAS to the right. • **Production efficiency** – if labour productivity increases, perhaps through the introduction of new technology, SRAS will shift to the left. • **Taxation** – a rise in VAT will see production costs rise for many products. • **Import prices** – government introducing new tariffs on imported goods will also increase production costs and shift SRAS to the left.	• **Natural disasters** – a natural disaster could lead to a sudden fall in aggregate supply as firms struggle to access the raw materials or components they need, affecting the price of raw materials. • **Food prices** – the price of imported foodstuffs used in the production of supermarket products or restaurants could rise sharply. • **Energy prices** – the UK imports a significant amount of its energy and any change in the cost of electricity or gas can significantly affect production costs and the costs of raw materials. • **Oil prices** – the world price of oil is one of the most significant factors in production costs for UK firms because it is used in a vast range of industries for the production of goods and transportation. • **Exchange rates** – a rise in the value of the pound will reduce import costs for UK firms and lower production costs.

Now try this

1 What will be the impact on SRAS if the government cuts corporation tax?

2 What will be the impact on SRAS if world oil prices increase by US $5 per barrel?

Classical and Keynesian AS curves

In the long run, it is assumed that the economy will move towards an equilibrium where all resources are being used to full capacity, also known as **full productive capacity**. In this model, the price level does not affect aggregate supply, as represented by a vertical AS curve. However, there are contrasting views on LRAS.

Classical view of LRAS

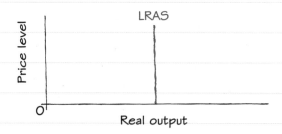

In the long run, the economy will move towards equilibrium output where all resources are being utilised and the economy is at full employment. The productive capacity of an economy can change (shift) (see page 73).

At low levels of output, aggregate supply is completely elastic (where the line is horizontal) as there is spare capacity in the economy so output can increase without a rise in the price level. The spare capacity comes from under-utilised resources and unemployment.

Keynesian view of LRAS

The Keynesian LRAS curve is L shaped.

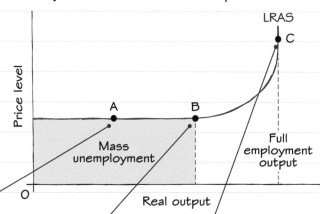

When the curve begins to slope upward, the economy starts to experience bottlenecks which will lead to additional costs to firms. For example, shortages of labour and raw materials.

As the curve becomes vertical, supply is completely inelastic. As in the classical view of LRAS, the economy has reached its productive capacity and output can't increase anymore.

A modern solution to AS

To solve the problem of the Keynesian and classical AS curve, modern economists tend to separate the short-run AS (SRAS) curve from the long-run AS (LRAS) curve. The short run is assumed to begin immediately after an increase in the price level, and ends when input prices (costs of production) have increased. Hence, during the short run producers are experiencing an increase in their 'real' prices and produce more output – and the supply curve slopes upwards. Any increase in input prices (costs) which may follow is assumed to lag behind increases in the general price level.

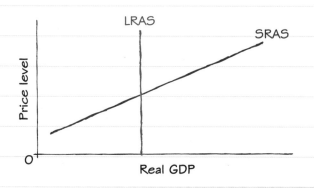

The long-run aggregate supply (LRAS) curve is shown as a vertical curve at full employment. LRAS can shift if the economy's productivity changes, either through an increase in the quantity of scarce resources, such as inward migration or organic population growth, or improvements in the quality of resources, such as through better education and training.

Now try this

1 Why is the Keynesian AS curve horizontal at low levels of output?

2 In the Keynesian model of AS, why might costs rise as output reaches full capacity?

Factors influencing LRAS

The productive capacity of an economy, as expressed by LRAS, is not fixed. Changes in the factors of production can lead to a shift in LRAS. The following may influence LRAS.

1 **Technological advances** – the internet has improved communication and access to trade. Individuals and small firms can set-up without the need for expensive overheads. Factor mobility has improved, as workers can now operate from home using the internet. Computer-aided manufacturing has also increased accuracy, efficiency, productivity and reduced human error.

2 **Changes in relative productivity** – specialisation increases productivity. If UK productivity of a good increases in relation to the same good in another country, then production of the good in the UK will attract investment. LRAS curve will shift to the right as more output of the specialised good leads to an overall increase in economic output.

6 **Competition policy** – governments in free market economies will encourage competition between firms. They can do this by regulating markets in a way that encourages open competition. In order to operate in competitive markets, firms must become more efficient and productive, leading to more efficient output in the economy.

Influences on LRAS

3 **Changes in education and skills** – investment in education and skills by firms and the government can increase labour productivity in the long run by improving the knowledge and skills of the workforce.

5 **Demographic changes and migration** – demographic changes are likely to impact the productive potential of an economy. Should the size of the population increase, such as a rise in immigration, so will the size of the workforce. However, an ageing population could also reduce the productive capacity of an economy if the number of people of working age falls.

4 **Changes in government regulations** – market regulation might include making it easier for entrepreneurs to start new businesses, giving support to businesses opening in areas of high unemployment and relaxing regulations around the market, making it easier to operate and run businesses.

Shifts in the LRAS

The LRAS curve is likely to shift over time. This is because the quality and quantity of economic resources will change, whether that be the size and skills of the workforce, technology, access to natural resources or policies affecting the efficiency and effectiveness of the economy.

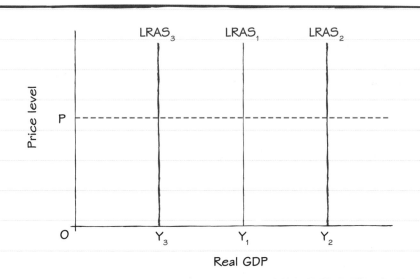

A shift from $LRAS_1$ to $LRAS_2$ shows an increase in the productive capacity of an economy. A shift from $LRAS_1$ to $LRAS_3$ indicates a fall in the productive potential. For example, through the depreciation of capital goods and lack of investment.

Now try this

How can government policy increase the productive capacity of an economy?

National income

The **circular flow of income** is the economic model that explains the relationship between national income, national output and national expenditure. This concept is linked to aggregate demand and aggregate supply and explains how money, goods and services, land, labour and capital flow within an economy. There is a difference between wealth and income.

Measuring national income

Three alternative methods of measuring the level of economic activity in the circular flow model are:

- national output (O)
- national income (Y)
- national expenditure (E).

Triple identifications

national ≡ national ≡ national
output   income   expenditure

or

O ≡ Y ≡ E

means 'equal and same as'

Wealth

Wealth is not the same as income. Wealth (the ownership of physical goods, assets, land and factories) is used to generate a flow of production or income. In this sense, wealth should be considered a stockpile of resources that can be used to create output and income. Over time, income can be amassed as wealth when stored in assets and not spent as expenditure in the circular flow.

The circular flow of income

The circular flow of income can be expressed as a diagram. The straight lines in the diagram below represent a physical flow or transfer of real things such as goods, land, capital and labour. The circular arrows show the flow of money between firms and households.

1 In an economy, firms produce goods and services. The total value of these goods and services (GDP) makes up the **national output**. Even where firms pay other firms for land and capital, they are ultimately owned by individuals so the flow of money counts as income.

2 'Households' refers to people who are also consumers and owners of wealth. Households in a country provide the land, labour and capital that firms use to produce the national output. The money paid to households by firms to use these factors of production makes up the **national income**.

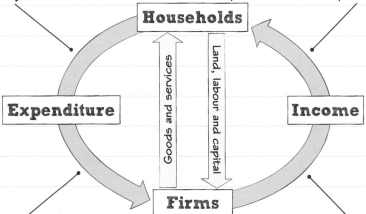

3 Households spend the money they get from national income on the goods and services that are produced by firms and this spending makes up the **national expenditure**. This three step process creates a circular flow of income.

4 Firms produce goods and services (output) using the factors of production that are owned by households (income). The goods and services are then bought by households (expenditure).

Now try this

1 Why does national output equal national income?

2 Why does national income equal national expenditure?

Injections and withdrawals

The circular flow of income does not remain constant over time. National income will change over time as money, goods and services flow in and out of the cycle. Where there are additional flows into the economy these are referred to as **injections** and where there are flows out of the economy these are known as **withdrawals**. Injections and withdrawals impact on the circular flow of income.

Injections

Injections are inflows of money into the economy that do not come from households. They include:

- **exports** – when uk goods and services are sold abroad they leave the country, but money from another economy enters the UK creating an addition to the circular flow

- **investment** – expenditure on additional capital stock such as factories and machinery used to produce other goods

- **government spending** – building a new hospital creates an additional inflow because money is used to pay households for land, labour and capital.

Withdrawals

Withdrawals are outflows of money from the economy (also known as leakages) and can come from firms or households.

- **Imports** – although goods and services flow into the economy, expenditure from the circular flow leaks out and becomes expenditure in other economies.

- **Savings** – when households (or firms) do not spend their income it becomes savings. This adds to wealth but detracts from the circular flow.

- **Taxes** – these are deducted from the national income, from both households and firms.

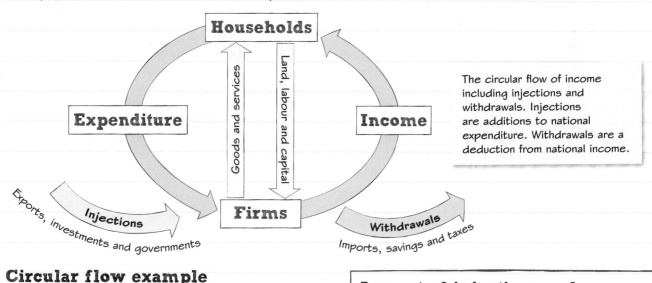

The circular flow of income including injections and withdrawals. Injections are additions to national expenditure. Withdrawals are a deduction from national income.

Circular flow example

The diagram below shows one aspect of the circular flow model in detail and how households contribute to withdrawals from the economy.

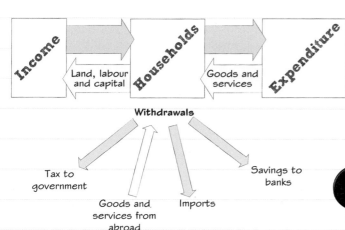

Impact of injections and withdrawals on the economy

If injections and withdrawals are equal, then the economy is in equilibrium. If withdrawals are greater than injections then there is a reduction in national output. Where injections are greater than withdrawals there will be an increase in output and the economy will grow. For example, if governments run a deficit budget (where spending is greater than taxation), *ceteris paribus*, this will contribute to greater national output.

Now try this

Why do exports lead to an injection into the circular flow of income?

Changes in AD and AS

Macroeconomic equilibrium occurs at the point where aggregate demand equals aggregate supply. This is the point where AD and AS curves intersect.

Macroeconomic equilibrium

At point OY the economy is in equilibrium. Here, derived demand will be the same as national output. At this level of output the general price level will be P. Although in theory equilibrium is possible, it is unlikely to be the case in reality. The most important factor is whether total demand for goods and services (AD) is close to actual production from domestic and external sources. When we compare AD to LRAS, this means how close the economy is to operating at full capacity. The relationship between AD and SRAS/LRAS affects national income, unemployment, inflation and the balance of payments.

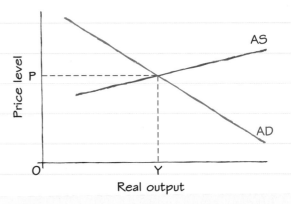

The SRAS aggregate supply curve. We can show macroeconomic equilibrium with both SRAS and LRAS.

Short-run impact of changes in AD

In the short run, an increase in AD will increase real output as there will be an expansion along the SRAS curve (Y_1 to Y_2). In the diagram (right), the increase in the price level from P_1 to P_2 is relatively small in comparison with the increase in real output. This is because in the short run, excess capacity in the economy will be used up with little impact on prices. The opposite is also true: if AD shifts to the left, perhaps through lower consumption, real output will fall and so should prices.

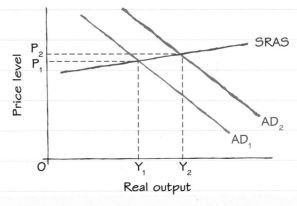

A shift from AD_1 to AD_2 leads to a rise in both equilibrium real output (Y_1 to Y_2) and the general price level (P_1 to P_2).

Changes in SRAS

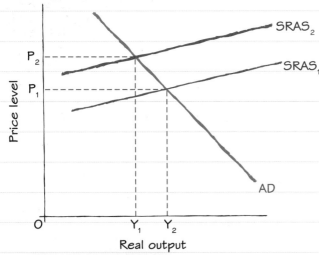

An economy can experience a fall or a rise in aggregate supply in the short-term. For example, this may come from changes in global oil prices, the level of taxation or a rise in wage rates.

A fall in short-run aggregate supply will shift the SRAS curve upwards and to the left. Not only will this reduce real output, but the price level will also rise. The aggregate supply curve shifts to the left as the price of key inputs rises, making possible a combination of lower output, higher unemployment and higher inflation. The opposite is also true of a rise in SRAS.

Now try this

1 What do the axes on a macroeconomic diagram represent?

2 What is the point where AD meets AS?

Perspectives on changes in AD

The impact of a shift in the AD curve will depend on the slope of the AS curve. The SRAS curve slopes upward and is relatively elastic, whilst the LRAS curve is vertical in the classical model.

Long-run impact of changes in AD

In the long run, the AS curve is vertical in the classical model. This is because LRAS represents the productive capacity of the economy when all factors of production are employed. In the short run, changes in AD can only cause a temporary change in total output. In the long run, an increase in AD represented by a shift to the right (AD_1 to AD_2) will only increase the equilibrium price level (P_1 to P_2) as real output cannot exceed Y. Therefore, in the long run, the impact of an increase in AD is only inflationary.

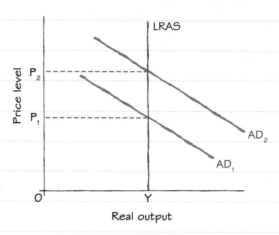

The Keynesian model

The Keynesian model suggests that when the economy is not at full capacity, such as during a recession, an increase in AD will increase real output with no impact on the price level (AD_1 to AD_2). As the economy starts to reach full capacity, then the factors of production become harder to come by, such as workers and raw materials. As such, prices start to rise (AD_2 to AD_3). When the economy has reached capacity (Y_2), then any increase in AD will only increase the price level.

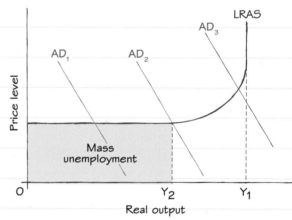

Above: the impact of changes in AD on the Keynesian model. If the economy is slightly below full employment (intermediate point) an increase in AD will increase real output and the price level.

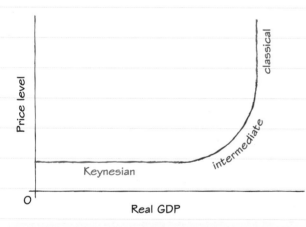

The Keynesian model can be divided into three sections (Keynesian, intermediate and classical) to help understand how changes in AD can affect the economy at different points.

The link between AD and AS

Unlike microeconomics, one factor that initially shifts AD could also shift AS. For example, investment and government spending are components of AD. An increase in either will shift AD to the right. The investment and spending will eventually lead to improved productivity so AS will also shift to the right. Real output increased, and prices may have fallen, due to improvements in production efficiency. (The link between AD and AS is explored further on page 82.)

Now try this

1 Why might an increase in AD only have the impact of raising the price level?

2 Why might a rise in AD have limited impact on the price level?

Changes in LRAS

In the long run, aggregate supply is fixed unless the potential output of the economy increases or decreases. A fall in LRAS will lower the equilibrium level of national output. A rise in LRAS suggests that an economy has greater potential output, possibly as a result of improved production efficiency, a larger working population or capital goods.

The classical model

The classical model, represented by a vertical LRAS curve, suggests that an increase in the productive capacity of an economy increases real output, whilst at the same time lowering pressure on the price level whilst the equilibrium level of national output rises.

The Keynesian model

In the Keynesian model, if the economy is at full employment or near full employment (AD_1 and AD_2) then an increase in AS will have the same benefits as in the classical model. Real output will rise and the price level will fall. However, when AD is low (AD_3) such as during a recession, an increase in AS will have no impact.

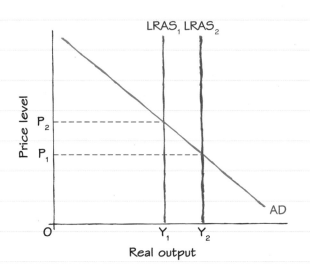

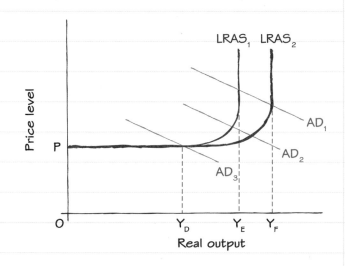

Benefits of increasing LRAS

The benefits of increasing LRAS are clear. These include increasing the productive capacity of an economy, reducing inflationary pressure and reducing types of unemployment. Increasing LRAS is the aim of supply-side policies explored on pages 91–92. Types of supply-side policy include:

- market-based policies
- interventionist policies
- incentive-based policies.

Correcting a recession

Keynesian economists would argue that supply-side policies are little use in correcting a recession. Instead, demand-side policies are key to taking an economy out of recession (see page 90). Examples of demand-side policies include:

- monetary policy (interest rates and quantitative easing)
- fiscal policy (taxation and government spending).

Now try this

1 What impact does a rise in LRAS have on the price level?
2 How does the classical model and Keynesian model of AS differ?

The multiplier

When there is an injection into the economy, aggregate demand will increase (see page 75). The effect of an injection has a **multiplier effect**. One person's expenditure becomes another person's income, which in turn is spent again. This multiplier effect continues until it has all leaked out of the circular flow. The **marginal propensity to consume** can be used to find the multiplier.

The multiplier shown using the circular flow of income model

 1 An initial investment of £10m flows into firms from government subsidies. Firms then spend this investment to build new factories, develop new product lines and expand production. This expenditure then flows into households as income. However, households do not spend all this income.

2 Only £9m is spent in the form of consumption as 10% leaks out in the form of savings, taxation and imports. Consumption flows through firms back into households as profit and wages. Again, further leakages of 10% leave the circular flow and £8.1m becomes consumption in the economy.

3 This process continues with smaller and smaller amounts being added to the national income. The total value of the multiplier of the initial £10m investment and a leakage of 10% is £100m – a multiplier of 10 (see calculating the multiplier below and on the next page).

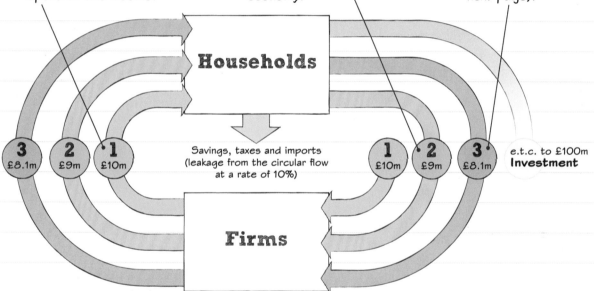

Households

| **3** £8.1m | **2** £9m | **1** £10m |

Savings, taxes and imports (leakage from the circular flow at a rate of 10%)

| **1** £10m | **2** £9m | **3** £8.1m |

e.t.c. to £100m
Investment

Firms

The multiplier process. The MPC is calculated by $\dfrac{\text{change in consumption}}{\text{change in income}}$ or $\dfrac{\Delta C}{\Delta Y}$

The multiplier ratio

The value of the multiplier is important as it helps the government to estimate the impact on aggregate demand of any investment in the economy. There are several ways that the multiplier can be calculated. One way is to use the value of the **marginal propensity to consume** (MPC). This is the proportion of any extra income spent on the consumption of goods and services. In the scenario above, the MPC is 0.9 (90%). The 10% that is therefore not spent does not contribute to the multiplier and becomes a leakage (withdrawal) from the circular flow of income.

 Maths skills **Calculating the multiplier: method 1**

$$\text{Multiplier} = \frac{1}{1 - \text{MPC}}$$

For example, in the above scenario the MPC is 0.9

$$= \frac{1}{1 - 0.9} = \frac{1}{0.1} = 10$$

Initial investment of £10m × 10 = £100m

Now try this

1 What is the formula for the marginal propensity to consume?

2 What would be the final impact on GDP of an initial investment of £50m if the marginal propensity to consume is 0.6?

Marginal propensity to withdraw

The **marginal propensity to withdraw (MPW)** can also be used to find the multiplier. Instead of looking at the proportion of extra income spent, the MPW considers the proportion of extra income that is withdrawn from the economy. The greater the MPW, the smaller the impact of the multiplier on aggregate demand in the economy. The MPW is made up of several withdrawals from the economy, each of which has an effect on the multiplier.

MPW

The marginal propensity to withdraw is made up of several withdrawals from the economy:

1. The proportion of an increase in income which is saved – **the marginal propensity to save (MPS)**.

2. The proportion of an increase in income which is taxed – **the marginal propensity to tax (MPT)**.

3. The proportion of an increase in income which is spent on imports – **the marginal propensity to import (MPM)**.

 Maths skills **Calculating the multiplier: method 2**

MPW = MPS + MPT + MPM

All extra income must either be spent or withdrawn. Therefore, MPC + MPW = 1

The multiplier can be calculated using MPW with the formula:
$$\frac{1}{MPW}$$
For example, on page 79 the MPW is 0.1 because MPC is 0.9
$$\frac{1}{0.1} = 10$$
This is the second way that the multiplier can be calculated.

The impact of MPS, MPT and MPM on the multiplier

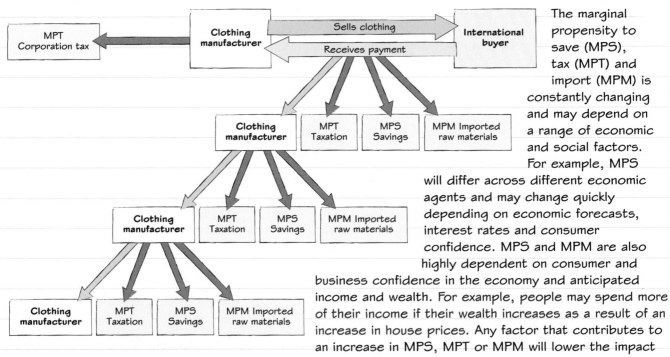

The marginal propensity to save (MPS), tax (MPT) and import (MPM) is constantly changing and may depend on a range of economic and social factors. For example, MPS will differ across different economic agents and may change quickly depending on economic forecasts, interest rates and consumer confidence. MPS and MPM are also highly dependent on consumer and business confidence in the economy and anticipated income and wealth. For example, people may spend more of their income if their wealth increases as a result of an increase in house prices. Any factor that contributes to an increase in MPS, MPT or MPM will lower the impact of the multiplier.

Now try this

1 What contributes to the value of MPW?
2 Define what is meant by marginal propensity to import.

The impact of the multiplier on the economy

You need to know how to calculate the multiplier and also how the multiplier impacts on an economy. You should also be familiar with the factors that may change the size of the multiplier.

Maths skills **Three ways to calculate the multiplier**

Each of the following three formulas can give us the multiplier.

1 $\dfrac{\text{Change in real GDP}}{\text{Initial change in spending}}$

An initial investment of £5billion led to a change in real GDP of £20billion... the multiplier is 4

If the MPC is 0.75 then $\dfrac{1}{1 - \text{MPC}} = \dfrac{1}{1 - 0.75}$

2 $\dfrac{1}{1 - \text{MPC}}$

$= \dfrac{1}{0.25}$ ... the multiplier is 4

If the MPC is 0.75 then MPW must be 0.25

3 $\dfrac{1}{\text{MPW}}$

$\dfrac{1}{\text{MPW}} = \dfrac{1}{0.25}$ ... the multiplier is 4

Impact of multiplier of aggregate demand

An initial increase in AD (through either investment, government spending or exports) will shift AD to the right. A shift from AD_1 to AD_2 with real output increasing to Y_2. If the initial injection was to the value of £500m and the value of the multiplier is 2.2, then there would be a subsequent increase in AD of £600m, a further shift to the right in AD from AD_2 to AD_3 and a further increase in real output from Y_2 to Y_3.

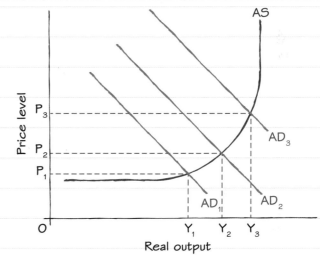

Factors that will change MPC and MPW

Both MPC and MPW are constantly fluctuating. Factors contributing to these fluctuations are:

- interest rates
- household wealth
- exchange rates
- the quality and availability of imports
- the rate of direct and indirect taxes
- the performance of the economy – stage of the economic cycle.

Estimating the impact of the multiplier

It can be very difficult for a government to estimate the impact of any additional spending on national income because there are so many factors contributing towards consumption, such as savings, taxation and imports. It also takes time for the impact of the multiplier to increase GDP. Any investment today may take months to have an impact on real output. In developed and wealthy countries it is estimated that the impact of the multiplier is relatively low, perhaps 0.5 in countries such as the UK and the USA.

Now try this

1 How might interest rates affect MPS?

2 How can the multiplier be calculated without using MPC or MPW?

Causes of growth

Economic growth is an increase in the productive potential of an economy. Any factors that contribute to an increase in aggregate demand or long-run aggregate supply will lead to **actual** or **potential economic growth**. There is a distinction between actual and potential growth. International trade is essential for export-led growth.

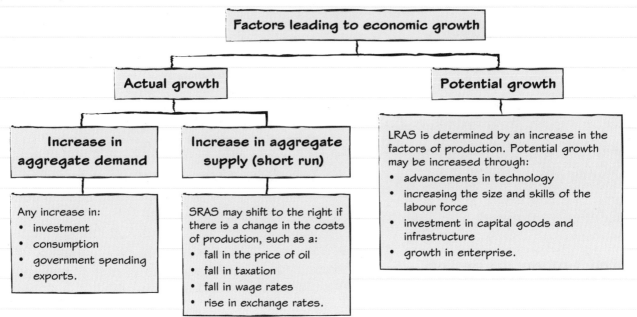

Factors leading to economic growth

Actual growth

Increase in aggregate demand

Any increase in:
• investment
• consumption
• government spending
• exports.

Increase in aggregate supply (short run)

SRAS may shift to the right if there is a change in the costs of production, such as a:
• fall in the price of oil
• fall in taxation
• fall in wage rates
• rise in exchange rates.

Potential growth

LRAS is determined by an increase in the factors of production. Potential growth may be increased through:
• advancements in technology
• increasing the size and skills of the labour force
• investment in capital goods and infrastructure
• growth in enterprise.

Actual growth

In the short run, economic growth is measured by the change in real national output (GDP). This is a measure of actual (real) growth as a result of growth in the quantity of goods and services produced, where the effects of inflation are removed from the figures. Actual growth tends to fluctuate up and down over time depending on the performance of the economy as measured by the trade (business) cycle (see page 84). Actual growth fluctuates up to the potential output of the economy and is shown through a movement from A to B on a PPF (below).

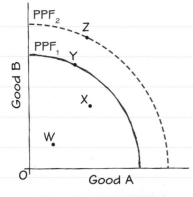

Short-run (actual) economic growth and long-run (potential) economic growth can be shown on a production possibility frontier

Potential growth

Potential growth (also known as long-run growth) is caused by an increase in the capacity of the economy. Potential growth is indicated by the trend rate of growth over time. Potential growth occurs when there is a rise in the quality or quantity of inputs (the factors of production). Potential growth is illustrated through an expansion of the PPF (a movement from C to D) (see diagram below left).

Export-led growth

Export-led growth (international trade) allows an economy to raise aggregate demand beyond that of its domestic markets through trade with other nations. An increase in exports leads to an injection into the circular flow of income, which in turn can be used for investment to fuel further potential growth in the economy.

Now try this

1 What is actual growth?

2 What is potential growth?

3 How can net exports support economic growth?

Output gaps

The growth of an economy fluctuates over time. These fluctuations are known as the trade (business) cycle. They are different than the trend rate of economic growth. Fluctuations in economic growth are linked to real growth, whereas the long-term trend rate of growth is linked to the potential growth of the economy. The difference between the long-term trend rate of growth and fluctuations in real GDP creates **output gaps**.

Negative output gaps

A negative output gap occurs when actual output in the economy falls below the trend output. This may happen during a recession when the economy is underperforming due to a fall in aggregate demand. Characteristics of a negative output gap are:

- underutilised resources
- a high rate of unemployment
- downward pressure of inflation
- low business and consumer confidence.

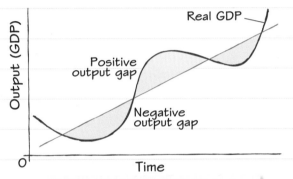

An output gap is the difference between real GDP and potential GDP

Positive output gaps

A positive output gap occurs when actual output is greater than the trend output. A positive output gap may occur during an economic boom period. For a period of time an economy can produce beyond its productive potential when the factors of production are being overused. Characteristics of a positive output gap are:

- over-utilised resources
- upward pressure on inflation
- low rates of unemployment
- high business and consumer confidence.

Measuring output gaps

Unlike actual output, the level of potential output (the difference being the output gap) cannot be observed directly. Potential output and the output gap can only be estimated. Estimating potential output assumes that output can be divided into a trend and a cyclical component. The trend is interpreted as a measure of the economy's potential output and the cycle as a measure of the output gap.

Illustrating output gaps through AD/AS diagrams

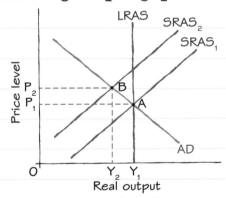

Positive output gap. At A the economy is operating at its full productive potential using all available resources. A fall in SRAS is represented by a shift from SRAS$_1$ to SRAS$_2$. At point B real output is below productive potential (Y$_2$) to create a negative output gap (Y$_1$–Y$_2$). A negative output gap could also be caused by a shift to the left in AD.

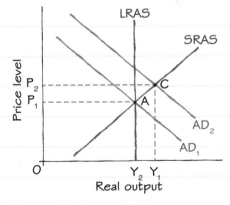

Negative output gap. At A the economy is operating at its full productive potential using all available resources. An increase in AD is represented by a shift from AD$_1$ to AD$_2$. At C real output exceeds productive potential (Y$_2$) to create a positive output gap (Y$_1$–Y$_2$). A positive output gap could also be caused by a shift to the right in SRAS.

Now try this

1 What is a characteristic of a positive output gap?   2 What is a characteristic of a negative output gap?

The trade (business) cycle

The actual growth of an economy fluctuates over time and goes through periods of boom and recession. These fluctuations are known as the trade cycle and are around the long-term trend growth path of output – the trend in the potential output of the economy.

Peak (or boom)

During a boom period, national income is high and the economy may be operating beyond its productive potential (overheating).

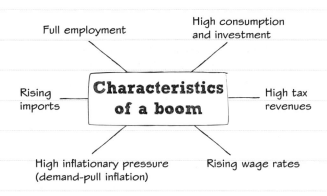

Full employment

High consumption and investment

Rising imports

Characteristics of a boom

High tax revenues

High inflationary pressure (demand-pull inflation)

Rising wage rates

Recession (or slumps)

A recession is characterised by negative economic growth over two consecutive quarters. During a recession a government may use supply-side policies and demand-side policies to stimulate economic growth (see pages 88–90 and 91–92).

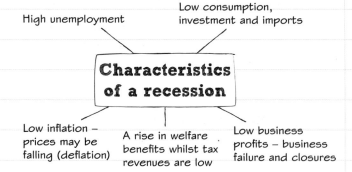

High unemployment

Low consumption, investment and imports

Characteristics of a recession

Low inflation – prices may be falling (deflation)

A rise in welfare benefits whilst tax revenues are low

Low business profits – business failure and closures

Downturn and recovery

As the economy moves from a boom into a downturn, aggregate demand will start to fall. Other features of a downturn are:

- consumption and investment fall
- tax revenues fall
- inflationary pressure eases
- unemployment starts to rise
- demand for imports falls.

During a period of **recovery**, leading to a boom, the reverse of the above starts to happen as the economy recovers from the recession.

Causes of the trade cycle

A number of factors can stimulate the economy to fluctuate between boom and recession. Factors that could lead to a recession include:

- housing market failure
- high interest rates
- a sharp rise in taxation
- world economic recession
- sharp appreciation of the pound
- a stock market crash.

A recession is not a bad thing for everyone. Discount retailers are one example of a sector that may benefit. Most firms will also become more efficient during a recession.

Now try this

1 What are three characteristics of a recession?

2 What are two drawbacks of a boom period?

The impact of economic growth

Over the past 50 years, global economic growth has averaged 2.5% annually. In the Euro zone this rate has been 1.8%. However, in parts of the developing world, economic growth has been much faster. In India economic growth was 7% in 2016. Economic growth is a key objective of all nations, but it can bring about both benefits and drawbacks for consumers, firms and the government. Overall, it leads to improved living standards but it can put financial pressures on an economy.

Benefits and costs of economic growth

👍 Higher wages and incomes

👍 Lower unemployment

👍 Increased tax revenue for the government

👍 Increased life expectancy

👍 Better housing and sanitation

👍 Better health

👍 Improved education – literacy rates

👍 Improved balance of payments on the current account – increasing exports

👎 When the growth rate is too high in an economy, production cannot keep up with demand – this is one reason for economic growth leading to **high rates of inflation**.

👎 **Negative externalities** such as pollution have to be corrected. This might mean governments have to spend tax revenue resolving these issues.

👎 Higher incomes lead to consumers importing more goods from abroad – this can create a **deficit on the balance of payments**.

Impact on current and future living standards

Economic growth leads to the development of industries through improvements in technology, capital stock and infrastructure. The result of this is better goods and services and an overall increase in the standard of living. Nevertheless, economic development can be unsustainable and contribute to falling living standards for some areas of society. Two major reasons include:

1 economic growth leads to **pollution** and damage to the environment (e.g. waste and greenhouse gases)

2 economic growth through capitalist systems can lead to **inequalities**. Although income differentials have decreased between the developing world and western countries. Income inequality between the richest and poorest has increased in the UK. In 2016 the wealthiest 10% of the UK owned almost half of all assets. The top fifth of the UK earned 40% of all income whereas the bottom fifth earned just 8%.

Specific impacts on economic agents

- **Firms** – increased demand leading to increased revenue and profits. However, as the economy changes some industries will decline and disappear, leading to business closures.

- **The government** – tax revenue will rise and benefit payments will fall as employment rates rise. However, governments will have to manage the rate of economic growth to minimise the impact of inflation, the balance of payments and negative externalities.

- **Consumers** – household incomes rise, leading to improved current and future living standards. However, the wealthiest in society benefit the most from economic growth. Those in relative poverty may see little difference. In developing societies, the benefits of increased GDP are felt by the poorest in society.

Human Development Index

One way to measure the standard of living is through the Human Development Index (HDI). The HDI demonstrates that the standard of living has improved across all world regions as a consequence of economic growth.

Synoptic link

For more on this look at Theme 4, page 177.

Now try this

1 What are three benefits of economic growth?

2 What are three drawbacks of economic growth?

3 Does everyone in society benefit from economic growth?

Possible macroeconomic objectives 1

Governments try to manipulate economic factors to improve the performance of the economy. In general, there are a number of common macroeconomic objectives that all governments will have. On this page and the next, you will revise these.

1 Economic growth

High-income nations such as the UK, Germany and the USA may look to achieve growth rates of up to 2.5% GDP, whilst less developed economies, such as Brazil, Romania and Zambia, may be able to achieve annual growth rates of 10% GDP because there is greater potential to develop underutilised land, labour and capital. Economic growth is linked to all other economic objectives and a fast rate of growth can also make it difficult to achieve some other objectives, such as a steady rate of inflation.

2 Low unemployment

Governments aim to achieve low levels of unemployment. Although zero unemployment is not possible, due to frictional and seasonal factors, low unemployment reduces poverty and the necessity for welfare benefits such as Jobseeker's Allowance. High rates of employment also increase government tax revenue through income tax, and support investment in other areas such as education and healthcare. There is a danger for inflationary pressure when an economy reaches full employment.

3 Low and stable rate of inflation

Most developed nations set inflation targets at around 2%. A 2% level of inflation is considered to be a low and stable rate as most economies can cope with this level of price rise. Consumers and businesses can adjust and keep up with this rate. Higher rates of inflation can cause problems such as wiping away the value of savings and can make an economy uncompetitive when trading internationally. Similarly, governments want to avoid deflation, which can lead to a recession and negative economic growth.

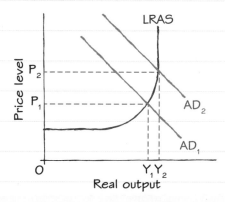

The Keynesian model suggests that as an economy reaches full employment, an increase in AD (AD_1 to AD_2) creates inflationary pressure without increasing real output.

4 Balance of payments equilibrium on current account

A government will want the current account to achieve equilibrium and broadly balance over time. Although economies running a current account surplus are generally seen as being strong, economies can maintain economic growth and hold a current account deficit at the same time. However, in the long term, running a current account deficit is dangerous and can cause problems if borrowers are unable to repay debt.

Deficit	Surplus
• High levels of importing	• Recession leading to domestic businesses focusing their attention selling to international markets
• Failure to compete with cheap foreign goods	
• A sharp rise in the value of the currency	• Fall in AD leading to a reduction in imports
• Protectionism leading to a fall in exports	• A fall in the value of the currency

Factors leading to balance of payments deficit and surplus

UK current account

The UK current account has been in deficit each year since 1984.

Now try this

1 Why would the government set an objective to lower unemployment?

2 How is inflation linked to the pace of economic growth?

Possible macroeconomic objectives 2

5 Balanced government budget

The government's fiscal budget (balance between tax revenue and spending) is another key economic objective. Following the 2008 financial crisis the UK government has been running a fiscal deficit. In March 2018 this deficit was 2% of GDP. Running a large fiscal deficit can help boost economic growth but a deficit is not sustainable in the long-term due to the interest that has to be repaid on the debt. There is disagreement on the rate at which a fiscal deficit should be cut as sharp cuts can lead to a fall in AD and increased unemployment.

 Real world **United Nations Sustainable Development Goals (SDGs)**

The United Nations Sustainable Development Goals (SDGs) is an agreement between the UN's 193 member states on a set of agreed measures and targets for a sustainable world. Many of the 17 SDGs focus on environmental targets but include global issues such as poverty and peace. The UN SDGs are closely aligned to the macroeconomic targets set by most governments.

 **Synoptic link** For more on this look at Theme 4, page 160.

6 Protection of the environment

Economic growth can create negative externalities in the environment. Therefore, governments may use a range of policies to reduce the impact on the environment, such as internalising negative externalities (see page 30). Apart from the depletion of natural resources, economic growth can lead to the destruction of wildlife habitats, pollution of the seas, poorer air quality in cities and global warming. This might be caused by an increase in transportation, the use of natural resources and conversion of green areas into commercial or industrial property. Governments set environmental targets around renewable energy, pollutants, recycling and greenhouse gas emissions.

7 Greater income inequality

Free markets tend to promote income inequality. Governments may therefore intervene and set policies that encourage a fair society and give all citizens a desirable standard of living. Policies to support income equality are the minimum wage, maximum prices, family benefits and tax relief for lower-income earners (see page 9).

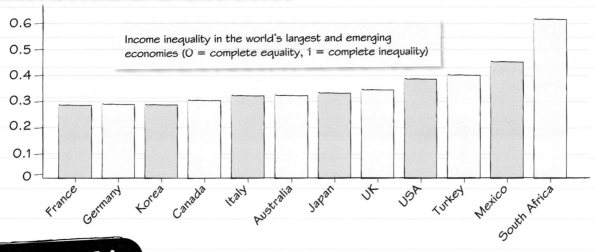

Income inequality in the world's largest and emerging economies (0 = complete equality, 1 = complete inequality)

Now try this

1 Identify two areas where the government might set environmental targets.

2 Why might a government set a deficit fiscal budget?

Monetary policy

In order to achieve a number of macroeconomic objectives, a government may use demand-side policies to boost aggregate demand in the economy. They include monetary policy instruments and fiscal policy (see page 89). Monetary policy instruments are the manipulation by government of monetary variables, such as interest rates and the money supply (quantitative easing).

Interest rates

The rate of interest in an economy has a direct impact on aggregate demand. The higher the rate of interest, the lower the level of aggregate demand.

	Impact of rate of interest
Consumer durables	Some big ticket items, such as cars, white goods and computers, are often bought using credit. The higher the rate of interest, the more these goods cost consumers.
Housing market	The largest expense for most households is the mortgage repayment on their homes. As interest rates rise, household disposable income will fall because more is taken in mortgage repayments.
Wealth effect	Falling interest rates can increase asset prices due to higher demand for houses, government bonds and company shares. If the value of assets rises, people are wealthier and may be encouraged to spend more. The opposite is also true.
Savings	Higher interest rates make saving more appealing. When people save, aggregate demand falls. The opposite is also true.
Exchange rates	A fall in interest rates leads to a fall in the value of a currency. A fall in the exchange rate (the value of a currency) leads to fewer imports and more exports (an increase in net exports equals increased AD).

Quantitative easing

Quantitative easing (QE) is a method used by a central bank to increase the supply of money in an economy to boost AD. The central bank (such as the Bank of England) makes asset purchases which involves buying bonds from banks in exchange for money. Fewer bonds and loans are therefore held by the banks. Instead, they then have more money, which can be made available to consumers and businesses. QE also helps lower interest rates further and is a strategy used when interest rates are already very low.

Bank of England and the MPC

In the UK, the Bank of England has control over monetary policy.

- The Monetary Policy Committee (MPC) – comprises nine members, including the Governor of the Bank of England and the Bank's Chief Economist. There are four independent members appointed by the Chancellor of the Exchequer. All members have expertise in economics and monetary policy.

- The MPC is responsible for making decisions about the Bank Rate – the **base rate of interest** that influences other interest rates across the UK. The MPC can raise, lower or leave the base rate unchanged in order to influence the economy.

- Key objective is to control inflation (target = 2%).

- After controlling inflation, the MPC may aim to achieve other economic objectives such as economic growth and employment.

The process of QE

Money created by central banks

⬇

New money used to buy bonds from financial institutions

⬇

Interest rates fall

⬇

Consumers and firms borrow more

⬇

Spending rises and jobs are created

⬇

AD rises, leading to economic growth

Now try this

What is the relationship between interest rates and savings?

Fiscal policy

Fiscal policy is a second aspect of the demand-side approach to stimulating aggregate demand. Fiscal policy instruments include the use of taxes, government spending and debt to achieve its economic objectives. There are two types of tax: direct and indirect.

Government revenue and expenditure

The government generates revenue from taxation, which is then spent on public services such as roads, healthcare, defence and nationalised industries. Government spending and taxation rarely balance.

How the government spends tax revenue has a significant impact on all economic objectives. The UK **fiscal budget** is announced in autumn by the Chancellor of the Exchequer.

A fiscal policy used to stimulate AD (increase spending and lower taxation) is referred to as **expansionary fiscal policy**. A fiscal policy used to reduce the budget deficit and lower pressure on prices in referred to as a **contractionary fiscal policy**.

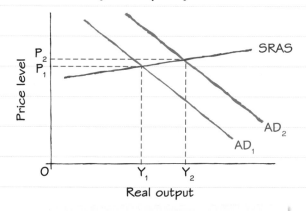

Since 2010, the UK government has been using fiscal policy to reduce national debt

Budget deficit and surplus

There is either a budget (fiscal) surplus or a budget deficit. A budget deficit leads to the government borrowing money. This borrowing is known as the national debt. The balance of any debt is known as public sector net debt. When a budget surplus is set, the government will attempt to reduce the size of the national debt.

Synoptic link For more information on the national debt, see Theme 4, pages 192–194.

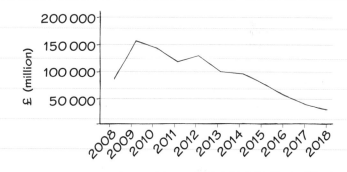

Public sector net borrowing, 2008–2017. The budget deficit is the annual amount the government has borrowed to meet the shortfall between current receipts (tax) and government spending. At the height of the 2009/10 recession net borrowing was £152bn.

Direct and indirect taxes

```
                    ┌──────────────────┐
                    │   Types of tax   │
                    └──────────────────┘
                      │              │
          ┌───────────▼──────┐   ┌───▼──────────────┐
          │   Direct tax     │   │  Indirect tax    │
          │ Levied directly  │   │ Levied on a good │
          │ on an            │   │ or a service     │
          │ individual or    │   │                  │
          │ organisation     │   │ Examples: value  │
          │                  │   │ added tax (VAT), │
          │ Examples: income │   │ excise duties,   │
          │ tax, national    │   │ council tax      │
          │ insurance        │   │                  │
          │ contributions,   │   │                  │
          │ corporation tax  │   │                  │
          └──────────────────┘   └──────────────────┘
```

Now try this

What is an example of a direct tax?

Real world # Historical examples

Economists have learned a lot about **demand-side policies** through key economic events, such as the **Great Depression of the 1930s** and the **Global Financial Crisis of 2008**.

The Great Depression

In the 1930s, the world experienced falling output, deflation and high unemployment. The Great Depression started with the Wall Street Crash in the USA in 1929 which then spread across the globe and had a huge impact on the UK economy. In the UK, government revenue fell, the cost of unemployment benefits rose and the government faced significant budget deficits.

The Global Financial Crisis

The Global Financial Crisis of 2008 started in the USA with subprime mortgage lending. This type of mortgage was offered to people who had low credit ratings and who were likely to have difficulty paying back the loan. To spread the risk, the mortgages were packaged up by the banks and sold on to other financial institutions. When many subprime mortgage borrowers failed to make their repayments, this led to a major financial crisis that spread across the globe.

Economic policy

Expansionary fiscal policy (using government spending and taxation to stimulate demand) became popular as traditional economic policy failed in the USA and the UK.

Economic policy

As with the Great Depression, both the USA and the UK adopted Keynesian fiscal policies to stimulate economic growth.

— The US government had a relaxed approach to economic policy, relying on market forces.

— Low tax rates rose to avoid a budget deficit.

— The depression got worse. Government criticised for not intervening.

— 1933: President Roosevelt introduces the 'New Deal' expansionary fiscal policy.

— Unemployment and poverty fell. Defence spending during Second World War led to full employment.

— UK government policy focused on matching government spending with government revenue. Deflationary fiscal policy applied.

— Cuts to public sector spending and unemployment benefits compounded the effect of the recession.

— The UK leaves the Gold Standard in 1931, leading to the lowering of interest rates and devaluation of the pound.

— Expansionary policy followed with investment in housing and defence spending ahead of Second World War.

— The US government had a relaxed approach to economic policy, relying on market forces.

— Interest rates lowered.

— The depression got worse. Government criticised for not intervening.

— Government funding of banks and motor industry.

— Expansionary policy with pressure on inflation phased out slowly from 2010, possibly leading to a faster recovery from the global recession.

— Jan 2010: Temporary cut to VAT from 17.5% to 15%.

— Monetary policy – base rate of interest lowered to 0.5%.

— Quantitative easing introduced to encourage lending by banks.

— Public money used to bail out failing banks to ensure they did not collapse. Banks returned to the private sector following the recovery.

— 2010: government policy focused on reducing the budget deficit with increase in taxation and cuts in spending. Slow recovery from the recession.

Benefits and drawbacks of demand-side policies

👍 Benefits	👎 Drawbacks
• Effective when economic resources are under-utilised and the economy is operating under its productive capacity to create a short-term boost (shift to the right) in AD.	• Has limited impact when there is a fall in AS and resources are not under-utilised. Here, demand-side policies will cause inflationary pressure.
• Helps smooth out the effect of the business cycle (the extreme impact of a boom or a recession).	• Increases the national debt, with a greater proportion of the national budget being spent on interest payments in the long-term. Too much debt can lead to economic collapse.
• Expansionary and contractionary policy can help stimulate growth through debt during a recession, and pay off the debt during a boom.	• In reality, governments are better at increasing debt than they are at paying it off in periods of strong economic growth.

Now try this

Describe the economic policy adopted by the USA at the start of the Great Depression.

Supply-side policies 1

The aim of government supply-side policies is to expand the productive capacity of the economy (increase the trend rate of economic growth). The basis of supply-side policies is about governments creating the right conditions for the economy to grow. Most supply-side policies are microeconomic because they target individual markets which then combine to affect AS. Supply-side policies may be market based or interventionist.

Market-based policies

These aim to remove factors that may get in the way of a market growing successfully, for example, by encouraging people to work, removing barriers to efficient production and encouraging innovation. Free market economists support these policies as they involve the state having minimum interference in markets.

Interventionist policies

These are designed to correct market failure (see page 29). This might include the under provision of a public good, lack of competition or reducing the negative externalities of markets. Interventionist supply-side policies are associated with command or mixed economies.

Supply-side policies explained through AD/AS diagrams

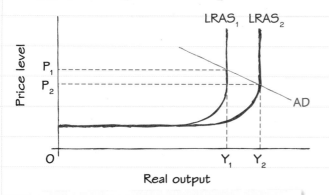

When supply-side policies are successful they will shift long-run aggregate supply (LRAS) to the right (LRAS₁ to LRAS₂). This will increase real economic output from Y_1 to Y_2 and reduce the average price level in the economy from P_1 to P_2.

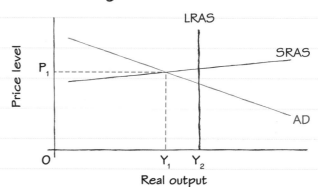

Where short-run aggregate supply (SRAS) equilibrium output is below LRAS, the economy is operating below its productive capacity. In order to achieve full employment, aggregate demand must rise at a faster rate than LRAS.

Policies to increase incentives

From a supply-side perspective, incentives in markets exist to encourage people to work and businesses to invest. Examples of ways the government can incentivise work and investment include:

- lowering the marginal income tax rate
- reducing welfare benefits
- subsidising workers – tax credits
- lowering tax on profits so firms have more to invest
- off-setting research and development investment against taxes on profits.

The right level of incentive

Incentives can be too small or too big. The **poverty trap** refers to a small or even negative gain a low-paid employee may experience as a result of a promotion that leads to the loss of benefits or move into a higher tax bracket. Similarly, the **unemployment trap** may occur when the benefits of working are outweighed by unemployment benefits. The solution of reducing benefits will ultimately have the impact of increasing poverty.

Now try this

1 What is a free market supply-side policy?

2 What are two examples of supply-side policies to incentivise investment?

3 What are the problems of supply-side incentives to work?

Supply-side policies 2

Promote competition

A lack of competition in markets leads to high prices, poor quality (both in terms or service and product quality) and a lack of innovation. The government can do a number of things to encourage competitive markets. However, there has to be sufficient profit incentive for firms to supply goods and services. Their actions can include:

- **privatisation** – associated with command and mixed economies (see pages 8–9)
- **deregulation** – removing government controls
- **competition policy** – aimed at reducing the power of monopolies
- **industrial policy** – supporting firms and industries that have a significant impact on economic growth (less common in the UK).

(For more on promoting competition, see pages 35–37 and 38–39.)

Improve infrastructure

Poor infrastructure in an economy, such as roads, rail, hospitals and broadband, can lead to low productivity and labour immobility. Capital expenditure in the economy can help boost short-term AD but can also shift LRAS too. Recent examples in the UK include:

- the free schools movement – funding for new schools
- a third runway at Heathrow airport
- HS2 rail network with faster connections between London and the North.

Reform – the labour market

LRAS is significantly influenced by the quantity of labour in markets and the productivity of that labour. The more flexible the labour market, the lower the level of unemployment. In order to reform the labour market and increase flexibility, governments can improve:

- **geographical flexibility** – increase transport links and provide affordable housing which can increase the willingness of workers to relocate or travel to find work
- **external numerical flexibility** – make it easier for firms to adjust their workforce, such as using flexible contracts
- **wage flexibility** – the ability to adjust wages based on supply and demand. This may involve curbing trade union powers in a given market.

Improve the quality of the labour force

The quality of a labour force can be improved by investment in human capital such as education and training.

- **Education** – standards can be affected by how long young people have to stay in formal education, the nature of the curriculum and how young people are taught.
- **Training** – firms may typically provide less training than is optimal in order to maximise short-term profits. Often, governments have to incentivise such human capital investment. The UK government's apprenticeship levy is one way the government can support businesses to invest in training.
- **Immigration** – encouraging immigration can help reduce skills shortages in a country and increase the overall size of the labour market.

The benefits and drawbacks of supply-side policies

👍 Benefits	👎 Drawbacks
• Increasing the trend rate of economic growth (shifting LRAS to the right) makes it easier to achieve macroeconomic objectives.	• Supply-side policies have little impact when there is a negative output gap. AD must increase in order for full employment to be achieved.
• Supply-side policies are effective at reducing inflation.	• Supply-side policies may not address low levels of consumer confidence associated with a recession.
• Unlike demand-side policies, supply-side policies can be targeted to deal with structural unemployment.	• It can take a long time to see the impact of investments in the economy.
• Supply-side policies will include an element of government spending which will also shift AD to the right, in addition to the impact on LRAS.	• Supply-side policies can lead to inequality and exploitation, for example, benefit cuts to incentivise work or deregulating a market leading to exploitation of customers.

Now try this

How can a government increase competition in a market?

Macroeconomic conflicts and trade-offs

A successful sustainable economy is one where a government is achieving all of its macroeconomic objectives. In reality, this can be very difficult to achieve as there are many conflicts and trade-offs that exist.

A successful economy

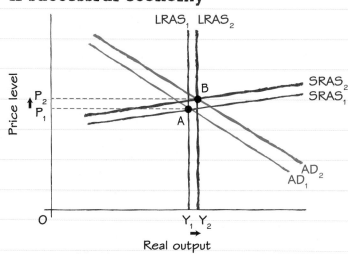

A successful economy is one which experiences steady economic growth, where AD is rising at a slightly faster rate than LRAS in order to maintain a steady rate of inflation. The government will manage a balanced budget and be able to address issues of inequality and environmental protection at the same time as investing in the future of the country and maintaining full employment. At point A the economy is in short-run and long-run equilibrium. The new equilibrium at B – AD has increased, the economy is close to full employment and there is mild inflation. For periods of time the economy may operate above its productive potential.

Reducing inflation through contractionary fiscal policy (used to 'cool down' economic growth and inflationary pressure).

- Could lead to cyclical unemployment
- Can lead to recession

Encouraging economic growth by raising AD.

- Creates inflationary pressure
- Increases imports lowering net exports

Lowering unemployment through supply-side reforms.

- Could create greater inequality
- Investment in infrastructure causing negative externalities in the environment

Conflicts between macroeconomic objectives

Improving the current account on the balance of payments by cutting imports.

- Could lead to higher unemployment if there is retaliation by other countries
- Any protectionist measures could lead to retaliation from abroad and a fall in exports

Reducing inequalities in income and wealth by redirecting income through taxes and spending.

- Disincentivising work, contributing to unemployment
- Reduce flexibility in the labour market and increase costs for businesses through an increase in minimum wages

Cutting a fiscal deficit through contractionary fiscal policy.

- Austerity will raise unemployment
- Lower economic growth and potential recession

Now try this

1 Identify two conflicts in economic objectives associated with raising AD.
2 Identify two economic conflicts associated with improving the environment.

Conflicts in economic policy

Different economic policies can have different effects which can conflict with each other or with economic objectives (see pages 86 and 87 for a reminder of macroeconomic objectives). One theory that explains the conflict between unemployment and inflation is the Phillips Curve.

The short-run Phillips Curve

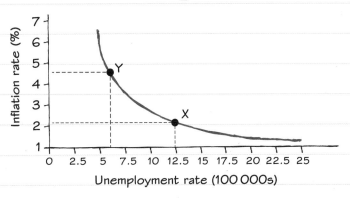

The short-run Phillips Curve demonstrates the macroeconomic trade-off between unemployment and inflation

The economist, A.W. Phillips studied the relationship between the rate of unemployment and the change of money wages (a key contributor towards the level of inflation in an economy). Phillips found that unemployment and inflation had an inverse relationship: as unemployment falls the rate of inflation rises. This trade-off can also be shown on an AD/SRAS diagram through a shift to the right in AD.

Expansionary fiscal policy

Expansionary or contractionary fiscal policy can be used to smooth out the impact of the business cycle.

Lowering taxes and increasing government spending will boost AD, but the trade-off is often one of inflationary pressure and a net trade deficit. Conversely, contractionary fiscal policy may help solve at least one of these problems and reduce a budget deficit. However, the opposite trade-off will exist as AD will fall, creating unemployment. Significant periods of austerity could even lower LRAS if capital resources are not replenished or there is a de-skilling of the labour market.

Changes in interest rates

As with fiscal policy, monetary policy can be used to influence AD. Lowering interest rates will boost spending but also has the potential to influence inflation in the short term. Low interest rates can also lead to the price of assets such as house prices increasing. High rates of interest may be desirable to curb inflation and 'cool down' the economy, but persistently high rates of interest can damage long-term investment and appreciate the value of a currency, weakening international competitiveness and the ability to export.

Environmental policies

Environmental policies may include investing in renewable energy, recycling, and protecting natural habitats or sites of heritage. Such policies may actually shift LRAS to the left and therefore lower economic growth. This is because environmental policies generally increase costs for businesses and lower productivity and efficiency. Nevertheless, environmental policies should also increase LRAS compared to a position where extensive market failure is caused through unsustainable business practices as a result of pollution and resource depletion.

Supply-side policies

Supply-side policies should increase the productive potential of an economy through investment in infrastructure and capital goods, creating effective conditions for markets to function efficiently. However, trade union intervention and deregulation can lead to inequalities in the economy. Short-term investment can also increase AD (a positive) but add to inflationary pressure, even if the long-term impact is to reduce it and increase output.

Now try this

What are the limitations of using interest rates to control inflation?

Exam skills 1: Section A

Section A of **AS** and **A level Paper 2** consists of **multiple-choice** and **short-answer** questions, often with stimulus material. These assess your knowledge and understanding of economic concepts and your ability to interpret economic data. You can use the data (such as tables, diagrams, graphs) to support your answers where relevant. Below are some exam-style multiple-choice questions with exemplar answers.

Worked example

AS/AL

1 The diagram below shows a shift in the long-run aggregate supply curve for an economy from LRAS$_1$ to LRAS$_2$.

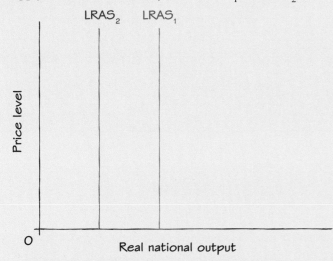

The shift in the long-run aggregate supply curve is most likely to have been caused by a fall in:

A the capital stock.   ☑

B income tax rates.   ☐

C the growth of labour productivity.   ☐

D interest rates.   ☐   **(1 mark)**

🔗 **Links** For more on shifts in the LRAS curve, see page 73.

Start by ensuring you understand what the data is showing you. You could annotate the data to highlight any trends or patterns. Look for options that you can rule out easily before you select the answer. The time you spend on a multiple-choice question should be comparable with the number of marks awarded – roughly 1 per minute.

Always clarify the direction of any shifts on a diagram. The capital stock includes factories and machinery. If these are not invested in then they will depreciate and their productive capacity falls, causing a fall in LRAS.

Worked example

AS/AL

2 The table below shows the index of gross domestic product (GDP) measured at current prices and the associated price index for an economy.

Year	Index of GDP at current prices (2008 = 100)	Price index (2008 = 100)
2005	80	80
2015	130	110

The table shows that between 2005 and 2015:

A real GDP rose by 50%.   ☐

B nominal GDP rose by 50%.   ☐

C real GDP rose by less than 50%.   ☑

D nominal GDP rose by less than 50%. ☐   **(1 mark)**

🔗 **Links** See page 52 for information on gross domestic product.

Make sure you are familiar with the definitions of the main economic concepts. The key difference between real GDP and nominal GDP is that real GDP is adjusted for inflation.

Exam skills 2: Section A

Section A of **AS** and **A level Paper 2** also contains short-answer questions. Remember, you can use the data provided where relevant.

AS Paper 2 covers **Theme 2**. A level Paper 2 covers **Themes 2 and 4**. Make sure you know which paper you are taking and the theme or themes it covers.

Worked example   AS

3 Define the term cyclical unemployment.   **(1 mark)**

Unemployment is associated with a general fall in the level of aggregate demand. Cyclical unemployment occurs as the economy moves through the economic cycle. As the demand for goods and services changes, so does the demand for labour and therefore the unemployment rate.

'Definition' questions feature on the AS exam papers. They are worth 1 or 2 marks and require a simple description of the term.

Worked example   AS/AL

4 The government of an economy plans to invest $30 billion over the next 10 years on a new airport and improvements to its docks.

Explain how the investment will impact on the price level in the economy. Use an aggregate supply and aggregate demand diagram in your answer.   **(4 marks)**

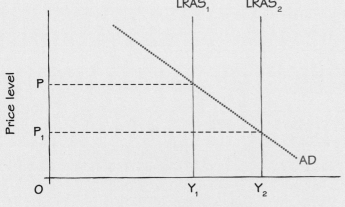

Explain

'Explain' questions expect you to apply your knowledge to a particular context. You are required to make a point to demonstrate your knowledge.

Some 'explain' questions will ask you to include a diagram. Make sure it is clearly labelled and drawn with a ruler. Specific points on the X and Y axis should also be labelled to demonstrate the direction of any shifts.

The investment of £30 million will improve the capital stock within the economy and increase the productive potential over the next 10 years. This is because a new airport and docks will not only create new jobs in the economy, but also increase the potential supply of goods in and out of the country. In the short term, AD will shift to the right as investment is a component of AD. Initially this is likely to increase the price level. However, the long-run impact will be for a shift from LRAS₁ to LRAS₂ increasing real national output from Y₁ to Y₂. This will create downward pressure on the price level from P to P₁ due to reduced demand-pull inflation.

The explanation has several linked strands of development. The answer makes reference to the context and refers to the supply and demand diagram that the student has drawn. Make sure you do this whenever drawing a diagram to support an answer.

Exam skills 3: Section A

Section A of **AS** and **A level Paper 2** also contain 'calculate' questions, which sometimes include data.

Worked example AS/AL

Country Z: trade accounts (£ million)	2015	2016
Trade in goods	−145,600	−160,300
Trade in services	90,400	105,200
Net primary income	−50,650	−30,700
Net secondary income	−25,000	−20,100
Current account balance	−130,850	−105,900
Current balance as % of GDP	−5.2	−3.9

Using the data on Country Z's trade accounts in 2015 and 2016, answer the following questions.

5 With reference to the data, calculate:

(a) the current account balances for Country Z in 2015 and

(b) the trade in goods for 2016. **(2 marks)**

(a) −45,600 + 90,400 + −50,650 + −25,000 =
−£130,850

(b) −105,900 − (150,200 + −30,700 + −20,100) =
−£160,300 deficit

 Maths skills Always ensure you use the **correct denominations** in your answers. For example, each of these answers should be expressed in £s.

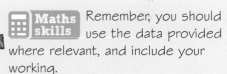 **Maths skills** Remember, you should use the data provided where relevant, and include your working.

Worked example AL

6 Using appropriate calculations, explain whether Country Z's economy performed better in 2015 or 2016. **(4 marks)**

2015: −130,850 / 0.052 = 2,516,346 or £2.51 trillion
2016: −105,900 / 0.039 = 2,715,384 or £2.71 trillion

In 2015 the current account balance for Country Z was a greater value and a greater percentage of total GDP than in 2016. This means that there was a larger current account deficit – more money leaving the economy in 2015 than 2016. Furthermore, in 2016 total GDP was £200m higher than in 2015 (not adjusted for inflation). Both these figures would suggest that Country Z's economy performed better in 2016.

 Maths skills As we know that the current account balance is a percentage of total GDP, we can divide it by the percentage to work out total GDP in 2015 and 2016.

Exam skills 4: Section B

Section B of **AS** and **A level Papers 1** and **2** contains a range of economic stimulus material based on a real-world topic. There may be up to three extracts. Following the extracts, there is one question, divided into sub-questions, based on the information. Always read the data carefully before you begin answering the question. Below is an example of an exam-style extract followed by an 'explain' question and answer.

Extract A: Nigeria's oil

Nigeria's economy grew by 1.5% in the third quarter of 2017. The growth was driven by increased oil output by the world's 13th largest producer of oil. Output of 2.03 million barrels a day was achieved – up from 1.87 million barrels a day average in the previous quarter. This growth is expected to continue into 2018. This period of economic growth comes after a recession in 2016 that saw Nigeria's economy shrink by 1.6%. A key component of Nigeria's economy, oil production, has always been uncertain in the Niger River delta region, where armed militants have attacked pipelines in the past.

5

Reference: Bloomberg

Worked example

7 (a) Nigeria is the world's 13th largest producer and net exporter of crude oil.

With reference to Extract A and using an appropriate diagram, explain the impact on aggregate demand of changes in Nigeria's oil output.   **(5 marks)**

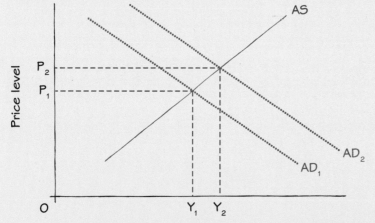

Real national output

> On an 'explain with a diagram' question, it is important that your diagram is representative of the data in the extract. The increase in the number of barrels of oil is represented by a shift to the right in AD.

Nigeria's oil output is expected to rise from 1.87 million barrels per day to 2.03 million, based on forecasts from the extract. As Nigeria is a net exporter of oil, export revenue would be expected to rise, contributing to an increase in aggregate demand as indicated by a shift from AD₁ to AD₂. Real national output will therefore rise from Y₁ to Y₂ with inflationary pressure increasing the price level from P₁ to P₂. However, as oil is a key component of AS, any increase in output is likely to lower the costs of producers in the economy. This could lead to an increase in SRAS, relieving pressure on inflation and shifting equilibrium output in the short-term to the right.

> The response draws on data from the extract and uses this to interpret a shift in AD. This is shown on the demand and supply diagram and clearly explained with logical chains of reasoning. The student has also used the context to suggest how increased production of oil may also increase SRAS.

Exam skills 5: Section B

Below is an example of an exam-style extract followed by an 'examine' question and exemplar answer. Look back at the extract on page 98 before continuing below.

Examine

'Examine' questions test the assessment objectives of knowledge (AO1), application (AO2), analysis (AO3) and evaluation (AO4). Application means that your response **must** be in the context of the question and should not be generic.

☑ Read the evidence provided and use this in your response.

☑ Identify at least two reasons, factors, etc.

☑ Use paragraphs.

☑ Evaluate each factor. One way to do this is to consider the drawbacks of each factor.

Worked example   AL

(b) With reference to Extract A, examine **two** factors that could impact on Nigeria's ability to increase production of oil. **(8 marks)**

One factor that could considerably impact on Nigeria's ability to increase the supply of crude oil in the future is **investment**. Investment would involve government spending and private investment from companies within Nigeria or FDI from international oil companies such as BP or Shell. Investment would introduce new production and refinery facilities (investment in capital goods) and through technological advancements increase the productive capacity of the industry. As oil is a significant export of Nigeria and factoring in AS, this could also improve Nigeria's balance of payments and shift LRAS to the right. However, any investment in oil production may take a number of years before an impact on supply is realised.

Another factor that could potentially limit Nigeria's ability to produce oil is **political instability**. Extract A identifies issues the country has had with armed militants attacking pipelines and this is a factor contributing to fluctuations in output and possibly the slump in 2016. Political instability such as the Iraq–Iran War can have a huge impact on the ability of countries to produce oil and uncertainty in the market, leading to significant price rises. However, political instability is less likely to impact on Nigeria's long-term ability to supply produce barrels of oil unless infrastructure is significantly damaged, which could result in a shift in LRAS to the left and a contraction in economic growth.

Overall, as political instability can be short-lived, investment would be the most significant factor in determining Nigeria's ability to increase oil output. However, oil output from oil producing nations will always depend on the strategy adopted by OPEC when attempting to influence the global market for oil.

Links This is a very open question. The two factors you choose could come from a range of topics covered in Theme 2, for example, investment (page 65), net trade (page 69), causes of growth (page 82) or the trade cycle (page 84).

Identify at least two different reasons or factors, then explain them before offering some evaluation.

The student has examined two clear factors: **investment** and **political instability**. The factors do not have to be linked, although comparing them may help when evaluating.

In an 'examine' question there are 2 marks for evaluation. You should include evaluative statements in your answer, such as commenting on the validity or significance of each factor.

Exam skills 6: Section B

Section B of **AS** and **A level Papers 1** and **2** contains a range of stimulus material based on a real-world topic.

Assess

'Assess' questions test the assessment objectives of knowledge (AO1), application (AO2), analysis (AO3) and evaluation (AO4). Your response **must** be in the context of the question and should not be generic. There are no right or wrong answers to these questions – it is up to you to present your arguments.

For an example of a 'discuss' question, see Theme 1 pages 45 and 50.

Extract B: UK lending

Recent Bank of England figures show a decline in the growth rate of money in the economy and lending to UK consumers. The outstanding balance of consumer credit – including personal loans, car finance and credit card lending – rose only £0.3bn in March, compared with an average monthly rise of £1.5bn over the previous six months, the biggest decline coming from car finance. Loan repayments jumped 14.5% this March compared with a year ago, suggesting that consumers are paying back loans on new cars purchased three years ago in March, a key month for new car sales. New car sales for March were also down 15.7% year on year.

5

10

Source: Financial Times

'Assess' questions require you to weigh up a scenario and apply economic concepts to the context. Make sure you use the context from the question and consider both sides of the argument. Aim to quote or use figures from the extracts.

Worked example   (AS/AL)

(c) With reference to Extract B, assess the impact on UK businesses of a decline in lending to consumers. **(10 marks)**

A reduction in lending is likely to reduce the demand for goods and services which are commonly purchased using loans or credit. This fall in demand is likely to result in lower revenues and, assuming costs remain constant, a fall in profit levels. A lack of credit may cause consumers to delay their purchases as they require more time to accumulate enough savings to make the purchase if no alternative is available. Consumers may also switch from purchasing new cars to used cars, which may be significantly cheaper. This may force firms to discount 'new' products to ensure they can sell stock, further reducing revenues.

However, it depends on the product/industry, large purchases of luxury items such as cars are likely to be more affected given that they are more commonly bought using a loan. Where items take up a lower proportion of household income, firms may be less affected as consumers do not require time to save. For the UK, a decline in lending may have a more significant effect than in other nations due to the reliance on and availability of cheap credit in recent years.

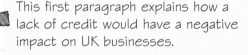

This first paragraph explains how a lack of credit would have a negative impact on UK businesses.

There is some evaluation in this last paragraph but your answers for 'assess', 'discuss' and 'evaluate' questions should show evaluation throughout with clear chains of reasoning.

Exam skills 7: Section C

Section B of **AS Papers 1 and 2** and Section C of **A level Papers 1 and 2** contain a choice of two extended open-response questions – you must answer **one** of them. The skills required are the same at both AS and A level. Below is an example of a Section C A level exam-style 25-mark open-response (evaluation) question and an exemplar answer. (You will find an AS Section B 20-mark exam-style question and exemplar answer on page 46.)

Worked example   AL

8 Evaluate the various policies that could be used to help an economy, such as that of the UK, to boost the rate of economic growth. Refer to real policy decisions in your answer.   **(25 marks)**

The Bank of England reduced the bank rate from 0.5% to 0.25% in 2016 in response to concerns about macroeconomic performance. A decline in the bank rate should lower the cost of borrowing and reduce the incentive to save. Consumers and firms should therefore increase borrowing and spend more on both household goods and capital goods. C and I are both components of aggregate demand which should lead to the AD curve shifting to the right. This causes an expansion along the AS curve and an increase in the output of goods/services in the economy, ultimately leading to economic growth, correcting the slowdown.

However, a reduction in the bank rate is only likely to be effective if commercial banks pass on the reduction to firms and consumers. Given that the bank rate is already at historically low levels, this is less likely to happen and the real cost of borrowing would actually remain constant. Firms are also only likely to increase borrowing for investment purposes if the economy is operating close to the full employment level of output. Given the economy is expected to experience a slowdown, this may signal to firms that they don't need to expand their productive capacity and firms may choose to cut back on planned investment irrespective of changes to interest rates.

Given that there does appear to be a clear correlation between the slowdown in growth and a reduction in household borrowing, this policy may be particularly effective as it directly addresses one of the main causes of the slowdown itself...

...On balance, although other components of AD may decline and could offset an increase in C, it is unlikely given that consumption is by far the largest component of AD. It is therefore likely that decreasing the amount of income tax paid would lead to increased spending but the effectiveness of the policy may depend on whether or not other taxes remain constant. Although the personal tax allowance may have been increased, a rise in national insurance contributions may offset any benefit to the level of disposable income. Households may not be left with any additional income to spend and therefore the slowdown would not be corrected.

🔗 Links You need to draw on your understanding of the concepts in Theme 2, in particular, demand-side policies for economic growth (page 90) and supply-side policies (page 91).

Evaluate

You need to weigh up a scenario, before offering some evaluation. This tests all four assessment objectives. Your response must be in the context of the question.

 It is important to provide specific examples of government policies and economic trends to support your analysis.
Here, a real example of UK monetary policy is used in the answer

When concluding a 25 mark question, it is important to draw on your analysis and identify what you believe to be the most important factor. In this case, which factor is the most significant in boosting economic growth. Your conclusion should also identify what the outcome may depend on.

 Next, this answer should discuss an alternative policy to lower interest rates, for example, raising the personal tax allowance. This might increase consumer ability and willingness to spend and increase the size of the multiplier. An appropriate demand and supply diagram could be used to support the analysis, showing a shift to the right in the demand curve. There should also be some balance, perhaps a discussion of how consumer spending is only one component of AD or the importance of consumer confidence for MPC.

Exam-style practice: Section A

These questions will help you to practise for Paper 2 of your AS or A level exams.

1 The economy is experiencing a balance of payments surplus on current account and high unemployment. Which policy is most likely to reduce both the balance of payments surplus on current account and unemployment? **(1 mark)**

A A cut in income tax.

B A rise in interest rates.

C An increase in the exchange rate.

D A fall in government spending.

> Think about which of these policies would lower government revenue from taxation and incentivise work.

2 The diagram below shows the aggregate demand (AD) and short-run aggregate supply (SRAS) curves for an economy. The economy is in equilibrium at point E.

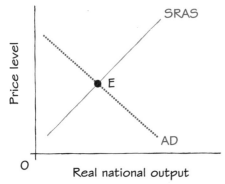

> Consider which of the options might contribute to AD shifting to the left or SRAS shifting to the right.

Which **one** of the following would be likely to lead to a new equilibrium position, with a fall in the price level? **(1 mark)**

A A fall in exports.

B An increase in government spending.

C A fall in productivity.

D An increase in wage rates.

3 Using the diagram below, illustrate a negative output gap by adding a trade cycle to the trend line. **(1 mark)**

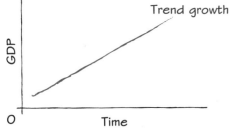

> Make sure you use a ruler and ensure your annotation is clear.

4 *It is estimated that there will be 76,000 drones in the UK's skies by 2030, and this will contribute to economic growth in the UK. Savings and efficiency could increase UK productivity by 3.2%.*

Explain **one** way that growth in drone technology could support the government's macroeconomic objectives. **(4 marks)**

> Think about the different themes within economics, such as transport, employment and so on, and also the industries that may benefit, such as delivery, manufacturing and retail.

5 Calculate the total increase in national income in Nepal of $28 million investment from the World Bank if the nation has marginal propensity to consume of 0.75. **(4 marks)**

> **Maths skills** Start your calculation by writing out the formula for the multiplier. Remember that the multiplier can be calculated using MPC.

Exam-style practice: Section B data

Use these data extracts to help you answer the Section B exam-style questions on page 104.

Energy

Extract A: Investment in Bangladesh

The World Bank has approved $55 million to increase renewable energy use in rural areas of Bangladesh where grid electricity does not reach.

The project will lead to the installation of 1,000 solar irrigation pumps enabling about 10 million people to access electricity. The funding will also help increase use of solar irrigation pumps, a cost-effective technology that maximises the sunny climate in Bangladesh. The move will reduce the dependence on diesel pumps. The Bangladesh government has previously had to heavily subside the import of diesel as a fuel for cooking in rural areas.

Reference: World Bank

5

Extract B: UK coal usage

Renewable energies such as offshore wind turbines continue to replace fossil fuels such as coal in many major economies. Recently, the UK went a record 55 hours without burning coal to produce electricity. Currently the UK leads many countries on its investment in wind turbines and fields of solar panels. Plans are to switch off all coal plants by 2025 in favour of renewable energy.

Reference: Bloomberg

5

Extract C: Biofuel growth

Palm oil is found in around half of food and consumer products on supermarket shelves, and its use is growing. There has also been significant growth in demand for the oil as a fuel substitute. Production of palm oil has required significant proportions of rainforest to be cut down to make room for the crop. Malaysia and Indonesia are two of the world's largest producers of palm oil, supplying almost 80% of global consumption. There are some concerns around the industry's ability to keep up with growing demand from both sectors. Significant efforts are being made to find comparable replacements for palm oil, but palm oil is one of the most economical sources of cooking oils, and also has the highest oil yield of any oil crop.

Reference: gro-intelligence

5

As you read through these extracts, look out for any factors linked to key macroeconomic objectives and note the impact they may have. For example, any point that could impact on GDP, employment, inflation of the balance of payments on the current account.

Exam-style practice: Sections B and C

Look at the extracts on page 103 before attempting the exam-style questions below, which will help you practise for Section B of your AS exam and Sections B and C of your A level Paper 2 exam.

Section B

6 Explain using a diagram the impact of investment in offshore wind turbines on the productive potential of the UK economy.   **(5 marks)**

AS/AL

> When drawing diagrams in an explain question, there will be one mark for an accurate diagram, a second for accurate labels and a third for demonstrating the appropriate change, e.g. a shift in LRAS.

7 With reference to Extract B, examine **two** consequences to the UK economy of a reduction in the consumption of coal.   **(8 marks)**

AL

> Two marks are also available for evaluation so you must include evaluative comments in your response to access full marks.

8 With reference to Extract C, discuss how the growth in alternative oil-based crops such as palm oil could impact on the balance of payments on the current account for countries such as Malaysia and Indonesia.   **(12 marks)**

AL

> Explain the factors that contribute to the balance of payments on the current account in the context of Extract C.

> Evaluative points could be made by explaining how any fall in demand for oil-based crops could be minimised by Malaysia and Indonesia.

9 With reference to Extract C, assess the possible trade-offs between macroeconomic objectives regarding the growth in biofuels in nations such as Malaysia and Indonesia.   **(10 marks)**

AS/AL

> You must demonstrate clear knowledge and analysis of economic issues, as well as some evaluation. This might include judgements about the most significant trade-off or identifying a limiting factor that could reduce the impact of the trade-off.

10 Discuss whether the growth in renewable energies is likely to lead to an increase in aggregate demand in the UK.   **(15 marks)**

AS/AL

Section C

11 Evaluate the impact of a decade of ultra-low interest rates on the macroeconomic performance of the UK economy.   **(25 marks)**

AL

> Consider the components of AD and discuss how growth in renewable energy could influence consumption, investment and government spending.

> Plan your answer and consider the concepts and diagrams you are going to use. Try to use a couple of real world examples linked to real markets or policies. Consider at least two factors in comparison to ensure a balanced answer. When concluding your answer, identify what you believe to be the 'most important factor' leading to your judgement.

Why some firms grow

A key assumption in economics is that firms aim to maximise profits. How firms do this can differ. In some industries, firms tend to be very large, for example, car manufacturers and water suppliers. In other industries, firms tend to be small, for example, window cleaners and newsagents. Where firms grow large, the principal–agent problem may arise.

Why do firms want to grow?

1 **Profits** – the larger the firm, the higher its sales will be, from which it can generate higher profits.

2 **Costs** – operating on a larger scale can lead to lower unit costs. (To revise economies of scale, see page 115).

3 **Market power** – a larger firm is more able to control its markets and reduce competition.

4 **Reducing risk** – larger firms can operate in different markets, and thus minimise the impact of one market or product becoming less profitable.

5 **Managerial motives** – the goals of owners and managers might be geared towards growth.

The divorce of ownership from control

When firms grow in size and become larger entities, the **divorce of ownership from control** can occur. Shareholders own the firm but appoint directors and managers to run it on their behalf. Shareholders want to maximise profits to maximise their dividends, whereas managers might have different motives, such as wanting to increase sales and revenue at the expense of profits. This may lead to the **principal–agent problem** where the principal (the shareholder) and the agent (the manager) have divergent aims. This may result in the business growing larger than a firm which simply aims to maximise profit.

Lack of finance for expansion (see page 109)   Avoids diseconomies of scale (see page 116)

May be a monopoly (see page 133)

Reasons for a firm opting to operate on a smaller scale

Provides a personal service

Barriers to entry are low (see page 127)   Supplies niche products (see below)

Niche products: a reason not to grow

Niche products have a low price elasticity of demand (PED) or a high income elasticity of demand (YED). Where a product has a low PED, a price change will cause a smaller percentage change in quantity demanded (see diagram right). As such, there is no great need for the business to expand to reduce unit costs.

Synoptic link To revise price, income and cross elasticities of demand, see pages 13–16.

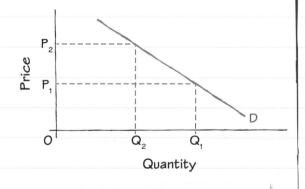

A niche product has a low price elasticity of demand of between 0 and 1

Now try this

1 Explain how growing in size will help a firm to reduce risk.

2 Give two reasons why a firm may not want to grow in size.

3 Describe what is meant by the principal–agent problem.

Public and private sector organisations

The objectives and motives of public sector and private sector organisations can be very different. Not-for-profit organisations have their own objectives.

Public sector organisations

Public sector organisations are owned and controlled by the state. Their purpose is to provide a service to society. Making a profit is not their main aim.

Civil service departments such as the Home Office and The Forestry Commission

Public corporations such as Highways England

Examples of public sector organisations

National regulatory authorities such as Ofcom and Ofgem

Local authorities

Trusts such as the NHS or education academies

Private sector organisations

Private sector organisations are owned by individuals or other companies. Their aim is almost always to make a profit. Not-for-profit organisations are part of the private sector but they do not have profit maximisation as their main aim. Charities, for example, use any profit they may make (known as a surplus) to further the causes they support.

Why there are different sectors

The public sector exists to provide services which may otherwise not be provided by the market. For example, street lighting cannot be provided by the market, so the public sector – in this case, the local authority – provides these as public goods. (To revise public goods, see page 33.)

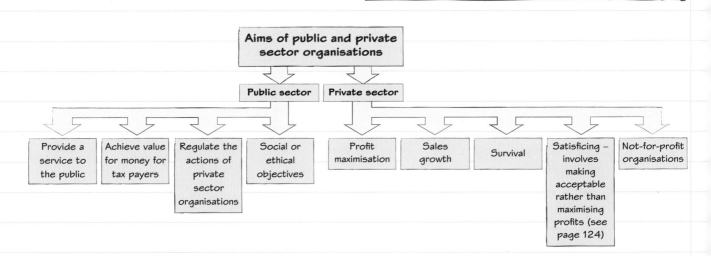

Aims of public and private sector organisations

Public sector — Private sector

| Provide a service to the public | Achieve value for money for tax payers | Regulate the actions of private sector organisations | Social or ethical objectives | Profit maximisation | Sales growth | Survival | Satisficing – involves making acceptable rather than maximising profits (see page 124) | Not-for-profit organisations |

Now try this

1 Explain the difference between the objectives of public and private sector organisations.

2 Describe the difference between profit and not-for-profit organisations.

How firms grow

Business growth can be achieved in a number of ways. Firms can grow internally by achieving higher sales, or externally through a process of **integration**.

How firms grow

Internal growth   External growth

Organic growth   Integration

Vertical integration –   Horizontal   Conglomerate
forward and backward   integration   integration

Organic (internal) growth

Organic growth is when firms increase their output, for example, through increased investment in new machinery or through an increased labour force. The term organic refers to 'internal' growth. The firm might choose to increase its output in this way due to increased demand for its product.

🌐 Real world   Organic growth at Wren Kitchens

Wren Kitchens is a privately owned manufacturer and retailer of fitted kitchens. Founded in 2009, the business has grown dramatically over recent years. The business is benefiting from the demand for fitted kitchens. It now employs over 4000 staff and has 78 showrooms nationwide. This is an example of organic growth.

Integration (external growth)

Growth can also be achieved by firms joining together. When two, usually larger, businesses are brought together through a merger or takeover, this is referred to as **integration**.

- A **merger** is when two or more firms join under one ownership.
- A **takeover** involves one firm buying another firm.

Vertical integration

Vertical integration is a merger of two or more firms at different production stages within the same industry. There are two types of vertical integration.

- **Backward vertical integration** – a firm merges with a business operating at an earlier stage in the industrial process, for example, a bread manufacturer purchases farms that produce wheat.
- **Forward vertical integration** – a firm merges with a business at a later stage in the industrial process, for example, in 2018 Coca-Cola bought the UK cafe chain, Costa Coffee, partly as a way of distributing Coca-Cola products to consumers.

Horizontal integration

Horizontal integration involves two firms at the same stage of production in the same industry merging, for example, a merger between two supermarket chains or two financial services companies.

Conglomerate integration

Conglomerate integration or a conglomerate merger is when two firms with no interests in common join together. This could also be in the form of a takeover. Google's purchase of the video-sharing website YouTube was an example of conglomerate integration.

A conglomerate has a large number of diversified businesses.

Now try this

1 Give two examples of forward vertical integration and backward vertical integration.
2 Describe how a merger and a takeover are different.
3 Explain which type of integration would be used if an aerospace company merged with an airline.

Advantages and disadvantages of growth

Organic growth and the different types of integration have both advantages and disadvantages for firms.

Type of growth	👍 Advantages	👎 Disadvantages
Organic	• Cheaper than other forms of external growth. Mergers and takeovers can be costly and time-consuming. • Can be financed through internal funds such as profits, rather than more expensive sources of finance. • Allows the business to grow at a more sustainable rate.	• Growth achieved may be dependent on the growth of the overall market and is therefore out of the control of the firm. • Slow method of growth – shareholders may demand more rapid growth.
Vertical integration	• Can take advantage of some economies of scale, such as financial economies, which can lead to lower prices for consumers. • Reduces risk as the firm is able to control its markets. • Backward vertical integration gives a firm more control and security over its supplies. • Forward vertical integration can give a firm more control over the prices it can charge.	• Communication and co-ordination problems can arise when a firm grows. This is an example of diseconomies of scale. • Problems can exist when merging firms with different corporate cultures. • Some workers may leave the firm – 'brain drain'.
Horizontal integration	• Reduces average costs due to economies of scale. • Reduces competition in the market. For example, if a car dealership merged with another car dealership, there is one less competitor in the market. • Allows a firm to grow in a market where it already has knowledge and expertise.	• Most horizontal mergers and takeovers fail. For example, a car manufacturer may have little experience of car retail. • Communication and co-ordination problems can arise when a firm grows in size – an example of diseconomies of scale. • Problems may arise when merging firms with different corporate cultures. For example, the merger may be poorly managed so that the two companies do not integrate well.
Conglomeration	• Reduces risk. The firm becomes less dependent on the movements within one market. • Easier to expand further due to access to finance. • Successful senior managers can be transferred to different parts of the organisation, leading to improved skill levels across the conglomerate.	• Lack of expertise in the new type of business. • Consumers may choose not to use the new firm as it has a different identity to the original firm. • Shareholders do not always get good value for money. Firms can pay too much when buying a new business.

Now try this

1 Identify two advantages of growth using vertical integration.

2 Describe one advantage for a firm of growing by backward vertical integration.

Constraints on business growth

Growth is not always straightforward. There exist some constraints – limits – on business growth.

 Size of the market

 Access to finance

Growth constraints

 Owner objectives

 Regulation

1 Size of the market

The fact that a firm is successful does not mean automatically that it can expand. The market it operates in may limit the chance for growth. Markets differ in size. Some markets are very small. For example, in a local area there may be a small number of hairdressers. Opportunities for expansion in this market may be very small.

2 Access to finance

Businesses need finance in order to grow. Many firms, especially large firms, use profits they have made in previous years. Firms can also use other types of finance such as bank loans and overdrafts. Larger firms are better able to borrow these funds as they have more equity and pose less risk to lenders. For smaller firms, access to funds can be a key constraint on growth.

3 Owner objectives

Not every owner wants their business to grow. Where a firm has more than one owner, their objectives may differ. One owner, or group of owners, may be satisfied with current profit levels, whilst others may prefer a more expansionary strategy. Such disagreements can limit opportunities for growth.

4 Regulation

Although most businesses can expand as they choose, some government regulation is intended to limit the growth of firms in certain sectors and areas. For example, in the UK the government regulates firms who may want retailers to charge a minimum price. This leads to the likelihood of greater price competition and ultimately lower revenue and profits for the firms involved. This can impact on growth plans for these firms.

🌐 Real world The CMA

The Competition and Markets Authority (CMA) is a UK government organisation. It aims to make markets competitive and that firms operate in the public interest. In 2016, mobile operators O2 and Three proposed a merger worth £10.3 billion. This would have been beneficial for both firms, through cost savings and economies of scale. However, the CMA criticised the merger as likely to limit competition in the market. It declared, in a letter to the European regulator, that the deal would lead to 'long-term damage to UK consumers'. The merger was blocked by the European Commission in response to the CMA's concerns.

Now try this

1 Give three different objectives of business owners.
2 Describe how regulation can limit the growth of firms.

Demergers

Sometimes, firms choose to reduce the size of their operation. One way they can do this is through a **demerger**. A demerger involves either splitting off a business into a separate company or selling one or more businesses to another firm. Demergers may have an impact on businesses, workers and consumers.

Why firms demerge

Cultural differences – where businesses with very different cultures come together, the result can be inefficiency and a lack of integration. In this case, demergers can be a desirable outcome.

To create more focused firms – smaller, more focused companies are often better able to recognise what specific consumers or markets want.

Lack of synergies – where the merger does not produce positive outcomes. It can mean diseconomies of scale, where higher unit costs occur because of the scale of the operation. Where there are no synergies from merging two parts of a business, a demerger may be the right course of action.

To reduce the risk of diseconomies of scale (see page 116). Very large organisations can suffer from rising unit costs due to the scale. A demerger reduces the size of the firm and therefore the risk of diseconomies.

Reasons for demergers

To raise money from asset sales and return to shareholders – sale of assets can mean funds returned to shareholders or used to increase investment in the core business.

To meet requirements of competition authority regulators – for example, BAA has been forced by UK competition authorities to sell off some airports, such as Gatwick.

Value – the value of the companies if demerged might be higher than the value of the single larger company.

To split a firm up into separate poorly performing parts.

To maximise profits.

Impact of demergers

Group	Impact
Businesses	👍 Allows focus on the core business
	👍 Raises funds from selling part of the business
	👍 Removes loss-making parts of the business
	👍 Increases efficiency/profitability
Workers	👍 Increased job security if loss-making parts of the business are demerged
	👍 Reduced conflict between cultures
	👍 Split may lead to creation of new jobs in the separated firm
	👎 Split may lead to job losses in the original company
Consumers	👍 Greater competition in the market leads to lower prices
	👍 More focused businesses are able to better meet consumer needs
	👎 Higher prices and reduced product range

 Real world **Prudential demerger**

In March 2018, life insurance company Prudential announced a demerger of its M&G Prudential fund management branch, forming two separate companies. The aim was to allow both companies to concentrate on specific parts of their market. M&G would focus on savings and retirement in Europe, whilst Prudential plc would focus on growth opportunities in Asia, Africa and the US.

Now try this

1 Explain what is meant by 'synergy', giving an example.

2 Give three reasons why demergers can occur.

Revenue 1

In a simple sense, revenue is the money a firm earns from the sales of its goods and services. In economics there are three types of revenue – **total**, **average** and **marginal**. They can be displayed as revenue curves on a diagram. On this page, you will revise what happens to revenue when the price of a good remains the same. You will also cover different calculations and formulae for revenue.

Revenue

- **Total revenue (TR)** is the income received from the sale of any given level of output.

- **Average revenue (AR)** is the average receipt per unit sold. Average revenue must be the same as price.

- **Marginal revenue (MR)** is the income gained from producing an extra unit of output.

🖩 Maths skills Revenue formulae

Total revenue (TR) = total quantity sold (Q) × average price (P)

Average revenue (AR) = $\dfrac{TR}{Q}$

Marginal revenue (MR) = $\dfrac{\Delta TR}{\Delta Q}$

Average revenue and price

These are the same. For example, a firm sells 100 units and receives total revenue of £750. Average revenue is £7.50 (£750 divided by the level of output). This is £7.50. It follows that price must also be £7.50.

Total, average and marginal revenue

The table gives information about a firm's total, average and marginal revenues.

Sales (units)	Average revenue (£)	Total revenue (£)	Marginal revenue (£)
1	2	2	
			2
2	2	4	
			2
3	2	6	
			2
4	2	8	
			2
5	2	10	

Note how TR is found by quantity sold (output) × price (AR). So, when 3 items are sold for £2 each, TR = £6. MR increases by £2 as price is constant.

TR, MR and AR when price is constant

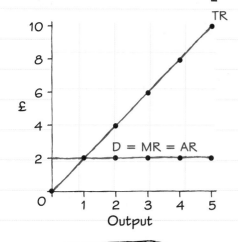

Assume that a firm receives the same price for each unit sold. This is shown in the diagram. As output increases, so does total revenue. Also shown are the MR and AR curves. Since the price of the good remains the same, both curves are identical. The AR line is also the demand curve because it shows the relationship between AR and quantity sold. So at any quantity sold, MR = AR = demand.

Now try this

1 What is marginal revenue?

2 A business increases its sales from 10 to 11. Total revenue rises from £150 to £165. What is the value of marginal revenue?

3 Give an example to explain why average revenue must be the same as price.

Revenue 2

A firm might decide to lower the price of a good to increase sales. This will have an impact on revenues – total revenue (TR); average revenue (AR) and marginal revenue (MR). There is also a relationship between revenue and price elasticity of demand. Both can be displayed using diagrams.

TR when price is falling

Assume that in order to increase sales of a good, a firm lowers its price. The total revenue (TR) curve shows that at first TR increases and then it begins to fall as price falls and sales rise.

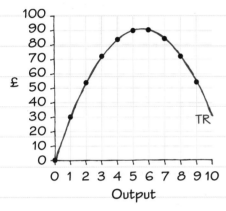

AR and MR when price is falling

From the diagram below, you can see that the average revenue (AR) and marginal revenue (MR) both fall as sales increase. The AR curve and the demand curve are the same as demand shows the average revenue received at each level of output. For example, when output is 8, price is £10. In this case TR = £80. Therefore, AR = £10.

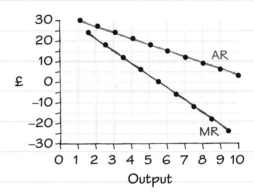

Revenue and PED

When the price of the good falls as sales increase, there will be a change in the price elasticity of demand (PED). In this example, TR is originally £2000 (£40 × 50 units). An increase in price to £50 results in TR falling to £1500.

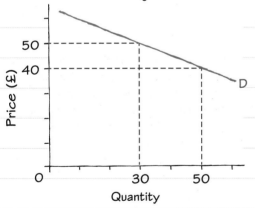

Remember this rule

When demand is price **elastic**, an increase in price results in a **fall** in revenue.

When demand is price **inelastic**, an increase in price results in a **rise** in revenue.

Positive/negative MR

- When MR is positive, demand is price elastic, that is, TR is rising.
- When MR is negative, demand is price inelastic.

Revenue and PID

In the situation shown in the diagram below, TR is originally £4000. An increase in price to £44 results in TR rising to £4180.

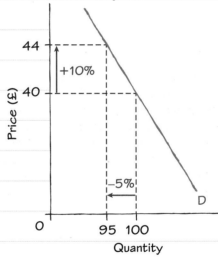

When the price for a product is constant, the demand curve and AR and MR curves will be the same thing and will be horizontal.

Now try this

1 Describe what happens to MR when demand increases due to falling prices.

2 Explain how the PED of a good can affect revenue.

Costs

All firms have one thing in common – they sell goods and services in order to make a profit. In order to do this, revenue must be greater than costs. Economists refer to a firm's fixed and variable costs.

Costs

Costs of production refer to the economic cost of producing the output. This includes the monetary cost of the factors of production but also includes the **opportunity cost** of production (look back at page 3 for more on this). Firms have two types of costs: fixed and variable.

Fixed costs do not change as output changes. Examples of fixed costs (which are sometimes known as overheads) include rent and salaries.

Firms' costs

Variable costs change with output. Examples of variable costs (which are known as direct or prime costs) include raw materials and packaging.

📝 Key terms and formulae

Total cost (TC) – the costs involved in producing a certain level of output.

Total fixed cost (TFC) – the part of total costs that does not vary with the level of output.

Total variable cost (TVC) – the part of total costs that vary with the level of output.

Average (total) cost (AC) – the cost per unit produced: AC = TC/Q

Average fixed cost (AFC) – total fixed costs divided by the number of units produced:

$$AFC = \frac{TFC}{Q}$$

Average variable cost (AVC) – total variable costs divided by the number of units produced:

$$AVC = \frac{TVC}{Q}$$

Marginal cost (MC) – the cost of producing one more unit of output:

$$MC = \frac{\Delta TC}{\Delta Q}$$

Costs in the short-run

In the short-run some costs are fixed. The short-run is the period of time when at least one factor of production is fixed. It is not a fixed period of time and can vary between industries. For example, a window cleaner might increase their stock of capital very quickly by buying a new set of ladders, but it might take a car manufacturer several years to increase its capital stock by building a new factory.

Short-run cost curves

The diagram below shows the shape of the TC, TFC and TVC curves in the short-run. TFC is a straight line showing that, as output increases, these costs remain unchanged in the short-run. Both TC and TVC rise as output rises. This is because as a firm increases its output, it uses more inputs, such as raw materials and labour. These variable costs rise, which lead to higher total costs, too. (See page 114 for short-run cost curves and diminishing marginal productivity.)

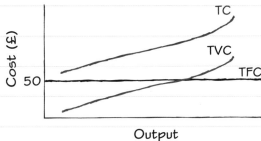

Now try this

1 Give three examples of fixed costs.

2 Why do variable costs change as output changes?

3 Explain why the TVC curve slopes upwards.

Short-run cost curves

Short-run cost curves are derived from the **assumption of diminishing marginal productivity**. The relationship between AC and MC curves will be covered.

The assumption of diminishing marginal productivity

Also known as the law of diminishing returns, the assumption of diminishing marginal productivity states that at a certain point, increasing a variable factor of production will eventually lead to a smaller output. By increasing the use of a variable factor (for example, labour) when one factor is fixed (for example, capital), the marginal returns – or marginal product – from the variable factor will begin to decrease. The point at which diminishing marginal productivity sets in can be seen where the MC curve begins to rise – see the short-run cost curve below.

Average cost and marginal cost in the short-run

In the short-run cost curve below, the AC curve is U-shaped in the short-run. This is because of the assumption of diminishing marginal productivity. In the diagram, AC initially falls as output increases as additional variable factor inputs lead to greater output at lower average cost. However, eventually AC starts to increase. Rising MC eventually causes overall AC to rise.

Derivation of the short-run cost curve

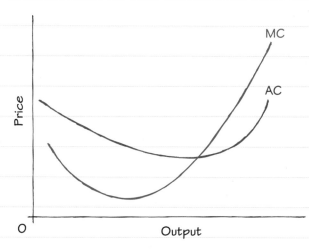

The MC line *always* intersects the AC line at the lowest point of AC. If the cost of producing one more unit – the marginal cost – is lower than the average cost, then overall average cost must be falling. Similarly, if the cost of producing one more unit is higher than the average cost, then overall average costs must increase.

Long-run average cost curves

In the long-run, all factors of production are variable. This means that the assumption of diminishing marginal productivity cannot apply. In such a case economists refer to **returns to scale**.
(See page 115 for more information on the relationship between short-run and long-run average cost curves and economies of scale.)

Now try this

1 Why does adding extra workers to a fixed stock of capital lead to diminishing marginal productivity?

2 Describe why, when MC is lower than AC, AC *must* be falling.

3 Describe why, when MC is higher than AC, AC *must* be rising.

Economies of scale

In the long-run, firms can increase the scale of their operation by varying all factors of production. Economies of scale are a fall in the long-run average costs of production as output rises. Both internal and external economies of scale are the advantages to be gained from producing on a large scale. You will also need to know about the long-run average cost curve.

Internal economies of scale occur when a firm increases the scale of production within the firm.	◁ **Economies of scale** ▷	**External economies of scale** involve changes outside of the firm. Average costs the firm fall due to changes in the industry in which the firm operates. For example, where an industry is growing the road network might be improved, which reduces delivery times and therefore the average costs of the firm.

Types of internal economies of scale

1 **Technical economies** – improved production methods that reduce average costs. Large firms can buy more efficient machinery.

2 **Managerial economies** – large firms can employ specialist managers with expertise in certain areas, leading to greater efficiency.

Economies of scale

3 **Financial economies** – the ability of large firms to borrow money at lower rates of interest as they are seen as less risky than small firms.

4 **Purchasing/marketing economies** – large firms can buy in bulk and therefore reduce average costs.

Long-run average cost (LRAC) curve

In the long-run, firms can move to a new short-run average costs (SRAC) curve. Looking at the LRAC diagram, each SRAC curve represents a different scale of operation. If the firm increases output from point A to B, then SRAC fall. However, this is not an efficient point in the long-run – remember all factors of production are **variable** in the long-run. By increasing the scale of production the firm could produce the same amount as B at a lower average cost, shown by C. Therefore, the LRAC curve of a firm shows the minimum or lowest **average total cost** at which a firm can produce any given level of output in the long-run.

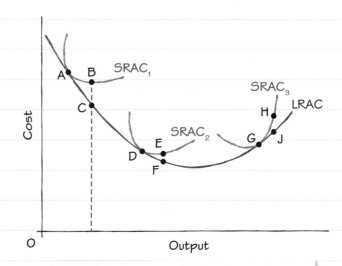

The lowest level of output at which LRAC is minimised is known as the **minimum efficient scale (MES)**.

Now try this

1 Why can larger firms borrow money more cheaply than smaller firms?

2 Explain why buying in bulk can lead to lower average costs.

Diseconomies of scale

Being a large firm does not only bring advantages in the form of economies of scale. There are cost disadvantages when a firm grows in size in the form of diseconomies of scale. There are various reasons for this. Diseconomies of scale cause a rise in the long-run average costs of production as output rises.

Diseconomies of scale – graphically

The diagram shows how, when output increases, average costs initially fall. This is an illustration of economies of scale. The LRAC curve is u-shaped. The lowest point (A) is the **minimum efficient scale** (MES) of production (the lowest level of output at which the long-run average cost is minimised). The range AB is the optimum level of production for the firm. Levels of output beyond point B lead to higher average costs as a result of diseconomies of scale.

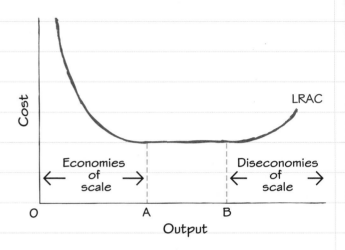

Reasons for diseconomies of scale

Area	Disadvantages
1 Control	👎 Larger firms become more difficult to manage. It may be more difficult to keep track of costs.
2 Communication	👎 There may be barriers to communication in larger organisations which may lower the morale of staff and reduce productivity.
3 Co-ordination	👎 It becomes more difficult in a larger firm to organise and co-ordinate the activities of different staff and departments, which may lead to lower productivity.

Productivity

Remember – productivity is a measure of the efficiency of factors of production. When productivity is falling, average costs are rising!

 Real world **Disadvantages of a large firm**

A small retailer served a local area and became very successful. The owner decided to expand the business by opening three new stores in surrounding areas. The result was that average costs increased due to the difficulties of communicating between the different stores, and that employees were not as responsive as when there was just one shop. The business also found it was less able to respond to local tastes and preferences with the result that stock was sometimes not sold and was wasted. Operating on a larger scale, rather than leading to efficiency gains, became less efficient due to communication and co-ordination issues.

Now try this

1 State two disadvantages of a firm growing in size.

2 Give one example of how poor communication within a large firm might lead to higher average costs.

Profit

A key assumption in microeconomics is that firms aim to maximise their profits. You need to revise the conditions required for this to happen – including the MC = MR rule – and that there are different types of profit.

(For more information on profit maximisation, see pages 120 and 121.)

Profit

Profit is the difference between the revenues of a firm (money received) and the costs it pays out. A firm will receive the maximum profit when the difference between revenues and costs are at their greatest.

 Maths skills **Formula for profit**

Profit = total revenue (TR) – total costs (TC)

The MC = MR rule

What is the level of output that will generate the maximum level of profits – the point of profit maximisation? We can find this by considering marginal cost (MC) and marginal revenue (MR). Where MC = MR, profits are maximised.

In the diagram, A is the profit maximising level of output. If the firm decides to increase output to B, the marginal cost of producing this extra output would be higher than the marginal revenue the firm would gain. Therefore, overall profit **must** decrease.

Normal profit

Normal profit occurs when the difference between a firm's total revenue (TR) and total costs (TR) is zero. Put another way, it is the profit needed by a firm to remain competitive in the market. (See page 118 for information on supernormal profit.)

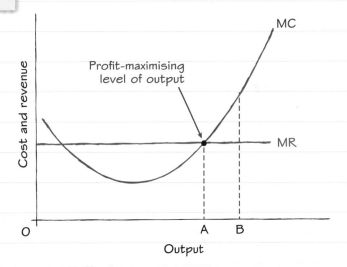

The profit maximising level of output is *always* found where MC = MR

The limitations of MC = MR

MC = MR is a very useful and versatile approach when considering the point at which a firm should produce. However, it does have some limitations.

👎 The model assumes firms accurately know their MC and MR, whereas in reality these figures are difficult to know with precision.

👎 The model does not consider how competitors will react. Increasing output or price may lead to a response by competitors.

👎 The effect of changes in price on quantity demanded might not be clear. Other factors can affect this, such as advertising.

Now try this

1 State three costs a firm must pay.

2 What is meant by normal profit?

3 Explain why a level of output lower than A in the diagram above would not be a point of profit maximisation.

Supernormal profit and losses

Firms may make **supernormal profit** – sometimes known as abnormal profit – which is where businesses make a profit over and above normal profit. They can also make **losses**. A firm cannot sustain losses indefinitely and may have to close – this is known as the **shut-down point**.

Supernormal profit

Supernormal profit means that the revenue generated from using factors of production is greater than it could have been if factors of production had been used in another way. In the diagram below, the firm produces at point A – the point where MC = MR. At this point average revenue is higher than average costs.

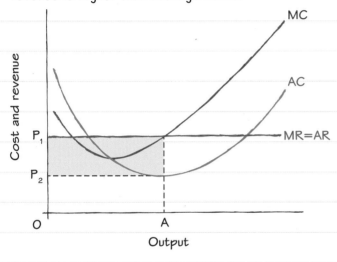

Losses and shut-down points

Losses occur when a firm's total costs are higher than its revenue. If a firm does not make normal profit it will close in the long-run because it is not covering all of its costs. This is known as the shut-down point. However, in the short-run a firm can accept some losses providing it can cover its variable costs.

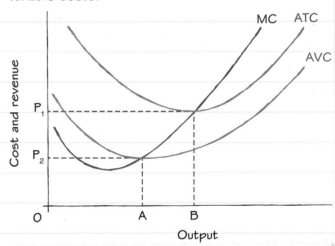

Short-run shut-down point. The firm will close down if the price it receives falls below P_2.

The effect on the market

Where firms in an industry are making supernormal profits, new firms will have an incentive to enter the market. This will have the effect of increasing supply and should, *ceteris paribus*, lead to a lower market price. Similarly, if firms in the industry are making losses, firms will have the incentive to leave the industry, which will lead to a reduction in supply.

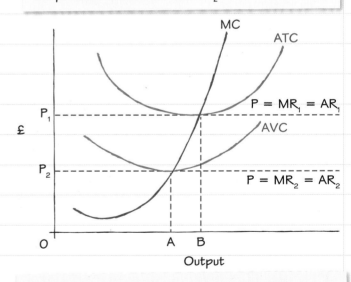

Here the firm will shut down if price falls below OP_1 because at this point it cannot cover variable costs. In the long-run, if price falls below OP_2 the firm will close down.

Now try this

1 State two reasons why a business might make a loss.

2 Why are normal profit and supernormal profit not the same thing?

3 Why might a firm make supernormal profit?

Business objectives

Firms can pursue different business objectives. Deciding which of these objectives to pursue is influenced by who controls the decision-making process.

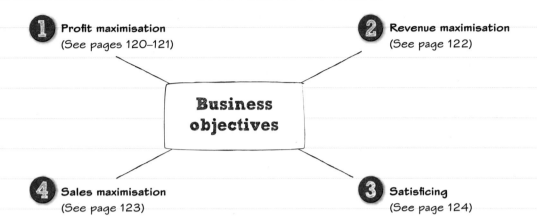

1 Profit maximisation
(See pages 120–121)

2 Revenue maximisation
(See page 122)

Business objectives

4 Sales maximisation
(See page 123)

3 Satisficing
(See page 124)

Who is able to influence the decision making?

The business objectives of firms are determined by who has control.
Stakeholders are groups that have an interest in the success of a firm.

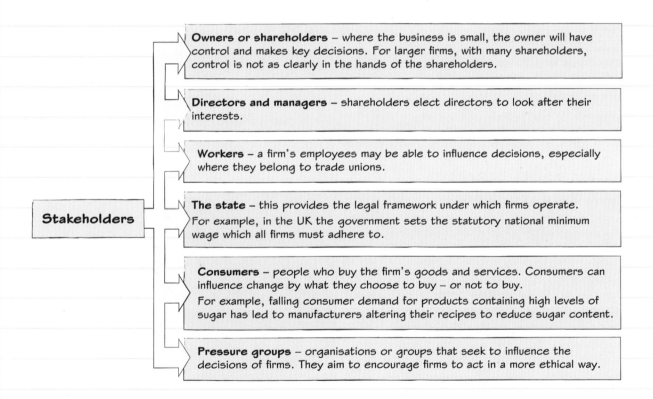

Stakeholders

Owners or shareholders – where the business is small, the owner will have control and makes key decisions. For larger firms, with many shareholders, control is not as clearly in the hands of the shareholders.

Directors and managers – shareholders elect directors to look after their interests.

Workers – a firm's employees may be able to influence decisions, especially where they belong to trade unions.

The state – this provides the legal framework under which firms operate. For example, in the UK the government sets the statutory national minimum wage which all firms must adhere to.

Consumers – people who buy the firm's goods and services. Consumers can influence change by what they choose to buy – or not to buy.
For example, falling consumer demand for products containing high levels of sugar has led to manufacturers altering their recipes to reduce sugar content.

Pressure groups – organisations or groups that seek to influence the decisions of firms. They aim to encourage firms to act in a more ethical way.

Now try this

1 State three objectives of firms.
2 Describe how workers might influence the decisions of the firm they work at.

Profit maximisation

Firms may pursue an objective of profit maximisation. This involves the firm making as much profit as it is able to. Some firms may seek to maximise long-run profits and may sacrifice short-run profits to do this. For more information on profit maximisation and the MC = MR rule, see page 117.

Short-run profit maximisation

Neo-classical economic theory assumes that the interests of owners or shareholders are most important. Whereas consumers aim to maximise utility and workers the rewards of working, owners aim to maximise profits. Short-run profit maximisation involves firms adjusting price and output in response to changes in market conditions.

Profits/losses

Firms aim to maximise profits or minimise their losses. These two statements are the same thing. If a firm cannot make a profit in the short term, its aim will be to keep its losses to a minimum. The condition for both is the same, where MC = MR.

Long-run profit maximisation

Maximising profit in the long-run may mean sacrificing profits in the short-run. Keynesian economists believe that firms will try to maximise their long-run rather than short-run profits. This idea is based on firms using cost-plus pricing where firms calculate the long-run average cost of production and then add a mark-up to represent profit. However, rapid price changes may affect a firm's position in the market. Consumers do not like frequent price changes and may see price reductions as signs of a firm's desperation and weakness. So rather than adjusting prices frequently the firm will continue to charge the current price and may make a loss in the short term but will adjust the price to the profit-maximising point in the long term.

 Key terms

The **short-run** is defined as the period of time when at least one factor of production is fixed.

The **long-run** is the period of time when all factors of production are variable.

Making a loss

In the short-run, firms may continue to operate despite making a loss, so long as they are able to cover variable costs. They may choose to do this if they expect sales to increase in the future. If a firm cannot cover variable costs, then it will close down as production is uneconomic.

 Savoury Foods

Savoury Foods produces a popular brand of ready-to-cook sauces. The firm employs 30 workers in a factory in the Midlands. The sauces were featured on a TV cookery programme and following this demand increased dramatically. Two large supermarket groups increased their orders by 200%. To meet the demand Savoury Foods introduced overtime for its existing staff. This is an example of a firm changing its mix of variable factors (workers) alongside its fixed factors (the factory).

If the increase in demand continues, the firm may decide to expand its factory, to allow profit maximisation in the long-run.

Now try this

1 What is the difference between the short-run and the long-run?

2 Describe why a firm may be able to continue production in the short-run, despite making a loss.

Profit maximisation: diagrams

Profit maximisation always occurs where MC = MR. Understanding this will help you to recognise profit maximisation on diagrams. You can also use diagrams to identify the area of profit.

(For more information on profit maximisation and the MC = MR rule, see page 117.)

Key steps to interpreting profit maximisation diagrams

You may be asked to identify the profit maximising level of output from a diagram. Remember, it is always at the point where MC = MR.

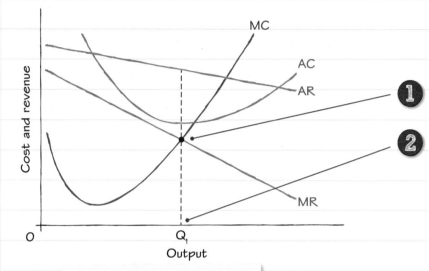

1 Find the point where MC = MR.

2 Drop a line to the x axis. This is the profit maximising level of output. It is the level of output required for the firm to maximise its profits (or minimise its losses).

Profit maximising is where MC=MR

Identifying profit

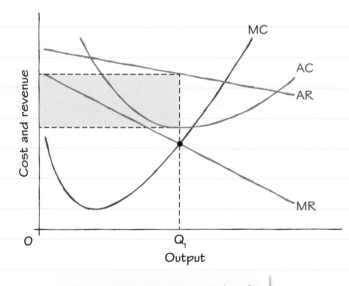

The actual level of profit is found by comparing average revenue with average costs. In the diagram on the left, the **area of profit** is shown by the shaded area. This is the area where the difference between average revenue and average costs is multiplied by the level of output. (See page 117 for the formula for profit.)

The shaded area is the area of profit

Now try this

1 Why does MC increase when output rises?

2 Explain why a business which has MR > MC when it produces an additional unit of output cannot be profit maximising.

Revenue maximisation

Some firms may seek to maximise their revenues as a business objective.

(For more information on revenue, see pages 117 and 118.)

Revenue maximisation

This objective arises from the idea of the **divorce of ownership from control** (see page 105 for more on this). Here it is assumed that the objective of managers is to maximise total revenue for the firm, subject to the profit satisficing constraint. The higher the sales revenue of a firm, the higher the salary and reputation of managers is likely to be. Revenue maximisation is a way for managers to justify their position and achieve their goals. (To revise profit satisficing see page 124.)

🖩 Maths skills

Revenue maximisation occurs where MR = 0. This can seem illogical. To understand you must be clear about the distinction between total revenue and marginal revenue. The table illustrates the point.

Price	Quantity sold	Total revenue	Marginal revenue
50	1	50	
45	2	90	40
40	3	120	30
35	4	140	20
30	5	150	10
25	6	150	0
20	7	140	–10

Selling the sixth unit of output achieves the same level of revenue as the fifth unit.

By selling a seventh unit, total revenue actually falls – resulting in MR of –£10.

📝 Key terms

- **Total revenue (TR)** is the income received from the sale of any given level of output.
- **Marginal revenue (MR)** is the income gained from producing an extra unit of output.

Revenue maximisation diagram

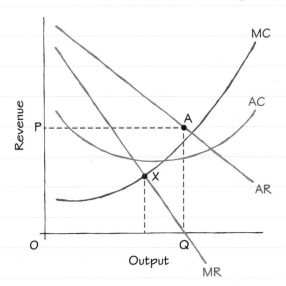

The information from the table above can be shown graphically (see left). The point of profit maximisation is where MC = MR (point X). The level of output for revenue maximisation – Q – is higher. If a firm is aiming for revenue maximisation it will increase output past the point where profit is maximised – as long as adding more output leads to greater revenue. Increasing output beyond Q leads to negative MR or, in other words, lower total revenue as a result of higher output.

Now try this

1 Describe why a business may have an objective of revenue maximisation.

2 Explain why revenue maximisation cannot be achieved if MR is not equal to 0.

Sales maximisation

A firm can have a range of objectives. Maximising sales is important for some firms.

What is sales maximisation?

Like shareholders, managers will also seek to maximise their utility. Some managers are paid a salary that is linked to the amount of sales they achieve. To maximise their own utility they will seek to sell the greatest number of products so they achieve a higher salary. Sales maximisation is where the business makes the maximum sales possible while still breaking even.

 Maths skills **Sales maximisation formulae**

Sales maximisation is achieved where:
average revenue (AR) = average cost (AC)

Remember also:

$$AR = \frac{TR}{Q} \qquad AC = \frac{TC}{Q}$$

Sales maximisation table

From the table it can be seen that, as output increases, total cost rises, as does total revenue, until 7 units are reached. At this point, total revenue falls. From this information it can be seen that sales maximisation is achieved at an output of 7.

Output	Total revenue (£000)	Total cost (£000)
1	50	23
2	90	48
3	120	63
4	140	83
5	150	99
6	150	116
7	140	140
8	120	175

Sales maximisation diagram

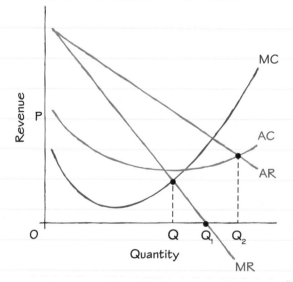

The point where AR = AC is the highest level of output the firm can sustain in the long-run

The information from the table above can also be shown graphically (see left). Note that the point of profit maximisation is where MC = MR. The level of output for sales maximisation – Q_2 – is higher. If output increased beyond Q_2 the firm would be making a loss (as AR < AC). If a firm is aiming for sales maximisation it will increase output past the point where profit is maximised – as long as adding more output leads to greater revenue.

1 What is the point where sales maximisation is achieved?

2 Explain why a business may have an objective of sales maximisation.

Satisficing

Sometimes firms choose profit **satisficing** as their business objective. Satisficing means doing just enough to satisfy stakeholders such as shareholders/owners.

Satisficing

Satisficing involves managers operating in such a way as to make sufficient profit to satisfy important stakeholders, such as shareholders, without aiming to maximise either profit, revenue or sales. A good way to think of this is aiming for the 'easy life'. Satisficing behaviour happens when businesses aim for minimum acceptable levels of achievement, such as in terms of revenue and profit. For example, a manager may recognise that a worker who does a reasonable job might be 'good enough'. By sacking such a worker, the impact on other workers, in terms of motivation, might be negative.

Maximisers vs satisficers?

Maximisers behave in a traditional economic way. They will always try to make the best possible choice from the available alternatives. For example, they make decisions on price, advertising and investments with the main aim of maximising profit. In a market this is at a point where profit maximisation is achieved – where MR = MC.

Satisficers, on the other hand, often aim to achieve a minimum standard of performance – a standard that will be enough to satisfy bosses, even though it is not the same maximising level of performance.

Profit satisficing diagram

The level of output – Q_2 – is higher than the profit maximising level of output, and higher than the revenue maximising level of output.

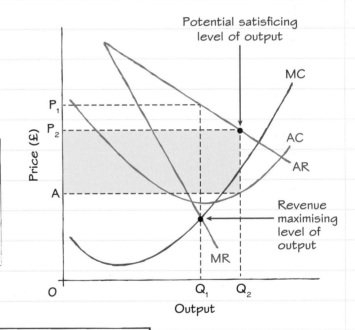

Remember

A good way to remember the idea of satisficing is to think of the idea of being 'satisfied' with something. For example, 'It's not the highest level of profit we might have achieved, but we're satisfied with it.'

Examples of satisficing

Managers choose to make enough profit to stop shareholders getting too concerned.

Satisficing examples

Managers show they are running the firm in an efficient manner to ensure they meet their performance targets

Managers choose to provide workers with an acceptable pay increase to ensure they do not take industrial action or decide to look for jobs with other firms.

Now try this

1 Why might firms decide not to pursue profit maximisation?

2 Describe why satisficing might be referred to as 'aiming for the easy life'.

Productive efficiency

Efficiency refers to how well resources, such as factors of production, are used to produce end results. In economics there are different types of efficiency. On this page, you will revise **productivity efficiency**. (See page 126 for other types of efficiency.)

Productive efficiency

Productive efficiency occurs when production is achieved at the lowest average cost. For example, if a firm produces 1000 units at a cost of £5000, this would be productively efficient as long as the same output could not have been produced for £4000.

Technical efficiency

For productive efficiency to occur there must be **technical efficiency**. This is where a given amount of output is produced with the minimum *number* of inputs. For example, an amount of output might be produced with five workers. However, it might have been cheaper to produce the output with machinery, such that the average cost was lower.

Productive efficiency – graphically

The diagram shows a firm producing at the bottom of the average cost (AC) curve. The firm cannot produce at a lower average cost in the short-run. This is because the AC curve shows the cost boundary that the business faces over the range of output. Remember that, in the long-run, all factors of production are variable and the firm may be able to invest in new machinery which would lead to lower AC. This would be caused by a downward shift in the SRAC curve (see page 114).

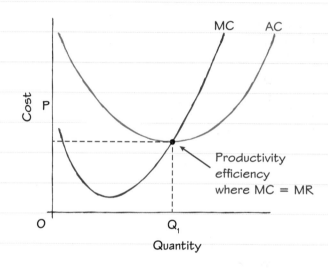

Productive efficiency and the economy

For the economy as a whole there is productive efficiency if it is operating on its production possibility frontier. Points A and B are productively efficient. Point D is not, however, as more goods or services could be produced with no opportunity cost.

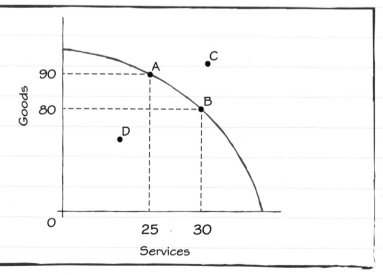

Now try this

1 Why is point C on the PPF above not an efficient point?

2 How can a firm become more productively efficient in the long-run?

Other types of efficiency

Efficiency is a concept which is important in economics. How well resources are used to produce the goods and services demanded is known as allocative efficiency. Efficiency can be static or dynamic. **X-inefficiency** is a type of productive inefficiency.

Allocative efficiency

Allocative efficiency occurs when resources are distributed according to consumer preferences. Think about this type of efficiency in terms of *how* resources are allocated. An economy could be productively efficient – where all firms are producing at the lowest point of their AC curves – but might not be producing goods and services that consumers want. In other words, resources are not being allocated efficiently.

🖩 Maths skills Formula

Allocative efficiency is found at the point where:

$$\text{price (P)} = \text{marginal cost (MC)}$$

For example, if the price of a t-shirt is £5 but the MC of producing it was £3, then this means the consumer places more value on the product – as reflected in the price they are willing to pay – than it costs to produce. This is not a point of allocative efficiency. More could be produced to the point where P = MC and in doing so increase the total amount of utility.

Static vs dynamic efficiency

- **Static efficiency** occurs at a particular point in time. Productive and technical efficiency are static efficiency concepts, for example, a firm producing an amount of output for the cheapest cost given its combination of factor inputs.

- **Dynamic efficiency** is concerned with the productive efficiency of firms over a period of time. For example, an economy could become more productive over time if more resources were devoted to investment in new technology.

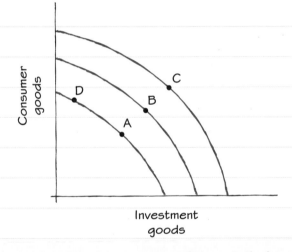

Dynamic efficiency – improving efficiency in the long term

X-inefficiency

X-inefficiency refers to the inefficiency caused by a firm not minimising its average costs. In the diagram (right), the difference between the two AC curves is the amount of inefficiency that exists. For larger firms, diseconomies of scale may mean that it is more difficult to co-ordinate and control activities, which leads to higher average costs than might exist in a more efficient firm.

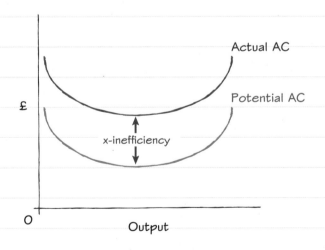

Now try this

1 Give two reasons why a firm might be inefficient.

2 Why is P = MC the point at which allocative efficiency is achieved?

Perfect competition

In the real world, all markets exist on a spectrum of competition, from the most competitive to the highly non-competitive. Over the next few pages, you will revise how firms in different types of markets behave.

Perfect competition　　Monopolistic competition　　Oligopoly　　Monopoly

Most competitive ⟷ No competition

Every type of market is somewhere on this spectrum.

What is perfect competition?

Perfect competition is one type of market structure. As the name suggests, it is based on lots of firms operating in a highly competitive environment. Perfect competition is a hypothetical market structure, although some markets do exhibit many of the key characteristics (see diagram below). For example, commodities markets exhibit the characteristics. Coal is mined in many countries with many suppliers. A tonne of coal is effectively the same wherever it is sourced. With perfect competition, no firm will make supernormal profits in the long-run, although profits and losses can be made in the short-run.

Characteristics of perfect competition

Many buyers and sellers	Perfect information	Homogeneous products	Freedom of entry and exit	Profit maximisers
No single firm can influence market price. Firms are price takers.	Buyers and sellers posses perfect knowledge of prices and products.	All firms produce an identical product. There is no branding or differentiation of products.	There are no barriers to entry or exit to the industry. This means firms can enter and leave the industry with ease.	All firms are assumed to be profit maximisers. (Remember – this is the point where MC = MR.)

 Fruit and vegetable markets

In the UK, food markets with traders selling fresh fruit and vegetables are very popular. This market exhibits the characteristics of perfect competition. Visit a market and you will see lots of sellers, each selling similar products. Prices tend to be very similar. Customers can check the products – they have perfect knowledge. Setting up such a business is relatively cheap as expensive premises are not required. There is therefore easy entry and exit into the market.

Now try this

1 Why is the demand line for a perfectly competitive firm horizontal?

2 Describe why AR = MR for the perfectly competitive firm.

3 What is meant by the term homogeneous product?

Perfect competition in diagrams

Below you will revise the diagrams which show the perfectly competitive firm in different situations.

Short-run supernormal profit

In the short-run, firms in a perfectly competitive industry can make supernormal profit. However, in the long-run these profits are competed away. In the diagram (right) the market price of P results in the individual firm making supernormal profit. As a result of this, new firms are attracted into the industry by the prospect of high profits. The assumption of freedom of entry and exit to the market makes this possible. As a result, market supply increases, as shown by the rightward shift in supply to S_2. The new market price of P_2 restores equilibrium. This is a long-run position (note the AC curve is LRAC).

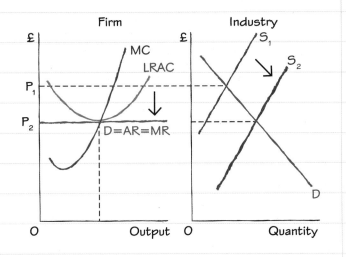

Losses: short-run and long-run

In the same way that supernormal profits are competed away, so losses under perfect competition are also short term. In the diagram (right) the market price of P means that the business is making a loss as AC > AR. As a result, firms will leave the market (freedom of entry and exit) leading to a shift in market supply to S_2. In the long-run this causes an increase in market price to P_2, which restores equilibrium for the firm.

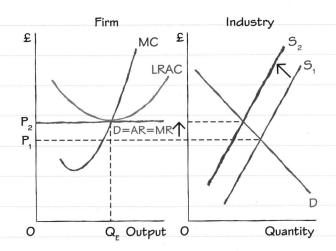

Long-run equilibrium

In the long-run, firms operating in a perfectly competitive market will reach equilibrium. This is shown in the diagram (right). The firm is productively efficient as it produces at the point where AC is at its lowest. It is also allocative efficient as output is at the point where P = MC. This firm produces at point Q – the profit maximising level of output. At this level of output the firm will make normal profit.

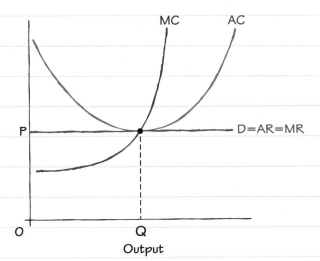

> A perfectly competitive firm has a perfectly inelastic demand curve. A change in output will not change the price. This is because the demand curve for a perfectly competitive firm is horizontal.

Now try this

1 Give two reasons why new firms might enter a market.

2 At what level of output will a perfectly competitive firm produce?

Monopolistic competition

On the spectrum of competition (see page 127), monopolistic competition occupies a more central position, suggesting it does not have the same pure level of competition as under perfect competition. It is also a more realistic market structure.

What is monopolistic competition?

Monopolistic competition is a market structure where a large number of small firms produce non-homogeneous products and where there are no barriers to entry. The key difference between monopolistic and perfect competition is the production of non-identical products.

Short-run

In the short-run, firms in monopolistic competition can make supernormal profits and losses.

Monopolistic competition: long-run equilibrium position

The monopolistic competition diagram, below, appears more complex than those for perfect competition – but it is actually quite easy to interpret. Notice how the demand curve is now downward sloping. This is because the firm does not produce a homogeneous product. Its product is differentiated in some way and this means the firm has a certain amount of market power. For example, it will be able to increase prices without losing all of its customers.

Interpreting the diagram

The diagram shows the long-run equilibrium position for a firm in monopolistic competition. Follow these steps in number order to find the level of output, the price the firm will charge and the amount of profit.

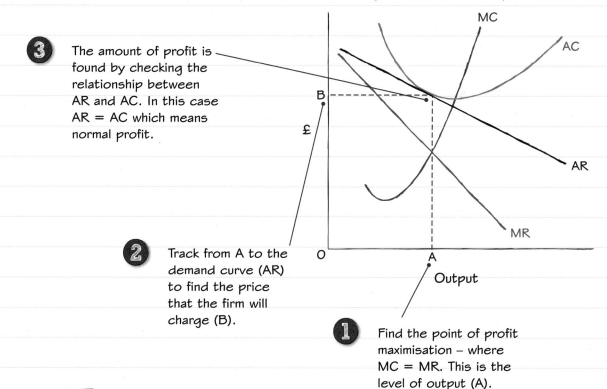

3 The amount of profit is found by checking the relationship between AR and AC. In this case AR = AC which means normal profit.

2 Track from A to the demand curve (AR) to find the price that the firm will charge (B).

1 Find the point of profit maximisation – where MC = MR. This is the level of output (A).

1 What is meant by non-homogeneous products?

2 Draw a diagram showing short-run losses for a firm in monopolistic competition.

3 Draw a diagram showing short-run profits for a firm in monopolistic competition.

Oligopoly 1

Like monopolistic competition, oligopoly is a more realistic market structure. It is found towards the centre of the competition spectrum (see page 127).

What is an oligopoly?

High concentration ratio – an industry where a small number of firms supply a large proportion of the market; sometimes referred to as a concentrated market.

Product differentiation – firms attempt to differentiate their products using techniques such as branding.

Characteristics of an oligopoly

Interdependence of firms – the actions taken by one firm in the market have an impact on the other firms, e.g. pricing. Interdependence creates uncertainty in the market.

High barriers to entry and exit – as firms in an oligopoly are typically large, the scale of operation is large and this deters competitors.

Concentration ratio

An oligopoly can be described as a concentrated market. Contrast this with a competitive market with lots of firms. This type of market is not concentrated. The level of domination in a market is measured by a **concentration ratio**. This is the ratio of the combined market shares of a given number of firms to the whole market size. It is most common to see the 3-, 4- or 5-firm concentration ratio, where the three, four or five largest firms dominate the market output.

Concentration ratios are used to assess the extent to which a given market is oligopolistic. They can be calculated using revenue, output, number of employees and profits.

 Real world **The UK supermarket industry**

The UK supermarket industry can be classed as an oligopoly. Here's why.

- **Dominated by a small number of firms** – Tesco, Sainsbury's and ASDA.
- **Interdependence** – firms likely to have price wars and react when others launch sales/ promotions.
- **High barriers to entry** – land and buildings are expensive and a deterrent to new entrants.

 Maths skills **Concentration ratio**

In the industry below there are five firms. In total, they have revenues of £98 million.

Firm	Output (revenue – £m)
A	12
B	24
C	10
D	22
E	30
Total	98

To calculate the 3-firm concentration ratio:

Largest three firms' revenue = 30 + 24 + 22 = 76

$\frac{76}{98} \times 100 = 77.55\%$

In other words, the largest three firms in this market control 77.55% of the market. The market can be said to be concentrated.

n-firm concentration ratio formula

The formula for calculating an n-term concentration ratio (where 'n' refers to the number of firms being considered) is:

$$\frac{\text{sum of market share of the number of firms}}{\text{total size of the market}} \times 100$$

Now try this

1 Identify three industries, other than supermarkets, which are dominated by a small number of firms.

2 For the following industry, calculate the 3-firm and 5-firm concentration ratio:
   Output: Firm A = 35 units; Firm B = 30; Firm C = 15; Firm D = 40; Firm E = 20; Firm F = 5

Oligopoly 2

Firms operating in oligopoly face some uncertainty. They must try to remove the risks associated with this uncertainty. One way they can do this is through **collusion**. Another way is to use game theory. There are three types of price competition.

Uncertainty

Uncertainty in oligopoly is created because firms do not know how rivals will react. This is different from perfect competition where rival firms – under the assumption of perfect information – know everything about other firms. There is a market price that all firms charge. However, in oligopoly, if one firm were to reduce prices, it does not know how others will react. Will they also cut prices, triggering a possible price war? Or will they maintain existing prices?

Collusion

One way firms can reduce the risk of uncertainty is collusion. This involves collective agreements between firms that restrict competition. For example, firms might agree to co-ordinate an increase in prices, or to charge the same price for the same products. Collusion is illegal. It restricts competition and is harmful for consumers.

👎 **Overt collusion** – is a formal, usually secret agreement between rival firms.

👎 **Tacit collusion** – is where firms accept the decisions, such as price changes, of a dominant firm.

Game theory

Game theory, such as the prisoner's dilemma (right), can be used to predict how firms might behave, for example, why firms may collude and why collusive agreements may break down. In this example, both prisoners have committed a crime together and are being held separately. They have been offered a deal by the police: confess and implicate the other and get a reduced sentence, while their accomplice gets five years in prison, or both deny and receive two years each.

		Prisoner B	
		Confess	Deny
Prisoner A	Confess	3 years/ 3 years	1 year/ 5 years
	Deny	5 years/ 1 year	2 years/ 2 years

The prisoner's dilemma. In this example, neither prisoner knows or trusts what the other will do. So, both plead guilty and take the lower prison sentence. If they could have discussed their options, they might have both denied the charge.

From prisoners to businesses...

In the example (right), two firms have the option of reducing prices or leaving them unchanged. There are risks for both firms. If Firm B reduces its price (and Firm A does the same), then it will lose £20 million (and Firm A will lose £10 million). Here the risk free option is for both firms to leave prices unchanged. This is one reason why oligopolists engage in non-price competition.

		Firm B	
		Lower price	Leave price unchanged
Firm A	Lower price	−£10m/ −£20m	+£5m/ −£27m
	Leave price unchanged	−£13m/ +£5m	0

Now try this

1 Explain why uncertainty exists in conditions of oligopoly.

2 What is meant by collusion?

Competition in oligopolistic markets

Firms in an oligopolistic market compete in different ways. They may compete on price but may also use non-pricing methods to stay ahead of their rivals.

Types of price competition

1 **Predatory pricing** – a pricing strategy where a firm lowers its price when a new firm enters the market in order to force them out of the market.

2 **Limit pricing** – setting a price just low enough to prevent new entrants into the market.

3 **Price wars** – where firms in a market repeatedly lower their prices to gain an advantage over rivals.

Types of non-price competition

Non-price competition involves oligopolistic firms using techniques other than price to increase sales, revenue and profit. The key here is that by competing using techniques other than price, firms are avoiding the risks associated with the kinked-demand curve, where an increase in price might result in competitors not following suit and the firm therefore losing sales. Non-price competition can be seen as a safer strategy for firms in oligopolistic markets.

Type of non-price competition	Explanation
Advertising	Advertising spending can be extremely high for some firms. Where these firms operate in an oligopoly market structure, spending can be extremely high. For example, in 2017 Procter and Gamble, a consumer goods conglomerate, spent over $7 billion on advertising.
Loyalty cards and schemes	Loyalty schemes are provided by a wide range of businesses, such as supermarkets, coffee chains, banks. These schemes provide discounts and gifts to encourage repeat purchases. They help each firm to stand out from rivals.
Branding	Many markets where a small number of firms exist are dominated by brands. Firms spend large amounts promoting and enhancing their brands. Brands are products which appear to have unique characteristics.
Packaging	Unique and distinctive packaging is used by some firms to differentiate their product from that of competitors.
Better quality customer service	Firms can offer services such enhanced after-sales support, guaranteed delivery times, 24-hour helplines to help customers to feel like they have a superior service.

🌐 **Real world** **Loyalty schemes**

UK petrol stations often have high-profile loyalty schemes. These reward customers with points which can be redeemed. Such schemes encourage repeat purchase and entice customers to stay loyal. As a result, petrol suppliers often do not need to compete on price. Prices of fuel at different petrol stations in the same area, often on the same street, are often identical – to the same decimal place!

Identical petrol prices are a clear sign that oligopoly exists in this market

Now try this

Give three examples of non-price competition.

Monopoly

A monopoly is when a firm is the sole producer in an industry. In the UK, monopoly power is said to exist when a firm supplies at least 25% of the market. Being the sole producer has some important implications for the decisions taken by such firms.

Characteristics

Only one firm in the market – the **monopolist**.

Barriers to entry prevent new entrants to the industry.

The monopolist is a profit maximiser in the short run.

Natural monopoly

A natural monopoly is one where the high cost of starting-up means that competition is impossible. For example, the water industry is a natural monopoly as the cost of competition in the same local area is inefficient and impractical.

Profit maximising equilibrium

The point of profit maximisation for the monopolist is where MC = MR (see page 129). Follow the steps below to understand the profit maximising equilibrium diagram.

Monopolist AR and MR curves

As the firm is effectively the industry, the demand curve for the monopolist is the same as for the industry – see diagram below. The AR curve for the firm is its demand curve. MR lies below the AR curve. To increase quantity sold, the firm needs to reduce price. By reducing the price for all buyers, MR falls by proportionally more.

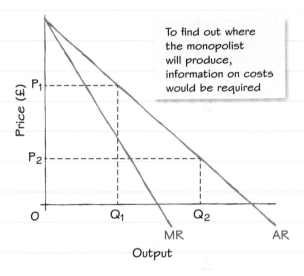

To find out where the monopolist will produce, information on costs would be required

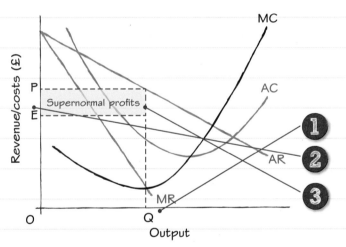

1 Identify the level of output (Q) – where MC = MR.

2 Read up to the demand curve (AR) to find the price (P).

3 Identify the difference between AR and AC to find the level of profit (or loss). In this case, AR is greater than AC, which means the firm is making supernormal profit.

This is an equilibrium position. The supernormal profits cannot be competed away (as they would be under perfect competition). This is due to one of the assumptions – high barriers to entry. If an established brand name was making high profits, it is difficult for a less well-known firm to establish itself in the market. This is a barrier to entry.

This is the long-run equilibrium under monopoly. Remember that, in the short-run, abnormal profits or losses can be made.

Now try this

1 Why does the MR curve for a monopolist lie below its AR curve?

2 Give two examples of barriers to entry in a monopoly.

3 Explain why high barriers to entry might prevent profits being competed away.

Price discrimination

As a monopolist is effectively the industry, they do not need to accept a market price, and can charge different consumers different prices.

Third degree price discrimination

This occurs when a business charges different groups of customers different prices for the same product, for example, discounted rail fares for people aged 16–25. The assumption is that there are two markets: one with demand that is price inelastic, the other where demand is price elastic (16–25 year olds). The different customers have their own demand curves.

Necessary conditions

1 **Market power** – price discrimination can only take place when the firm has the ability to vary the price.

2 **Different price elasticities of demand** – for the different products.

3 **Information** – it must be possible to distinguish between different customers' willingness to pay.

4 **Limited ability to resell** – consumers cannot resell the product. For example, a young person buying a cheap rail ticket with their 16–25 Railcard cannot sell this to other people.

Price discrimination in diagrams

To maximise profit the seller in each market would set the price at the point of profit maximisation (where MC = MR). This is shown in the diagram below. A higher price is charged in the market where demand is more price inelastic. This is price P_1 in diagram 1. The higher price will not result in a large reduction in price. A lower price – P_2 – is charged in the market where demand is more price elastic as seen in diagram 2. The shaded areas show the supernormal profit earned in each market. The total amount of supernormal profit is found by adding together the two shaded areas – this amount of profit is greater as a result of charging different prices (of price discriminating) than by the firm charging the same price for all consumers.

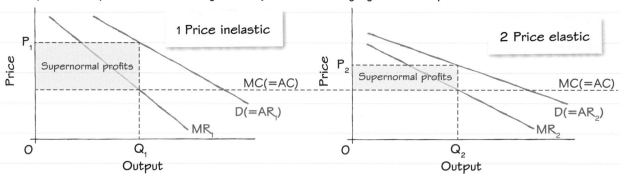

Costs and benefits of monopoly

👎 Less incentive for producers to be efficient and to develop new products.

👎 Higher prices for consumers than exist under competitive conditions.

👎 Do not produce at the most efficient point of production at the lowest point of the AC curve.

👎 Not allocatively efficient – produce where P > MC.

👎 Can abuse market power with suppliers and insist on lower prices.

👎 Ability to pay workers lower wages.

👍 Supernormal profit means finance available to firms to develop new products.

👍 Monopolists can take advantage of economies of scale. This leads to the ability to charge lower prices than firms under competitive conditions.

👍 Price discrimination helps different types of consumers.

👍 Large employers with lots of opportunities for career progression.

Now try this

1 Using an example, explain what is meant by third degree price discrimination.

2 Give two conditions required for third degree price discrimination.

Monopsony

In a similar way to monopoly meaning 'one seller', you also need to revise the idea of 'one buyer'. This is **monopsony**.

Characteristics and conditions

- Monopsony exists in a market when there is only one buyer.
- Monopsonists exist in both product and labour markets. Whereas pure monopoly is rare in the UK, examples of monopsony are more common. For example, the NHS is the main employer (buyer) of nurses and doctors. British Sugar is virtually the sole buyer of UK sugar beet.
- Monopsonists are **profit maximisers**. They pay lower prices to suppliers than they would under competitive conditions.

Price and quantity supplied

Under monopsony, both price and quantity supplied are lower than would exist if the industry were competitive.

Equilibrium under perfect competition and monopsony

Under perfect competition, equilibrium output exists at point OB. But under monopsony, the firm will aim to buy at a lower price (OE). At this price, however, sellers will not wish to supply as much as under perfect competition. As a result, equilibrium output falls to OA.

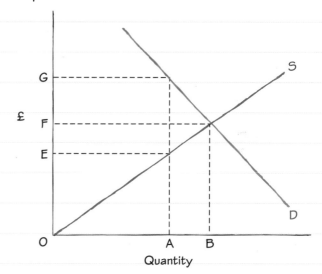

Costs and benefits

Agents	Benefits	Costs
Firms	👍 Lower costs as the firm is able to buy at lower prices. This will shift the MC curve downwards.	👎 Relationship with suppliers may be poor. 👎 Suppliers may be encouraged to find other buyers.
Consumers	👍 Lower prices – due to the lower costs the monopsonist can ensure.	👎 Quality – the supplier may have to cut corners to remain profitable.
Employees	👍 By reducing costs of raw materials, for example, the firm has greater funds for investment and wages.	👎 Monopsonists employ fewer workers than under competitive conditions.
Suppliers	👍 When the supplier has market power as a monopolist it can counteract the monopsonist buyer.	👎 Lower prices – the monopsonist may exploit the supplier, which will reduce their income.

Now try this

1 Why is the NHS an example of a monopsony?

2 How might the existence of a monopsonist in a market benefit consumers?

Contestability

Contestability is an important concept when considering the theory of the firm. It refers to how open a market is to competition, rather than how competitive it is at the current time.

Characteristics

A contestable market is one where there is:

- freedom of entry to and exit from the industry
- low exit costs.

Barriers to entry and exit are key to understanding this idea. Some market structures – such as monopoly and oligopoly – are characterised by high barriers to entry. These barriers stifle competition and lead to higher prices than would exist under competitive conditions. In contestable markets, these impediments do not exist.

Assumptions behind the concept

1 No barriers to entry or exit. There are low sunk costs (see below).

2 Firms are profit maximisers – produce where MC = MR.

3 The number of firms in a contestable market can vary from one (monopoly) to many.

4 No collusion between firms.

5 Perfect knowledge exists in the market – firms have access to the same technology.

Sunk costs

Sunk costs are those costs which, once they have been incurred, cannot be recovered. Advertising is an example. If a new entrant has to spend lots of money on advertising, and then leaves the industry, this cost is sunk. Compare to the machinery or equipment the firm purchased. These can be sold on if the firm leaves the industry, meaning some costs can be recovered. Other examples of sunk costs include rent and specialist equipment. Having to purchase highly specialised equipment, possibly made especially for the purpose, might deter new entrants as the equipment cannot be easily sold to other firms if it chooses to leave the industry.

The existence of sunk costs reduces the contestability within markets.

Staying competitive

A contestable market may only contain a small number of firms, but they act in similar ways as they would in a perfectly competitive market. They do this because of the threat of rivals entering the market. It is the contestability of the market that keeps firms competitive. Examples of barriers of entry include the need for advertising and branding, the existence of sunk costs and high entry/exit costs.

Hit and run competition

Low barriers to entry and exit in a market raise the possibility of 'hit and run' competition. Therefore, contestability will affect the behaviour of firms. High levels of contestability can encourage firms to look for opportunities in different markets.

Stage 1
Supernormal profits are made by incumbents in an industry.

Stage 2
New firms enter the market to earn high profits. They are able to do so due to low barriers to entry.

Stage 3
The new firms leave the market once prices have been driven down to normal profit levels.

Degrees of contestability

The lower the barriers to entry in a market, the higher the degree of contestability. Some markets are highly contestable, others less so. Technological change is generally improving the contestability of markets. For example, setting up new businesses using the internet is making incumbent firms (those firms already operating within a market) more responsive to the threat of competition.

Now try this

1 What does contestability mean?
2 Why do high sunk costs make a market less contestable?

Demand for labour

In the same way that markets exists for goods and services, so markets (and demand) exist for labour.

Derived demand

The demand for labour comes from firms.

It is a **derived demand**. This means that it is based on the demand for the goods and services that the labour produces. For example, if the demand for houses increases, the demand for construction workers will increase. The demand for these workers is derived from the demand for housing.

Demand for labour: short-run

In the short-run, the demand for labour curve is downward sloping (see diagram below). This is explained by the assumption of diminishing marginal productivity (see page 114). Marginal output will start to decline if more units of a variable factor – labour – are combined with a given stock of fixed factors.

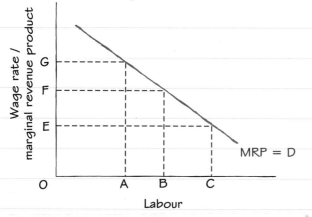

MRP = demand curve. This curve shows the maximum a firm would want to pay for an extra unit of a labour. So, it is the actual demand curve.

Elasticity of labour supply

This measures the responsiveness of the demand for labour to changes in the wage rate. This is influenced by:

 time – the longer a time period, the easier it is to substitute factors

 elasticity of demand for the product – as labour is a derived demand

 availability of substitutes – where few are available, the elasticity of demand for labour will be small

 proportion of labour costs to total costs.

Key terms

Marginal physical product (MPP) – the addition to output caused by an extra unit of a variable factor, such as labour.

Marginal revenue product (MRP) – the value of the physical addition to output from an extra unit of variable factor.

Productivity – measures output per factor per period of time.

Factors influencing the demand

Productivity is a major influence on the demand for labour. If productivity increases, unit labour costs fall. If an extra worker produced five units of additional output, and these were sold for £20 each, the MRP would be £100. As long as the worker costs less than this to employ, it is profitable to employ this worker. A further factor influencing demand for labour is the price of the product. If price increases, the demand for labour will increase.

Shifts in the demand for labour curve

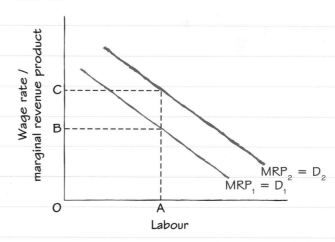

A rise in the MRP of labour at any given level of output will lead to a shift in the MRP (i.e. demand) curve to the right.

Now try this

1 Define marginal revenue product.

2 Use the idea of derived demand to explain why the demand for labour might fall.

Supply of labour 1

You need to understand the **supply of labour** and its determinants, as well as factors influencing the supply of labour.

Supply of labour

The supply of labour can refer to an individual, an occupation or the whole economy. For a particular occupation or industry, the labour supply is the number of workers willing to work in that occupation at each given wage rate.

The supply curve for labour is typically upward-sloping

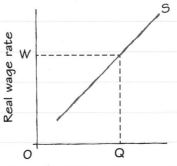

Quantity of labour/hours worked

Factors influencing labour supply

Factor	Effects on labour supply
Monetary (pecuniary)	The level of wage rates (the amount paid to workers in return for their labour), includes wages as well as additional benefits. Also important is how wage rates in one industry compare to other industries. For example, if wage rates rise in the car manufacturing industry, this will attract workers from other industries and therefore increase supply of labour in the car industry.
Size of the working population	If the population of working age is falling, labour supply will fall.
Information	How effectively job vacancies are publicised and promoted will influence how quickly posts are filled.
Changes in migration	Where there are few limits on migration, the supply of labour can increase – and can be more responsive to changes in demand.
Trade unions	Trade unions can influence the wage rate in particular industries. This can lead to higher labour supply in these industries in preference over non-unionised industries.
Income tax	Marginal tax rates will influence the willingness of individuals to supply their labour to the jobs market. High marginal tax rates have the effect of reducing the supply of labour.
Welfare payments	Where payments are relatively high, the effect can be to provide a disincentive for individuals to enter the labour market.

Elasticity of labour supply

This measures the responsiveness of the supply of labour to changes in the wage rate.

Level of skills and qualifications – where lots of workers have the skills and qualifications needed for an occupation, supply will be more elastic.

Influences on elasticity of supply to an industry

Level of unemployment in the economy – where there is high unemployment, elasticity of supply of labour will be high as there is a plentiful supply of labour that will respond to changes in wage rates.

Time – elasticity of supply is lower in the short run. Training workers can take time.

Now try this

1 Describe what the opportunity cost might be for a worker.

2 Why is the supply of low-skilled labour likely to be elastic?

Supply of labour 2

Geographical mobility relates to how easily workers can move from one area to another to find work.
Occupational mobility relates to the ability of workers to move from one job to another. Where there is geographical or occupational immobility, there is market failure. You need to understand the supply curve and marginal cost curve of labour for a monopsonist employer.

Market failure in labour markets

Examples of market failure

Geographical immobility – is one example of market failure in the labour market. This is where workers find it difficult to move from one area to another. One reason for this is the cost involved. Moving home can be expensive.
Some areas – such as the South East of England – are very expensive. Another reason might be the reluctance to leave behind family and friends.

Occupational immobility – occurs when a worker cannot easily change jobs, perhaps due to not having the skills and qualifications to take up another job. This leads to market failure because it makes it more difficult for demand for labour to equal supply. If workers cannot easily switch between jobs, this leads to an impediment.

Supply of labour to a monopsonist employer

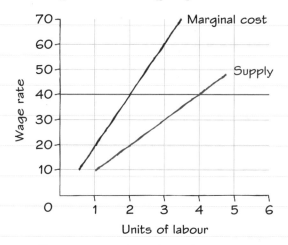

A monopsonist is a sole employer within an industry. The supply curve is upward-sloping. The marginal costs curve lies above the supply curve because the higher wage rate paid to the marginal worker needs to be paid to all existing workers. (To revise monopsony, see page 135.)

Access to labour supply

As a member of the European Union, before Brexit UK firms had access to a supply of labour from all 28 member states. In some industries, EU workers are vital for firms as there is an insufficient supply of labour from within the UK. From 1995 to 2015 the share of EU nationals working in the UK rose from 1.8% of the labour force to 6.3%. EU immigrants are on average younger and more qualified than UK-born workers. The effect of this access to EU workers is to increase the supply of labour, which should lead to lower wages for firms. Access to large numbers of workers from abroad should also lead to the supply of labour being more elastic.

Note that as a result of the UK's departure from the European Union (EU) – so-called Brexit – the ability of workers to move freely between countries in the EU to work, may be more difficult. This could limit UK firms' access to labour and reduce the supply of labour.

Now try this

State two ways a government could reduce occupational immobility.

Wage determination 1

In a competitive market, wages are determined by market forces. Workers who are highly skilled and in short supply can command high wages. Workers lacking specialist skills are in more plentiful supply and their wage rate reflects this. Demand (page 137) and supply (pages 138–9) in the labour market can be brought together to show how wage rates are determined in competitive markets.

Wage determination and elasticity

Wages rates can – and do – change. These changes are caused by changes in the demand and supply of labour. In the example on the right the demand for labour has increased and caused the demand curve to shift to the right. This could be a result of:

- increased productivity (increasing MRP)
- price of capital increase.

As supply is inelastic, an increase in demand from D_1 to D_2 leads to large increase in real wages from W_1 to W_2.

Labour supply is inelastic

Remember

The lower the elasticity of supply, the greater will be the change in wages and the less will be the impact on employment.

Wage determination and elasticity of demand

In the market shown in the diagram below, the demand for labour is inelastic. The supply of labour has increased. As demand is inelastic, an increase in supply from S_1 to S_2 leads to large fall in real wages from W_2 to W_1, but only a small increase in employment (E_1 to E_2).

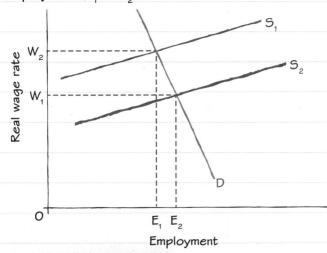

Perfectly competitive labour markets

In a perfectly competitive labour market there are a large number of small firms hiring large numbers of individual, homogeneous workers. The demand curve for labour – the MRP line – is downward-sloping (see diagram below). The supply curve is perfectly elastic, meaning it is horizontal. It is also the MC line. The firm can therefore hire as many workers as it likes at the going wage rate. The firm will employ the number of workers where the MC is equal to the MRP of labour – point B.

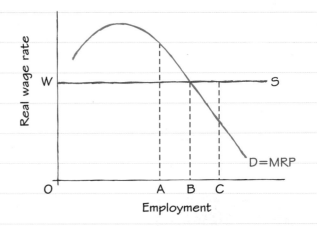

Now try this

1 State three things that would cause the productivity of workers to increase.

2 Explain one reason why wage rates might fall.

Wage determination 2

As in the markets for goods and services, so there are factors which reduce competitiveness in labour markets.

Why wage rates differ

Wage rates differ for a number of reasons. These factors influence either the demand for labour or the supply of labour. They include:

- age – young, middle-aged, old
- sex – male/female
- ethnic background
- education, training, experience
- ability to perform tasks.

Wages also differ because some workers do not work to maximise wages but instead for other aspects, such as satisfaction.

> **Real world** **One in a million**
>
> Cristiano Ronaldo is a football player of rare talent. Some say he is one in a million. For the 2017–18 season, playing for Real Madrid, his salary was equivalent to £17.5 million per year (after tax). Economic theory can explain this. Supply of players like Ronaldo is very low. Indeed, supply of Ronaldo himself = 1. Demand, on the other hand, is very high. Lots of rich football clubs would love to sign the player. In this case low supply plus high demand equals £17.5 million per year.

Non-competitive labour markets

Not all labour markets are competitive. These are labour markets where:

- the firm is a dominant buyer of labour – a monopsonist – such as the NHS being the main 'buyer' of doctors and nurses

- there is a monopoly supplier of labour, such as a trade union.

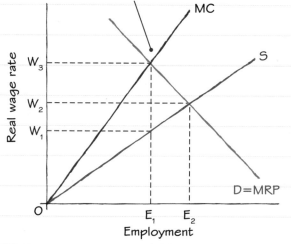

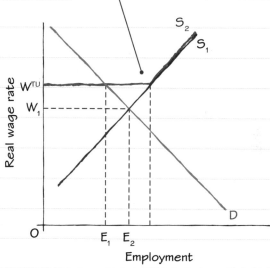

Here the NHS hires to the point where MC = MRP, shown by W_1. If the industry had been perfectly competitive the equilibrium wage rate would be W_3, higher than the wage rate under monopsony. Employment would be higher were the market perfectly competitive. Where a monopsony exists, wages and employment are *both lower* than if the market had been competitive.

The trade union has the effect of charging a minimum wage for its members. This effectively 'kinks' the supply curve of labour and creates the wage rate W^{TU}. Employment falls from E_2 to E_1 while wage rates rise from W_1 to W^{TU}.

Current labour market issues

- **The gender pay gap** – there is an ongoing discussion about how women are paid less than men for carrying out the same job.

- **Executive pay** – some executives are paid large multiples of the wages of regular employees and there is debate about whether executive pay should be capped.

- **Automation and the future of employment** – the rise of robotics threatens traditional types of employment.

Now try this

Describe one disadvantage of increased automation in a manufacturing industry.

Government intervention 1

Governments may intervene in the labour market in order to set minimum and maximum wages. Government policies can have an effect on wage rates in the public sector and the mobility of labour.

Minimum wages

Low wages can be a problem for several reasons. For workers who earn low incomes, the result can be a lower standard of living than other workers. Low wages can give rise to relative poverty. For governments, low wages impact on the economy through the effect on AD. There are strong equity arguments for the government to intervene to ensure workers do not suffer as a result of earning low incomes. A minimum wage, imposed by the government, means employers cannot pay below a certain amount.

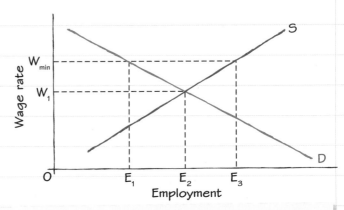

The minimum wage – W_{min} – is imposed above the market wage rate. For workers in the industry this results in higher incomes. However, note how at the new minimum wage, unemployment will be created, shown by the difference between E_1 and E_3.

Maximum wages

A maximum wage places a limit on a worker's wage rate. To be effective it must be set below the equilibrium wage rate. This will reduce wage rates in the market. Effects of a maximum wage include:

- less inequality in society – top income earners cannot earn excessive market wages
- lower labour costs for firms – they now pay lower than the market equilibrium wage rate.

However, problems with maximum wages exist. Higher wages act as a motivation for employees and can lead to increased productivity. Maximum wages can limit this effect. Also, by placing limits on wage rates, governments are impeding the market which would reward talent and scarce skills with higher wages.

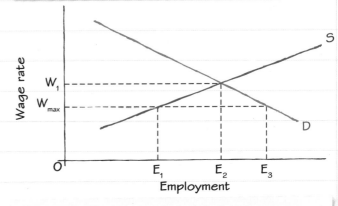

The effect of this maximum wage – W_{max} – is to create excess demand. This is because fewer workers want to work at the lower wage rate, meaning the supply of labour is shown by E_1, but the demand for labour is shown by E_3.

Public sector wage setting

The government can have an impact on the labour market through the setting of wages in the public sector. In many economies across the world, the state employs millions of workers. In some industries – such as education and health in the UK – the government is a monopsonist (the main buyer of labour in the industry).

Policies to tackle labour immobility

Government intervention may be required in labour markets because they do not behave like many other (product) markets. Labour markets deal with people. Market equilibrium is not always easily restored. One reason is that labour is not always very mobile (see page 139). The government can play a key role in helping to improve mobility through:

- **training programmes** – to provide workers with skills which may be in demand in some areas and industries
- **relocation subsidies** – providing workers with cash incentives to move to different areas.

Now try this

Referring to the diagram at the top of the page, explain why a minimum wage must be set above the equilibrium wage to be effective.

Government intervention 2

Governments are involved in all areas of the economy. One area in which governments intervene is the control of **monopolies and mergers** to ensure consumers are not disadvantaged by their dominance.

Controlling monopolies

A monopoly is a firm that controls over 25% of a market (see page 133). In the diagram (right) you can see that the monopolist produces at point OA – where MC = MR, which is below the level of output that would occur if this industry were competitive (OB). The monopolist is producing a lower output and at a higher price than would exist under perfect competition. Therefore, there is a clear case for government intervention.

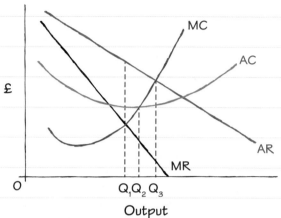

Government intervention to control monopolies

Price regulation – prices might be capped in an industry to prevent monopolists charging excessively high prices due to their market power (see below).

Profit regulation – the maximum amount of profit that a monopolist can earn is set so that the level of profit is no more than could have been earned if the firm operated under competitive conditions. For example, this model has been used in the USA to limit the profits of utility industries. Regulators need detailed knowledge of costs and rates of return in the industry. The approach gives monopolists no incentive to reduce costs.

Types of government intervention

Quality standards – minimum standards set by government to ensure that all firms, even those with market power, deliver a minimum standard to ensure consumers are not disadvantaged.

Performance targets – set by government regulators for monopoly industries such as utilities. For example, the water industry has targets on how quickly water leaks are repaired.

Price regulation in a monopoly industry

The diagram shows how the government can fix a maximum price in a monopoly industry. For example, this can be used by the government to fix prices in the private rental sector. The maximum price is set by the government at E. This makes the average and marginal revenue curves horizontal for part of their curves. This results in a higher output at OB and a lower price of OE compared to the profit maximising price (OF) and output (OA) of the monopolist.

Remember: the firm, as a profit maximiser, will produce where MC = MR!

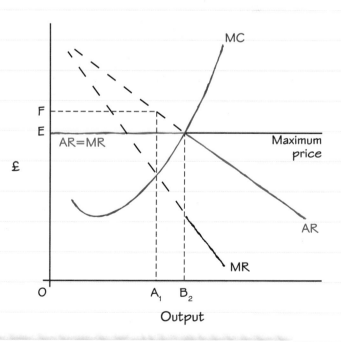

1 Define monopoly.

2 Explain why it is necessary for the government to set quality standards of monopolies.

Competition and contestability 1

As well as controlling the behaviour of monopolies, the government can also try to improve the level of competition in a market. On this page, you will revise **deregulation**. You also need to understand the difference between competition and contestability.

Promoting competition

Regulating the prices monopolists can charge, or the profits they make, can be effective strategies. However, an alternative approach, favoured by free market economists, is to increase the amount of competition that exists in a market. In this situation, the invisible hand of competition will limit the excesses of monopoly without the need for inefficient government intervention.

Key terms

Competition – refers to the number of firms in an industry. If there are lots of competitors then the market is competitive.

Contestability – refers to the threat of competition. A firm might have a monopoly but will act as if it were in a competitive market if the threat of new entrants existed. Contestable markets have low barriers to entry and exit.

Deregulation – the process of removing government controls from markets.

Government intervention

Government intervention to promote competition and contestability			
Enhancing competition between firms through the promotion of small businesses.	**Deregulation** The process of removing government control from markets.	Competative tendering for government contracts.	**Privatisation** Selling state-owned firms to private sector owners.

Real world Deregulation of the bus industry

In the 1980s the UK bus industry was deregulated as a way of improving the efficiency of the industry

Until the 1980s, UK bus companies operated as local monopolies. Different companies served different areas. The government deregulated the market to encourage firms to compete for local routes. As a result, more competitors entered the market. However, as profit maximising firms, many bus companies bid for the most profitable routes – an attempt at 'creaming the market'. Less popular – often rural – routes were typically left with poorer service as they were not as profitable for the new companies. Deregulation can bring efficiency gains and better service – but there are often more negative consequences.

Now try this

1 State three ways the government can improve contestability in a market.
2 Describe how contestability in a market might be encouraged.

Competition and contestability 2

Governments can improve competition and contestability through encouraging the growth of small businesses, **competitive tendering** and **privatisation**. (For information on deregulation, see page 144.)

Encouraging growth

There are a variety of ways that a government can encourage the growth of **small businesses**. By reducing the level of welfare benefits for the unemployed, the government can encourage people to start small businesses. This can be challenged on an ethical level, however.

Alternatively, the government might provide incentives to individuals. These include:

- lower taxes for business start-ups
- small business grants
- training grants.

 Real world **Outsourcing**

In the UK, Serco is a large service provider to the public sector. It provides air navigation services, healthcare services, citizen services and many more. Governments outsource services rather than provide these services themselves.

Transport for Edinburgh, the University of Edinburgh and Serco worked together to introduce a new cycle hire scheme for the city

Competitive tendering

This occurs when the government invites private firms to bid for the contract to produce a public good or service. The firm bidding the lowest cost, subject to quality, wins the contract. In the UK, contracts to supply the NHS, schools, the army and so on have to be done through competitive tendering. Financial regulations ensure that this happens. Organisations, when seeking a supplier, must obtain quotes from at least three suppliers. This encourages competition between suppliers who know they will be tendering against at least two other rivals. The aim is that public sector organisations obtain efficiencies from this process.

Privatisation

Privatisation means the transfer of assets from the public (government) sector to the private sector. This is another method to improve competition in a market. This will work if a previously nationalised industry is broken up into smaller, competing parts. In the UK governments over the past 30 years have embarked on a process of privatisations in areas such as the rail industry. In June 2018, 16.5% of people in paid work in the UK were employed in the public sector and 83.5% in the private sector.

 Key term **Key terms**

Competitive tendering – introducing competition between private sector firms that bid to provide services to public sector organisations.

Outsourcing/contracting out – using private sector firms to provide goods and services on behalf of the state.

Protecting suppliers

Some firms have monopsony powers – they are the sole buyer of a firm – and can potentially exploit suppliers. The government has a number of strategies it can use to protect suppliers in this situation.

 Appoint independent regulators that have the powers to force the monopsonist to act in a competitive manner.

 Introduce self-regulation through an industry code of practice.

 Nationalisation – taking industries into public ownership.

Now try this

1 Describe one disadvantage of competitive tendering.

2 Why might the government outsource services that the state sector could supply?

Impact and limits of government intervention

All economic decisions have consequences. **Government intervention** has impacts in a range of areas but there may also be limits to government intervention.

Government intervention

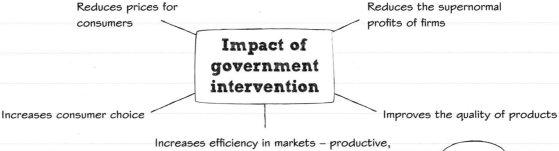

Reduces prices for consumers

Reduces the supernormal profits of firms

Impact of government intervention

Increases consumer choice

Improves the quality of products

Increases efficiency in markets – productive, allocative and dynamic (see page 126)

Asymmetric information

Asymmetric information is where imperfect information exists in a market – where one party has different information to another party. If the government does not have the 'right' information, decisions may be made which do not lead to efficient outcomes. In this case, the true value of the car is known by the seller only, as they know the condition of the car. The buyer does not have the full picture!

Car value is actually £3500

Seller

Buyer

FOR SALE £4,500

In economics, information is key: consumers and firms make decisions based on the information they have

Regulatory capture

Regulatory capture is an example of government failure and occurs when firms in an industry are able to influence a regulatory body to their own benefit. Firms achieve this by developing positive relationships with the government regulator with the aim of ensuring they are not dealt with harshly. Firms may also not give complete information to regulators. The presence of this asymmetric information in the relationship also means that regulators may never know the full picture.

 Real world **Gas and electricity markets**

In the UK, Ofgem regulates firms in the gas and electricity markets. In 2016, with falling gas wholesale prices, the big energy companies were able to increase their profit margins. This translated into £120 profit per customer, according to the regulator Ofgem. According to some reports, the information was quietly removed. Since then it has been difficult for households to know whether providers are making a fair return. However, the growth of information and switching tools has improved the situation for consumers.

Now try this

1 Give two methods the government could use to reduce prices to consumers.

2 What is meant by asymmetric information?

Exam skills 1: Section A

Section A of **A level Paper 1** consists of multiple-choice and short-answer questions. Each question starts with some stimulus material, such as tables, statistics or short case studies.

A level Paper 1 covers **Theme 1** and **Theme 3**. Make sure you know which paper you are taking and the themes they cover.

Worked example

1 Identify a defining feature of monopoly.   **(1 mark)**

A Firms are price takers. ☐
B Operates at point of productive efficiency. ☐
C Lots of small producers. ☐
D High barriers to entry. ☑

The key here is your knowledge that a monopoly is a single supplier in a market, so C is ruled out straight away. Since monopolies are generally not efficient, you can rule out B. A refers to a situation where there are lots of competing forms, which leaves D as the correct answer.

Worked example

2 Explain **one** advantage of organic growth for a business.
   (2 marks)

An advantage of organic growth is that it can be funded from internal funds. <u>As a result</u>, the business does not need to use external sources of finance, such as loans, which can increase risk.

 Links Revise advantages of growth on page 108.

You are required to make **one** point to demonstrate your knowledge before offering some linked development to support your point. There is more about how to answer 'explain' questions on page 150.

Use the phrase 'As a result...' to link your points in 'explain' questions.

Worked example

3 Explain the effect of increased income on the demand for a normal good. Use a supply and demand diagram in your answer.
(5 marks)

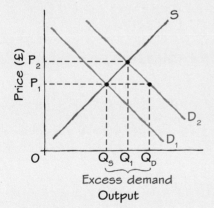

 Links Revise shifts in the demand curve on page 14.

Use a ruler to draw legible diagrams. Remember to label them clearly and refer to them in your answer.

Use technical language.

A rise in income will, <u>ceteris paribus</u>, lead to <u>an increase in demand to D_2</u>. This can be seen in the diagram by a right shift in the demand curve. As a result, an <u>excess demand</u> is created and this causes price to increase.

The answer is clear and well developed, using phrases such as 'As a result...'

Exam skills 2: Section A

 Maths skills 'Calculate' questions require you to use your knowledge of formulae and economics and apply this using the statistics provided (AO2 application). You may also be asked to calculate answers based on a chart or diagram, or to complete information in a table (see page 149).

Worked example

 AL

4 A report by a consumer trends organisation found that when household incomes rose by 5% in the UK, the demand for HD TVs increased by 8%.

Calculate the income elasticity of demand for HD TVs.
You are advised to show your working. **(2 marks)**

$$\frac{8}{5} = 1.6$$

 Links Revise income elasticity of demand on page 15.

Maths skills The question reminds you to show your workings. Only the calculation is required. You do not need to include the formula or provide an explanation.

The topic – income elasticity of demand – is from Theme 1.

Maths skills Remember, the formula for income elasticity of demand is:

$$\frac{\% \text{ change in quantity demanded}}{\% \text{ change in income}}$$

Worked example

 AL

5 In April 2018 the UK government increased the amount of landfill tax to almost £89 per tonne. The purpose of this tax is to reduce the amount of waste being dumped in landfill. The diagram below shows the effect of this tax.

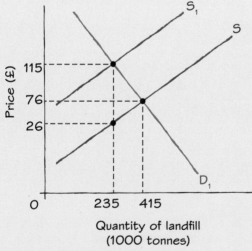

Calculate the total incidence of tax on producers. You are advised to show your working. **(2 marks)**

£76 – £26 = £50

£50 × 235,000 = £11,750,000

Links Revise shifts in supply on page 17.

You may be required to calculate answers based on an economics diagram, using the figures from the diagram. Read the information on the diagram carefully.

The student has demonstrated good understanding of the incidence of tax and has correctly identified the impact on the producer.

 Maths skills 1 mark can be earned from your working, for example, £76 – £26 = £50.

 Maths skills This is the new equilibrium price, £76, from which you deduct £26, the point on the original supply line.

Exam skills 3: Section A

Maths skills You may be required to calculate information given in a partially completed table in order to complete the table, and then to do some additional calculations using the data from the completed table. Below is an exam-style 'calculate' question with exemplar answer.

Worked example

AL

6 The table below shows demand and supply for solar roof panels, which are used to generate renewable electricity.

Price £	Quantity demanded per month (000)	Quantity supplied per month (000)	New quantity demanded per month (000)	New quantity supplied per month (000)
1500	11	8	14 (11 + 3)	10 (8 + 2)
2000	12	10	15	12
2500	13	12	16	14
3000	14	14	17	16
3500	15	16	18	18

As a result of greater consumer awareness, demand increased by 3000 units at every price. At the same time the government has introduced a subsidy which increases supply by 2000 units at all prices.

(a) Calculate the new equilibrium price and quantity as a result of the changes. Use the last two columns for your working. **(4 marks)**

New equilibrium price is £3,500

New equilibrium quantity is 18,000

Revise equilibrium price on page 20. **Links**

Some questions will require you to calculate answers and add these to a table that is partially completed.

Maths skills Make sure your working is clear in the table.

Maths skills To calculate the correct answers for each price, add 3000. For example, when price was £1500, original QD was 11, so the new QD is 14, and so on.

Remember to answer the question! It isn't only about completing the table. Read the question carefully.

Maths skills Don't forget to include any units. Here, the equilibrium price should be in £.

Maths skills You must show your answer using the correct scale. For example, if the student had answered '18' for the new equilibrium quantity, this would have been incorrect and not received any marks. This is because the correct answer is '18 000'. Be accurate in your answers!

Exam skills 4: Section A

'Explain' questions require a particular technique to answer them, involving making a point followed by one or more strands of linked development. Find out more below about the skills required to respond to 'explain' questions. There are two exam-style 'explain' worked examples.

Worked example (AL)

7 Explain **one** type of price competition that a firm could use to help it dominate a market. **(2 marks)**

Price competition involves a business changing its prices to gain a competitive advantage.

One type of price competition is predatory pricing. This involves a business setting a low price in the short term in order to force a competitor out of business.

This is a strong answer because a type of price competition is identified (AO1 knowledge) which is supported by a strand of linked development in which the student shows how predatory pricing helps a business. The linked development is evidence of AO3 analysis.

🔗 Links Revise price competition on page 132.

The question asks you to 'Explain **one**...' You just need to make one point which shows knowledge and then develop this with one strand of linked development. Use phrases such as 'this leads to' to help you structure your response.

It is not necessary to provide a definition of the term in the question (price competition).

The question asks for the 'likely effect' (singular), not 'effects' (plural). Identify one point and develop it.

Worked example (AL)

8 Explain the likely effect of a large number of new entrants into a perfectly competitive market. **(4 marks)**

A large number of new entrants will have the effect of increasing overall market supply. As a result, the supply curve will shift to the right, which will create an excess supply in the market, which will cause the market price to fall.

The question is worth 4 marks – make one point (1 mark) and support it with 3 strands of linked development (1 mark per strand).

A point is made – the effect is identified (AO1).

1st strand of development (AO3).

2nd strand of development (AO3).

3rd strand of development (AO3).

Exam skills 5: Section B data

Section B of **A level Papers 1** and **2** contains a range of economic data and information based on a real-world topic. Read Extracts A–C carefully before looking at the worked examples on page 152.

The steel market

Extract A: Tata Steel and Thyssenkrupp merger announced

In June 2018 the merger was announced between Tata Steel and Thyssenkrupp, a German-owned steel producer. The merger would create Europe's second largest steelmaker. Tata is an Indian-owned company which owns some plants in the UK, including the Port Talbot steelworks in Wales. The new company will be called Thyssenkrupp Tata Steel, will have annual sales of about £13bn and be based in the Netherlands.

Reference: The Guardian

 Any reference to mergers should get you thinking about economies of scale.

5

Extract B: What's behind the Tata–Thyssenkrupp merger?

The steel industry has suffered in recent years from both over-capacity and from low prices inthe market. There are a number of reasons for these changes. One is a fall in demand for steel. Another is the excess supply created from Chinese steelmakers. Between 2000 and 2014 global steel production rose from 800 million tonnes to 1600 million tonnes, mainly delivered by Chinese firms.

However, world steel prices are gradually increasing. Some Chinese producers have been reducing their output, and there has been a small rise in the price of steel.

For steel producers, mergers make sense: fewer companies in the market means less competition, and, eventually, better prices. Mergers are also a way to reduce average costs as firms take advantage of economies of scale. However, mergers can result in job losses, with steel workers losing out when operations are combined.

One of the main issues in this industry is that the total costs of running steel factories are very high. That means that when they're not being used, or they are underused, steel producers may sell their steel at lower prices to offload their excess supply – and that could push prices down again.

Source: The Economist

 You should be able to illustrate excess supply with a demand and supply diagram.

5

10

Extract C: Steel market data

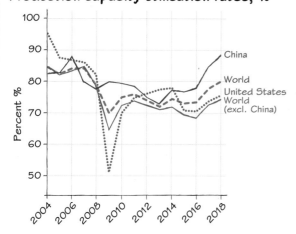

Production capacity utilisation rates, %

China
World
United States
World
(excl. China)

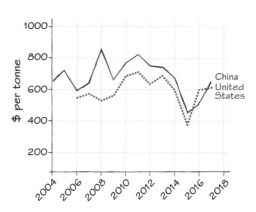

Price, hit-rolled coil, $ per tonne

China
United States

The left-hand chart shows capacity utilisation in steel plants increasing. World prices for steel are starting to increase, as shown in the right-hand chart.

Source: The Economist

Exam skills 6: Section B

Section B in **A level Papers 1** and **2** consists of one question, divided into several part questions. The question will enable you to demonstrate all four of the assessment objectives. The exam-style 'examine' question below is based on the information on the steel market on page 151. Read the extracts carefully before looking at the worked example.

 Links In the exam, the data-response question covers a range of economic concepts and topics. For the exam-style question on this page and the next you may find it helpful to revise mergers (page 107), profit maximisation (pages 120–121), economies of scale (page 115).

Examine

In 'examine' questions you need to identify at least two different reasons or factors, then explain them before offering some evaluation which should consider the drawbacks of each factor.

Remember to refer to the evidence provided in your response, as your response must be in the context of the question and should not be generic.

Worked example

AL

9 Examine **two** benefits to steelmakers of merging with rival firms.
(8 marks)

One benefit is that steelmakers will be able to close inefficient steel plants. This will mean they will be able to reduce the average costs of producing steel which, all other things being equal, will increase profitability. As firms are assumed to be profit maximisers, this decision is rational. However, closing capacity at this stage might cause problems at a later date as the demand for steel is rising and once steel plants are closed down they cannot easily be reopened.

A second benefit is the firms can take advantage of economies of scale. Both Tata and Thyssenkrupp have expertise in steelmaking and by joining together will be able to share knowledge which will lead to lower average costs. However, by becoming a very large firm – the second largest in Europe – the new firm may suffer from diseconomies of scale as it is operating in more than one country and may suffer from co-ordination problems. For example, managers in Germany may find that instructions to managers in UK factories are misunderstood and not followed accurately, perhaps because of language or communication issues.

 You may be awarded up to 8 marks in an 'examine' question.

 The response is logical in its approach. Two benefits have been identified and explained. The response is very clearly in the context of the steel industry and uses evidence from the stimulus material.

 Structure your answer using paragraphs.

 Each benefit is evaluated, with the drawbacks of each benefit considered. Note that each drawback is also in context – refers to the difficulty of reopening steel plants once they are closed, and the fact that the new firm operates in a number of countries.

To complete the response, you should go on to suggest another benefit before explaining this with linked strands of development, and then consider the drawbacks of the benefit.

Exam skills 7: Section B

The exam-style 'discuss' question below is based on the information on the steel market on page 151. Read the extracts carefully before looking at the worked example.

Discuss

In 'discuss' questions, you need to weigh up a scenario before offering some evaluation. Your response must be in the context of the question; for example, you could quote or use figures from the extracts. Remember, there are no right or wrong answers to 'discuss' questions – it is up to you to present your arguments.

Worked example

(b) Discuss the likely impact of mergers between steelmakers on an industry and an economy.　**(15 marks)**

By merging together, Tata and Thyssenkrupp will be able to take advantage of economies of scale, which will reduce average costs and therefore increase productive efficiency. Productive efficiency occurs when firms are producing at the lowest average cost. This is important given the intense competition from low-cost Chinese steelmakers. By reducing average costs the new firm will be able to reduce prices and pass these on to consumers. The users of steel are most likely to be other producers, such as car manufacturers. This is because the demand for steel is a derived demand – it depends on the demand for other products. By other industries having lower prices, so low costs in other industries can be spread. This improves the level of efficiency throughout the economy.

However, mergers can have drawbacks. By merging, Tata and Thyssenkrupp will create a large company which will reduce the amount of competition in the steel industry. If the firm has 25% or more of output of an industry, it will have a degree of monopoly power. <u>Monopolies are neither productively or allocatively efficient.</u> Allocative efficiency occurs where P = MC. But in a monopoly price is above MC and higher than would exist in a perfectly competitive industry.

'Discuss' questions may have a mark allocation of either 12 or 15 marks.

There is no need to provide an introduction or definitions. Get straight to the point by considering, in this case, how mergers benefit firms in this industry.

The answer is in the context of the steel industry. You need to show that you can link your knowledge to the context and use relevant examples.

This paragraph considers the drawbacks of mergers. This is where AO4 evaluation occurs. Again, this is in the context (AO2 application) of the steel industry.

Key terms are correctly used. This clearly demonstrates AO1 knowledge.

A balanced argument (assessment) is provided through discussion of how the merger might not be efficient.

Exam skills 8: Section C

A level Paper 1 Section C consists of two extended open-response questions. The questions are stand-alone and are not based on the extracts Section B. You must answer **one** of them.

Links Recap the following topics: nationalisation (page 145), economies of scale (page 132) and monopolies (page 133).

Evaluate

'Evaluate' questions require you to weigh up a scenario, before offering some evaluation. These questions may ask you to 'evaluate the likely extent...' or 'evaluate the factors...'. They test all four of the assessment objectives. There are no right or wrong answers to 'evaluate' questions – it is up to you to present your arguments and a conclusion.

Worked example   AL

11 In 2017, John McDonnell, Labour Party shadow chancellor, re-stated his party's plans to begin a programme of rail nationalisation in the UK.

Evaluate the likely economic effects of increased nationalisation of industries in the UK.   **(25 marks)**

Nationalisation is the process of taking privately owned businesses into public ownership. These organisations are then under the control of government.

There are a number of arguments in favour of nationalisation. Firstly, where industries are very large there are efficiency gains to be had from single, state ownership. The rail industry, for example, is a <u>natural monopoly</u> which is well-suited to being controlled by the state. Such an industry has extensive economies of scale and this is certainly the case with the rail industry. Therefore, by being taken into state ownership the government would be able to more readily take advantage of these economies of scale. One benefit of these economies of scale is that prices can be reduced for consumers. The rail industry is often criticised for very high fares, usually rising by more than the rate of inflation. In fact, the train companies effectively have a monopoly on the lines they operate, and one feature of monopoly is that these firms can charge prices above what would exist under perfectly competitive conditions. There is therefore a strong **equity** argument that the industry is nationalised so that government can ensure fair fares are in place.

However, these arguments can be challenged. Whilst it is true that such large industries have opportunities for economies of scale, there are possible drawbacks with large organisations, such as diseconomies of scale. By being on such a massive scale, the rail industry is very difficult to manage and to co-ordinate. Before parts of the industry were privatised, the UK rail industry was often criticised for inefficient and late trains – it was something of a laughing stock. X-inefficiency can exist in large organisations, and such inefficiencies are best dealt with by businesses with a profit motive...

Although the rail industry is referred to in the scenario, the question is not specifically about the railways.

Analysis and evaluation make up the majority of the marks but there are marks available for knowledge and application.

The response starts well, with a clear definition of nationalisation.

A good use of and understanding of economics concepts, such as natural monopoly.

Having set out the arguments in favour of nationalisation, the student goes on to evaluate the points discussed previously. This is an important element in 'evaluate' questions.

The response is well structured and set out into paragraphs. The plan for the remainder of the response could be:

- another argument in favour, e.g. profits go direct to taxpayer and can be used for re-investment
- evaluation of this argument, e.g. profits might not be very large
- a final conclusion which brings the argument together. Use the 'it depends' rule a is a way to do this, where the conclusion suggests that an option 'depends' on a perspective, point of view, etc. For example, 'Nationalisation is perhaps best where natural monopoly exists but not in other types of industry.'

Exam-style practice: Section A

On this page, you will find exam-style multiple-choice and short-answer practice questions for **A level Paper 1** Section A. There are answers on page 217.

1 Which of the following will cause a shift to the right of the demand curve for a normal good? **(1 mark)** **AL**

A The imposition of an indirect tax. ☐

B The launch of an advertising campaign. ☐

C A fall in consumer incomes. ☐

D The introduction of a subsidy. ☐

Which of these affect the demand curve, and which affect supply?

Links Recap shifts in demand curve on page 11.

Maths skills You will need to know the formula for calculating price elasticity of demand. Formulae are not provided in the exam.

2 One supermarket reported that the price of parsnips has fallen by 12%. As a result, quantity demanded had increased by 18%. **AL**

Calculate the price elasticity of demand for parsnips. You are advised to show your working. **(2 marks)**

Links Check out the formula for PED on page 13.

3 Which of the following is the point where profit maximisation occurs for a firm? **AL**

A Where AC = AR ☐

B Where MC = MR ☐

C Where AR > AC ☐

D Where MC = 0 ☐

You need to understand how profit maximisation is achieved for a firm.

Links Check out the theory on page 120.

Exam-style practice: Section B data

On this page, you will find exam-style stimulus material for **A level Paper 1** Section B data response. Before you answer the exam-style questions that follow on page 157, make sure you read the extracts carefully, highlighting any key terms and annotating useful points.

The fruit and vegetable market

Extract A: The problem of rejected vegetables

Supermarkets have been criticised for setting unnecessary cosmetic standards for fruit and vegetables before they can be sold in their stores. The result is that 'wonky vegetables', which are perfectly fit for human consumption, are either not being sold or are being sold at discounted prices. It is estimated that 5–25% of apples, 9–20% of onions and 3–13% of potatoes are rejected on their appearance, not their nutritional value. Making small changes to specifications could, it is estimated, reduce food waste by 15%. This would reduce costs to farmers, with a net welfare gain to society.

5

Source: Environment, Food and Rural Affairs Committee

Extract B: Inefficiency of rejecting food

Rejecting food is wasteful. It is also inefficient. Costs involved in rejecting food includes:

- labour costs

- costs of growing food which is later discarded

- opportunity cost – farmland could have been used for other purposes which did not lead to wastage.

5

Extract C: Supermarket benefits from sale of 'wonky' fruit and vegetables

Some supermarkets have developed strategies to get around the problems associated with this inefficiency. One solution has been to sell misshapen fruit and vegetables. Sales of 'wonky veg' has increased in recent years.

Booming sales of 'wonky' fruit and vegetables have enabled UK supermarkets to achieve in the region of £500m of extra sales in recent weeks. Morrisons, which has championed the sale of so called 'wonky' vegetables – smaller or misshapen fruit and vegetables – said its popularity has helped make it the fastest-growing of the UK's big four supermarkets. The Bradford-based chain increased sales by 1.9% in the last three months and said sales of wonky greengrocery – which it sells at a lower price as a way to cut down waste – have more than tripled, according to Kantar. A spokesperson at Kantar said that the wonky produce was now bought by 12% of shoppers at Morrisons, boosting its own-label sales by 18%.

5

10

Source: The Guardian

Exam-style practice: Section B

On this page, you will find exam-style practice questions for **A level Paper 1** Section B data response. Before you answer the questions, make sure you read the extracts on page 156 carefully. There are answers on page 217.

4 Explain the effect of the increased supply of vegetables on the market price. Use a supply and demand diagram in your answer.

(5 marks)

AL

There are two parts to this question – the diagram and the answer. Make sure your diagram is clear – use a ruler and label the axes, price, quantity and curves. Ensure you refer to your diagram as part of your answer.

 Revise demand and supply diagrams on page 21.

5 Assess the possible impact on consumers of supermarkets having monopsony power over farmers that produce fruit and vegetables.

(10 marks)

AL

'Assess' questions require you to provide a balanced argument. There is no right or wrong answer here.

 Revise monopsonies on page 135.

 Recap perfect competition on page 127.

6 Discuss the likely impact on the farming industry of supermarkets deciding to accept and sell 'wonky' vegetables.

(12 marks)

AL

Aim to spend 12–15 minutes on your response. Think about the impact on the farming industry of increased demand for its produce. Remember to use evidence from the extract in your answer.

Try to show some original thinking, in addition to demonstrating your knowledge of economics.
Where appropriate, support your explanation with a diagram. For example, you might consider how the PED for such products might affect their sales. A diagram showing a relatively elastic demand schedule can be used to point out the likely effectiveness of selling such a vegetable at a lower price than standard.

There are marks in 'discuss' questions for evaluation, which means you need to show that you have weighed up different points of view.

Remember, 'discuss' questions require you to consider both sides of an argument. For example, you need to consider both the advantages and disadvantages for farmers of supermarkets selling 'wonky' vegetables.

157

Exam-style practice: Section C

On this page, you will find exam-style extended open-response questions for **A level Paper 1** Section C. There are answers on pages 217–218.

 Links Recap monopoly on page 133.

7 'Monopoly is not always bad. In fact, for many, the benefits of monopoly outweigh the costs.'

To what extent do you agree with this statement? **(25 marks)**

This is one of two questions in Section C – in the exam, you will need to choose **one** of them.

Remember to consider at least two factors and provide a conclusion – make clear the extent to which you agree with the statement.

Aim to spend 20 minutes on your response. Think about weighing up the pros and cons of monopoly.

8 Evaluate the microeconomic impact of the government banning the use of zero hours contracts by firms. **(25 marks)**

Remember, 'evaluate' questions require you to write in an essay style, using paragraphs, before arriving at a conclusion.

You might use the 'it depends' rule in your conclusion (see page 154).

Begin by outlining some of the positive microeconomic impacts of zero hours contracts. Also, there might be an impact on productivity. In a separate paragraph, consider some possible negative impacts of such a ban. For example, negative impacts involve the impact on workers and firms. These might include less flexibility for firms and workers who rely on zero hours contracts. This might impact on productivity.

Why some firms grow

Globalisation involves the process of countries from across the globe becoming more linked and interdependent. Below you will revise the key features of globalisation and factors contributing to globalisation.

Characteristics of globalisation

Globalisation involves the ever-increasing **integration** of the world's local, regional and national economies into a single international market.

Increased foreign ownership of companies.

Increasing global media presence.

Characteristics of globalisation

Increased trade in goods and services.

Deindustrialisation in developed countries. This involves a decrease in the industrial (secondary) sector of the economy, such that manufacturing accounts for a smaller percentage of GDP. The service sector becomes more prominent.

Factors contributing to globalisation since 1970

Factor	Explanation
Improvements in transport infrastructure	The cost of transporting goods globally has fallen. Containerisation – the use of bulk ocean shipping – costs far less than in previous decades. This makes it possible for firms to produce goods in countries where costs are low, such as China, and transport them to foreign markets.
Improvements in communication technology	There has been rapid and advanced change in the area of communicating information, through the development of internet technology. Managers in global firms can run meetings through web-conferencing rather than through more face-to-face meetings, which brings down costs.
Trade liberalisation	Through organisations such as the World Trade Organization, far less protectionism exists between countries, which means trade can take place with fewer barriers and restrictions, such as tariffs. A tariff Is a tax imposed on imports.
Growing influence of global companies	As firms are profit maximisers, they have been able to grow globally, expanding into new markets to sell goods and services, and also to exploit lower cost regimes in less economically developed countries.
The end of the Cold War	The Cold War was a period of political tension between countries in the East and West between 1947 and the 1980s. The end of the Cold War led to the opening up of formerly closed economies in communist countries, such as Russia, Poland and Romania, and a subsequent increase in global labour supply.
The role of international financial markets	Finance is more globally available. This has led to domestic firms being able to access finance from foreign sources, which has contributed to business growth.

Now try this

1 Give three examples of firms that operate on a global scale.

2 Define the term tariff.

The impacts of globalisation

Globalisation has had impacts on a wide range of global stakeholders. Some of these impacts have been positive, some less so.

Impact on countries and governments

Countries can gain and lose economically from the process of globalisation. Globalisation can lead to rising incomes and therefore rising tax revenue for governments. It also can lead to better quality jobs as **multinational corporations (MNCs)** invest in new factories and facilities. However, it can lead to the decline of traditional industries, which leads to structural unemployment and lower wages. Many countries have also experienced increased migration as workers from poorer countries move to those where more job opportunities exist.

 UK shipbuilding

The UK was once famous for its shipbuilding industry. Many towns and cities were renowned for their shipyards. These included Sunderland, Newcastle, Belfast, Portsmouth and Glasgow. In 1976 the UK shipbuilding industry produced 134 vessels. By 2011 this figure was just 4.

Shipyards in Glasgow and elsewhere were forced to close as a result of intense competition from foreign producers in South Korea, Japan and China.

Impact on consumers

👍 Global competition has the effect of reducing prices as goods can be produced more cheaply. Prices are also forced lower due to competition that now exists globally. In addition, consumers have far greater choice than in previous generations. Globalisation has increased the availability of goods and services. For example, in the UK fruit such as strawberries used to be available only in the summer, but now they are a year-round product due to supplies from countries such as Spain, Morocco and Egypt.

Impact on producers

👍 Costs are lower as firms are able to obtain products and materials from a wide range of countries.

👍 Increased competition means firms need to aim for productive efficiency. Many UK high streets used to have local furniture stores but the arrival of large foreign competitors, such as Ikea, has put many out of business.

👍 Tax avoidance – if firms operate in more than one country they can decide which country to base their central operation in and therefore where they pay tax. Some firms have been criticised for locating where the lowest tax rates are payable.

Impact on workers

👍 Higher economic growth resulting from globalisation has led to rising employment and higher wages.

👎 However, traditional industries have suffered as a result of competition and workers in these industries have become unemployed. Wages as a share of GDP have been falling.

👎 Increased migration gives some workers opportunities to work in other countries but also affects workers in these countries, where wages might be forced down.

Impact on the environment

There are serious negative impacts on the environment resulting from globalisation.

👎 Resource depletion – greater production of goods leads to the use of finite resources. For example, refrigerators are made with materials such as iron ore.

👎 Climate impacts – the transportation of goods across the globe, plus increased travel by individuals, leads to higher carbon emissions.

👎 Rising world population is linked to globalisation and this places stresses on natural resources.

Now try this

1 Give two environmental impacts of globalisation.
2 Explain one benefit of globalisation for workers.

Specialisation and trade 1

Countries need to trade with each other because they cannot produce everything they want. Absolute and comparative advantage are used here to explain why trade takes place. Specialisation involves countries focusing on goods and services that they have an advantage in producing.

Absolute advantage

This exists when a country can produce a good at a lower cost per unit than another country. Imagine a world with two countries – A and B. They produce two products – bikes and bananas. They split their resources equally between the production of bikes and bananas. Output is shown below:

	Units of bikes	Units of bananas
Country A	100	500
Country B	200	300

Country A has an **absolute advantage** in the production of bananas and country B has an absolute advantage in producing bikes.

If both countries decide to specialise in the product where their absolute advantage lies, this is the outcome:

	Units of bikes	Units of bananas
Country A		1000
Country B	400	

If both countries choose to specialise, world production of both products increases. This then allows trade between the two countries to take place. The diagram (right) illustrates this position.

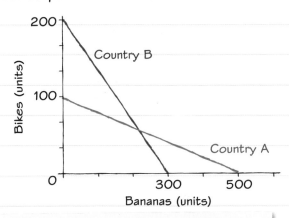

The production possibility frontier (PPF) for countries A and B. Country A clearly has an absolute advantage in the production of bananas while B has an absolute advantage in bikes.

Comparative advantage

This exists when a country can produce a good more cheaply relative to other goods produced domestically. A country has a **comparative advantage** if the opportunity cost of it producing a good is lower than the opportunity cost for another country. The example below assumes both countries use half their resources to produce bikes, the other half to produce bananas.

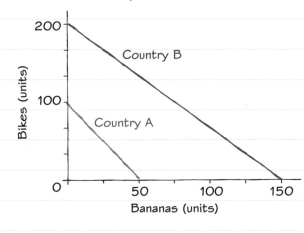

	Units of bikes	Units of bananas
Country A	100	50
Country B	200	150

Country B has an absolute advantage in both bikes and bananas. The theory of comparative advantage shows that specialisation and trade are still advantageous to both countries. This happens when a product has a lower opportunity cost than another. The opportunity cost of producing bananas for Country A is $\frac{100}{50} = 2$. For country B it is $\frac{200}{150} = 1.33$. Country A has to give up 2 bikes to produce a unit of bananas. Country B has to give up only 1.33 units.

Country A has to give up more bikes to produce more bananas so its slope is steeper. Therefore, country B has the lower opportunity cost when producing bananas. Country A has the lower opportunity cost when producing bikes so should specialise with this product. After specialisation, the figures are:

- Country A = 200 units of bikes
- Country B = 300 units of bananas

Now try this

Why might a country have an absolute advantage when producing a certain good?

Specialisation and trade 2

The theory of comparative advantage has some important assumptions. It also has some limitations. There are both advantages and disadvantages of trade and specialisation for countries.

Comparative advantage: assumptions

The following assumptions exist with the model:

1 Constant costs of production – there are no economies or diseconomies of scale.

2 Transport costs are zero.

3 Perfect knowledge exists.

4 Factors of productions are perfectly mobile – they can easily be switched from producing one good to another.

5 No tariffs or other trade barriers.

Comparative advantage: limitations

A number of the assumptions of the theory can be regarded as unrealistic:

1 Transport costs exist – and these may outweigh any comparative advantage that a country has.

2 Increased specialisation may lead to larger firms, which can give rise to diseconomies of scale (where average costs of production rise as the scale of production increases).

3 Governments may introduce tariffs or other barriers to trade.

Advantages and disadvantages of specialisation and trade

👍 Lower prices and more choice for consumers – as greater competition exists, so the benefits can be enjoyed by consumers.

👍 Countries can have access to goods and services they would otherwise not be able to produce or access.

👍 Innovation – free trade encourages competition, which leads firms to be innovative. The rewards for such investment and innovation are large global markets.

👎 Risk of **dumping** by foreign firms. This occurs when firms sell to foreign markets at below cost with the aim of putting rivals out of business.

👎 Increased unemployment due to competition and dumping.

👎 Increased economic integration might lead to countries becoming more exposed to external shocks.

👎 Growing influence of global monopolies, which might lead to higher prices.

👎 Environmental degradation due to increased transportation and the depletion of natural resources.

👎 Developing and emerging economies may face particular problems, for example, infant industries may be unable to compete and go out of business; the monopsony power of global companies may mean that low prices are paid for commodities from developing countries.

Now try this

1 What is meant by international trade?

2 Describe one criticism of the theory of comparative advantage.

Pattern of trade

The **pattern of trade** reflects the nature of trade between countries by considering the nature of imports and exports. Several factors influence the pattern of trade.

What is the pattern of trade?

The pattern of trade is something that changes over time. The UK used to be the major manufacturer in the world, exporting its goods globally. Today, manufacturing is less important in the structure of the UK economy (although it is still very significant). The UK is now primarily a service-led economy. Most of the manufactured goods that UK consumers buy have been produced abroad as other countries are better positioned to carry out mass manufacturing. The pattern of trade for the UK has changed.

Factors influencing the pattern of trade

Comparative advantage – where countries develop cost advantages in the production of certain goods, the pattern of trade changes to reflect these advantages. This is because lower costs of production, due to the comparative advantage, mean trade increases.

Impact of emerging economies – as countries grow in size they tend to import more. This growth can impact on the pattern of global trade. These countries will also need to export more, to pay for their foreign expenditure. The pattern of trade can change as a result. China is now the world's leading exporter, with a massive manufacturing sector, and yet 50 years ago it did not trade much with the rest of the world.

Pattern of trade: influencing factors

Changes in relative exchange rates (see pages 170–172) – an exchange rate is the value of one currency in terms of another. As exchange rates change they can affect how competitive countries are when importing and exporting.

Growth of trading blocs (see page 165) – these are designed to increase trade between countries. The European Union is an economic area that aims to encourage trade between member states. It originally had six member states in the 1950s but at the time of publication has 28 members. As a result, trade between member states has increased.

 Real world **Pattern of UK trade**

The table (right) shows how the UK, since the 1950s, has changed in terms of its pattern of trade from one where exports of goods far outweighed those of services, to a position in 2014 where exports of services were much more closely matched.

£ billion	Exports		Imports		National income
	Goods	Services	Goods	Services	
1955	3.1	1.0	3.4	1.0	17.6
1965	5.0	1.6	5.3	1.7	33.4
1975	19.5	7.7	22.8	6.0	102.8
1985	78.3	25.7	82.0	17.2	346.8
1995	153.6	59.1	166.6	42.9	703.6
2000	187.9	81.4	222.0	67.4	911.1
2005	212.7	128.9	282.4	94.0	1189.2
2010	270.8	176.2	368.2	115.9	1400.7
2014	292.2	207.7	412.1	122.6	1593.4

Now try this

1 From the table, calculate and compare the value of imports as a percentage of national income in 1955 and 2014.

2 Describe one factor that has contributed to the UK's changing pattern of trade.

Terms of trade

The **terms of trade** measures the ratio of export prices to import prices. Various factors may influence a country's terms of trade. You will also revise the impact of changes in the terms of trade.

Terms of trade

The terms of trade refers to the relative price of a country's exports compared to its imports. It is effectively a rate of exchange used between the country and the rest of the world. It measures the amount of imports the country can buy per unit of exports. You need to be able to calculate the terms of trade using the formula (right).

Maths skills — Calculating the terms of trade

The calculation is based on index numbers. Remember, an index number shows the relative value of one number to another using 100 as a base. Index numbers make comparisons more straightforward.

$$\text{Index of terms of trade} = \frac{\text{index of export prices}}{\text{index of import prices}} \times 100$$

Example

A country has the following information:

Year	2017	2018
Index of export prices	98	110
Index of import prices	103	105

In 2017 the terms of trade was 95.1 (98 ÷ 103 × 100). In 2018 this has changed to 104.8. This means that the country is effectively better off as it is exporting its goods and services at a higher price and can afford more imports.

Remember

If a country's terms of trade rises, it is **better off**. If it falls, it is **worse off**. One reason why a country will be better off is the reduced cost-push pressures in the economy, as import prices are lower compared to export prices.

Factors influencing the terms of trade

1 **Relative inflation rates** – if prices in the country rise, then the index of export prices is likely to rise and this will improve the terms of trade index.

2 **Relative productivity rates** – productivity measures the output per factor input per period of time. Rising productivity leads to lower unit costs which will lead to a worsening of the terms of trade if export prices are able to be reduced.

3 **Changes in exchange rates** – a rise in the exchange rate will lead to a fall in the price of imports. As a result the terms of trade will improve.

Impact of changes in the terms of trade

There are a number of impacts of changing terms of trade index. In terms of **living standards**, an improvement in the terms of trade caused by a rise in the index of export prices may lead to fewer exports and less demand for output from the export sector. This could lead to job losses and lower incomes in this sector, which will impact on living standards of workers in the sector. However, the improved terms of trade will also mean that the country is able to import more for the same level of exports, which improves living standards.

A further impact of changes in the terms of trade is on the balance of payments accounts. Improved terms of trade should lead to an improvement in the balance of payments, although the impact will depend on the price elasticities of demand for imports and exports.

Now try this

1 A country has an index of export prices of 108 and an index of import prices of 120. Calculate its terms of trade index.

2 How does a fall in the exchange rate affect the terms of trade index?

Trading blocs

Countries sometimes form **trading blocs**, which can have both positive and negative effects on trade. There are different types of trading blocs.

Trading blocs

- A trading bloc is an agreement between a group of countries that promotes and manages trade between member states. Members agree to remove protectionist measures, such as tariffs or quotas. The aim is for trade creation between members.

- Trading blocs are typically a **regional trade agreement**. This is an agreement between at least two countries to reduce or eliminate tariffs, quotas and other protectionist measures. For example, the Association of South East Asian Nations (ASEAN) is a trade bloc of 10 nations.

- **Bilateral agreements** exist between two countries or trading blocs. In 2018 a bilateral agreement between the EU and Japan was signed.

- **Multilateral agreements** exist between more than two countries or trading blocs. For example, the Pacific Alliance Free Trade Area was formed between Chile, Colombia, Mexico and Peru.

Types of trading blocs

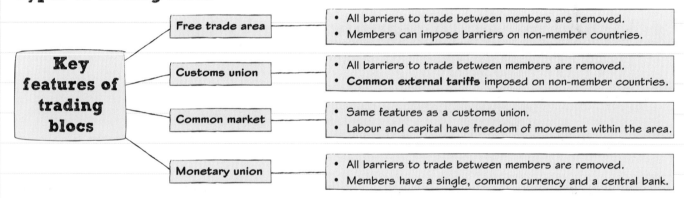

Key features of trading blocs	**Free trade area**	• All barriers to trade between members are removed. • Members can impose barriers on non-member countries.
	Customs union	• All barriers to trade between members are removed. • **Common external tariffs** imposed on non-member countries.
	Common market	• Same features as a customs union. • Labour and capital have freedom of movement within the area.
	Monetary union	• All barriers to trade between members are removed. • Members have a single, common currency and a central bank.

Costs and benefits of regional trade agreements

👎 Agreements often don't cover a wide range of goods and services, so the impact can be weak and therefore limit the economic benefits.

👎 Reduced national sovereignty. For example, the UK's decision to leave the EU was largely due to a belief that sovereignty would be lost by continued membership of the EU.

👍 Static benefits occur as a result of increased specialisation and include reduced average costs for firms.

👍 Dynamic benefits stem from the creation of increased competition within the area of the bloc and include increased innovation and knowledge transfer.

👍 Increased trade between member states.

Now try this

1 How does a common market differ from a free trade area?

2 Describe one benefit arising from a regional trade agreement.

World Trade Organization (WTO)

The **World Trade Organization** (WTO) is an international organisation which sets rules for trade between nations. There may be conflicts between regional trade agreements and the WTO.

Formation of the WTO

The WTO was established in 1995 and replaced the **General Agreement on Tariffs and Trade** (GATT), which was established in 1948. In the post-war period there was a belief that countries needed to work together to rebuild following the Second World War. There currently are 164 member countries.

Role of the WTO in trade liberalisation

The main role of the WTO is to ensure that trade flows as smoothly, predictably and freely as possible. Its two key functions are to:

1 facilitate the reduction or removal of protectionist barriers between countries – the aim is for **trade liberalisation**, where trade can be as free as possible

2 make sure that countries adhere to the agreements that they have signed up to, in other words, that they obey the rules – the WTO acts as a negotiator between countries to help resolve conflicts.

 Real world   **Resolving conflicts: WTO and Airbus**

Airbus moves to comply with WTO ruling on aircraft subsidies

In 2018 the European aircraft producer, Airbus, announced that it would take steps to comply with a WTO judgement that the firm was in breach of WTO rules regarding subsidies from governments. The USA had complained to the WTO that its aircraft manufacturers, such as Boeing, were disadvantaged by such subsidies and that the arrangements were not in line with WTO rules. Airbus has agreed with the French and German governments that the subsidy arrangement will be changed.

The Airbus A380

Possible conflicts between the WTO and regional trade agreements

- A common external tariff contradicts the principles of the WTO. Although there is free trade between members, protectionist barriers are imposed on those who are not members.

- Some argue that the WTO is too powerful and favours developed countries over developing countries. For example, it requires developing countries to lower their barriers to trade while richer countries can keep them.

- Setting up a customs union or a free trade area may be seen to violate the WTO's principle of having all trading partners treated equally.

- Some also argue that the WTO damages native cultures by adopting an American-style materialistic approach. However, the WTO does not have the power to force workers in less economically developed countries (LEDCs) to accept very low wages. This is a matter for the country and the workers involved.

Now try this

1 What is the WTO?
2 Describe one benefit of the WTO.

Restrictions on free trade

Despite the benefits that exist from trade, there are reasons why countries may want to avoid such free trade. Governments can use a range of methods to restrict free trade, including **tariffs**, **quotas**, **subsidies to domestic producers** and **non-tariff barriers**.

Reasons for restrictions

There are a wide range of methods that governments can use to restrict free trade.

- To protect infant industries (new industries at the early stage of their development) and sunset industries (those in decline), to protect employment.
- To retain self-sufficiency.
- To correct imbalances on the current account of the balance of payments.
- To retaliate against restrictions imposed by another country.
- To prevent dumping.
- To reduce competition from countries with cheap labour and poor labour/ environmental laws.
- To protect strategic industries, such as defence, essential foodstuffs and energy.

Tariffs

Tariffs are a tax on imported goods, also known as customs duty or import duty. Tariffs have the effect of making imports more expensive. This is shown below.

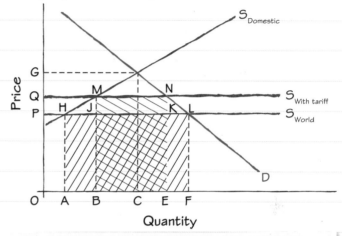

If the world price of a product is P, a tariff of GH will shift the supply curve upwards from S_W to S_{WT}. Consumption in this economy will fall by EF whilst production will rise by AB. Imports will fall from AF to BE.

Quotas

Quotas are physical limits on the quantity of a certain good that can be imported.

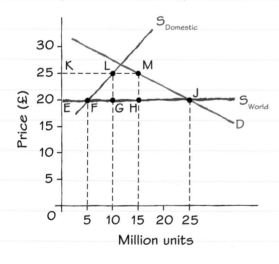

Other types of restrictions on trade

- **Subsidies to domestic producers** – grants given to domestic producers to enable them to lower production costs, therefore lowering prices, which should make the country's products more competitive internationally. Unlike tariffs and quotas, subsidies incur a cost to the public finances.
- **Non-tariff barriers** – include product specifications, health and safety regulations, environmental regulations and labelling of products.

In the diagram on the left, the introduction of the quota of 2 million units limits supply and raises price to £25. Domestic consumption will fall to 15 million units, whilst domestic production rises to 10 million. Importers of the units subject to quotas will see a windfall gain shown by GLMH.

Now try this

1 State three reasons why countries might choose to restrict free trade.

2 How does a tariff restrict free trade?

Impact of restrictions on free trade

Restrictions on free trade have impacts on consumers, producers, governments, living standards and equality.

Impacts on consumers

Consumers tend to be adversely affected by protectionist measures as they may face higher prices for imports (through tariffs) or limited supply of goods where quotas have been imposed.

Impacts on governments

Governments may benefit in the short run from restrictions on trade because they will receive tax revenue from tariffs. However, in the long run, if the protectionism results in a less efficient industrial sector, future economic growth might be lower.

Impacts on equality

Equality involves people being equal. Trade unions represent workers and often aim for greater equality, for example, through a more equal distribution of income. Trade unions are often in favour of greater restrictions on trade to protect their members. Free trade can mean some industries will face competition which might result in job losses or even closure.

Impacts on producers

Domestic producers can gain and suffer from protectionism. If their sales are affected by imports, then restrictions can be beneficial. However, if they are a producer that uses imports subject to tariffs, then they may suffer. For example, the UK car industry uses steel from foreign suppliers.

Impacts on living standards

In the short run restrictions on trade may protect living standards. For example, the imposition of a tariff on imported steel into the US will benefit workers, and their living standards, in this industry. Their jobs will continue as they are cushioned from some international competition. However, in the long run, the industry is likely to lose competitiveness and eventually may face contraction. As a result, unemployment in the industry may rise and therefore the living standards of its workforce will deteriorate.

 Real world **The UK motorcycle industry**

Until the 1970s the UK had a very large motorcycle industry, with producers such as Triumph and Norton. However, competition from Japanese manufacturers such as Honda, Suzuki and Kawasaki led to a great decline in the UK industry and the jobs it provided. By limiting competition, restrictions on trade can help to create equality. However, longer-run pressure means this often cannot be sustained.

British Triumph motorcycles have been produced in the UK since 1902.

Now try this

Outline one impact on consumers of quotas.

Balance of payments

The balance of payments is split into two main components: **current account** and **capital and financial accounts**. The current account records the sale of goods and services.

Synoptic link This topic builds on the content in Theme 2.1.4 on pages 61–62.

The capital and financial accounts

The capital account shows transfers of non-monetary and fixed assets.

The financial account involves the movement of fixed assets and includes:

- **foreign direct investment** – flows of money between countries where one firm buys or sets up business in another country
- **portfolio investment** – investment in financial assets such as shares in foreign companies
- **financial derivatives** – contracts whose value is based on the value of an asset, for example, a foreign currency

- **reserve assets** – those foreign financial assets that are available to, and controlled by, the monetary authorities such as the Bank of England for financing or regulating payments imbalances. Reserve assets include: monetary gold, Special Drawing Rights, reserve position in the IMF and foreign exchange held by the Bank.

Causes of deficits and surpluses on the current account

Causes of deficits	Causes of surpluses
👎 **Economic growth** – as consumers' incomes grow, demand for imported goods increases. This is explained by the income elasticity of demand.	👍 **Natural resources** – where countries have large reserves of natural resources, they can run large current account surpluses. For example, Russia has large reserves of oil and gas and has a large current account surplus.
👎 **Inflation** – high domestic inflation makes foreign goods more attractive for consumers.	👍 **Exchange rate manipulation** – where the exchange rate is kept low, imports are more expensive and exports cheaper.
👎 **International competitiveness** – if domestic firms struggle to compete, the level of exports will fall relative to the volume of imports.	👍 **High interest rates** – cause more saving and less spending on foreign goods and services.

Measures to reduce an imbalance

1 **Exchange rate changes** – a devaluation will make exports cheaper for foreign consumers and imports more expensive for domestic consumers.

2 **Deflationary policies** – higher interest rates will reduce consumer spending which will reduce spending on imports, given the high propensity of UK consumers to spend on desirable imported goods and services.

3 **Supply-side policies** – a long-term approach which will increase labour productivity and reduce unit labour costs. Such developments will improve international competitiveness.

4 **Protectionism** – see page 181.

Significance of global imbalances

Some argue that, since a country's balance of payments must always balance, any global trade imbalances are insignificant. But, the Global Financial Crisis of 2008 suggests that persistently large current account deficits may be unsustainable long term.

- Large and persistent **deficits** can be a problem because there is a need to finance the increasing expenditure on imports, usually through loans from abroad.

- In contrast, large and persistent **surpluses** can be a problem because resources are focused on producing to meet export demand rather than domestic demand, so consumer choice and resulting living standards could actually be low.

- Imbalances may also lead to large currency fluctuations, which can have a destabilising impact on world trade.

Now try this

How does the current account differ from the capital and financial accounts of the balance of payments?

Exchange rate systems

Exchange rates are the value of one currency in terms of another. Exchange rate systems can be floating, fixed or managed. You need to understand the difference between revaluation and appreciation and devaluation of a currency.

Exchange rate systems

In broad terms, there are two types of exchange rate systems: floating and fixed.

Synoptic link This topic builds on the content in Theme 2.2.5 on page 69.

Types of exchange rate system

Floating exchange rate – this allows the exchange rate to be set by the market forces of demand and supply for a currency.

Fixed exchange rate – this exists when a government or central bank sets the exchange rate they would like by tying the exchange rate to another currency, gold or to a basket of currencies.

A managed exchange rate system – this system is a combination of fixed and floating and is perhaps the most common system. It is characterised by the currency freely floating but where the government might intervene from time to time to change the value of the currency. A managed exchange rate is one which is floating but is affected/influenced through intervention by the central bank.

Floating exchange rate system

The exchange rate is shown on the y axis of the diagram (right). This rate is determined by the forces of demand and supply. Reasons for changes in demand and supply are:

* **A rise in UK exports** – to buy UK goods, foreign consumers need pounds. This shifts the demand curve for pounds to D_2. This causes the exchange rate to increase to P_3.

* **A rise in imports** – this will increase the supply of pounds onto the market as UK consumers buy foreign currency – using pounds – to be able to buy foreign goods.

* **A rise in UK interest rates** – foreign savers will buy more pounds enabling them to save in the UK. The demand for pounds rises to D_2.

* **Increase in investment** – if foreign firms decide to invest in the UK, such as Nissan building a new factory, they will need pounds to pay for this which will see an increase in demand for pounds and a rise in the exchange rate to P_2.

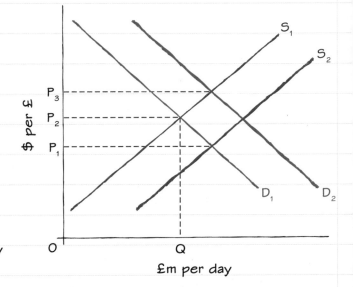

Fixed exchange rate system

Fixed and managed exchange rate systems have a target rate at which governments or central banks want to hold the exchange rate.

Key term **Key terms**

Appreciation and **depreciation** are the terms used under a system of floating exchange rates to describe increases and decreases in the value of a country's currency in relation to other currencies.

Revaluation and **devaluation** are the terms used under a system of fixed exchange rates to describe increases and decreases in the value of a country's currency in relation to other currencies determined by the country's central bank.

Now try this

Draw a diagram to show the effect in a floating exchange rate system of an increase in speculation in favour of buying the currency.

Exchange rate systems and competitive devaluation

The different types of exchange rate system have both benefits and disadvantages. Governments may attempt to manage exchange rates and may deliberately devalue the currency to give it competitive advantage.

Summary of exchange rate systems

System	👍 Advantages	👎 Disadvantages
Floating	• Correction of balance of payment deficits under an automatic adjustment mechanism. • Protection from external shocks – the exchange rate will change in response to shocks such as a rise in the oil price. • Less need for central banks to hold reserves of foreign currency.	• Instability – exchange rates can be volatile. This can make it difficult for firms – and governments – to plan ahead as uncertainty exists. • Speculation – leads to changes in exchange rates unrelated to the underlying pattern of trade.
Fixed	• Certainty over the exchange rate can encourage domestic investment and FDI. • Reduced speculation – dealers know that the central bank will aim for the exchange rate target and there will be little chance of devaluation or revaluation.	• Policy conflicts – a fixed exchange rate may be incompatible with an objective of low inflation or low unemployment. • Difficulty in responding to external shocks. In a floating system the exchange rate will adjust automatically in response to domestic and international shocks.
Managed	• Market forces determine the value of the currency from day to day. • Government intervention is only required to make adjustments when necessary. • Predictability – consumers and firms have a clear expectation of the value of the currency and can plan on this basis.	• Loss of control of interest rates – a central bank/government would still have control of the base interest rate but this would have to be set to ensure the currency was maintained at the desired level. Therefore it could not be used to control inflation.

Competitive devaluation/depreciation

A country may deliberately devalue its currency to give it a competitive advantage. Its exports will be cheaper to foreign consumers, which should lead to increased demand for exports (and a fall in imports) and therefore an increase in AD. However, this will only work if other countries do not similarly retaliate. This may be far from guaranteed and is one of the reasons why devaluation is a risky strategy.

Government intervention in currency markets

Attempts to manage the exchange rate by governments can be achieved by:

- **Changing interest rates** – if the central bank wishes to increase the value of the country's currency, it would raise interest rates, so making it more attractive for foreigners to place cash balances in the country's banks. This would increase the demand for the currency which would lead to a rise in its price. The exact extent of the increase will depend of the price elasticity of demand for the currency and what happens to supply.

- **Intervention on the foreign exchange market** – if the central bank wishes to increase the value of the country's currency then it would buy its own currency. Demand would increase for the currency which would lead to a rise in price.

Now try this

Outline two effects of changes in the exchange rate in an economy.

Changes in exchange rates

Changes in exchange rates can have a significant effect on the current account of the balance of payments. The **Marshall–Lerner condition** and the **J-curve effect** are used to explain why the anticipated impact on the current account may occur or not.

The current account of the balance of payments

If the exchange rate falls, exports become cheaper and domestic goods and services become more competitive. Therefore, the demand for **exports** will **increase** and the demand for **imports** will **fall**. The effect should be an improvement in the current account position, with either a reduced deficit or an improvement in the surplus, as shown in the table.

	Price of imports	Price of exports	Impact on current account
Value of currency increases	↓	↑	Worse
Value of currency decreases	↑	↓	Improved

SPICED

A way to remember the effect of changes in the exchange rate is through the acronym: S.P.I.C.E.D.

Strong **P**ound = **I**mports **C**heaper, **E**xports **D**earer

The Marshall–Lerner condition and the J-curve effect

- The Marshall–Lerner condition suggests that a devaluation in a currency will lead to an improvement in the current account position, **providing the combined elasticities of imports and exports are greater than 1**.

- The **J-curve effect** shows that, in the short run, a devaluation is likely to lead to a worsening in the current account position (see diagram right).

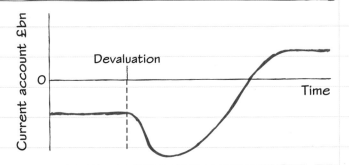

In the short run, demand for exports and imports is likely to be price inelastic. Reasons for this are that it takes time for firms to change to different suppliers and contracts might need to be renegotiated.

Other effects on the economy

Factor	Impact
Economic growth and employment/ unemployment	If exports rise and imports decrease due to a fall in the exchange rate, then economic growth will result due to an increase in AD (remember, net exports are a component of AD). Unemployment would decrease through the creation of jobs due to economic growth, for example, with firms involved in the export sector.
Rate of inflation	A fall in the value of a currency will lead to higher inflationary pressures as the cost of imports will rise. For example, a fall in the value of sterling will lead to the price of oil – denominated in dollars – rising. As oil is used throughout the economy, the impact is to increase the rate of inflation.
Foreign direct investment (FDI) flows	A fall in the value of sterling, for example, is likely to lead to a rise in foreign direct investment (FDI) flows. This is because the foreign firm will be able to spend less (in its own currency) to purchase the same UK assets. Effectively this type of investment is now cheaper. However, this may be less likely if the value of the currency is continually falling, as this suggests that the economy is volatile and a risky investment.

Now try this

1 What would be the effect on economic growth of a **rise** in the exchange rate?

2 Using the theory of the J-curve, explain the effect of a rise in the value of a country's currency on its current account of the balance of payments.

International competitiveness

International competitiveness refers to the ability of a country to sell its goods/services abroad. Competitiveness is usually determined by the price and/or quality of the good or service. Measures of international competitiveness include **relative unit labour costs** and **relative export prices**. Several factors influence international competitiveness.

Productivity

Relative unit labour costs – wages and non-wage costs relative to those of competitors

Factors influencing international competitiveness

Regulation relative to competitors

Rate of inflation relative to competitors

Productivity

Productivity is a measure of the output per worker per unit of time. If a country's productivity deteriorates relative to that of competitors, the effect is effectively an increase in unit costs which will lead to a worsening of competitiveness. In short, **higher productivity = improved competitiveness**.

 Real world **Super-fast broadband**

The UK government announced in 2018 that it would invest billions to roll-out the latest 5G broadband to every new home. The hope is that super-fast internet connection will increase productivity and the UK's competitiveness.

Relative unit labour costs

Unit labour cost measures the cost of labour required to produce output. To compare unit labour costs between countries it is necessary to convert each country's labour costs to the same currency. A rise in labour costs in a country, perhaps due to an increase in the minimum wage or a fall in unemployment which leads to less supply of labour, will feed through to higher export prices and therefore reduced competitiveness. Investment in **human capital** can improve productivity and help to reduce unit labour costs.

Regulation and rate of inflation

- If a government decides to increase the level of regulation on business, then the impact of this will be to increase costs on firms. Higher costs are likely to be passed on to consumers in the form of higher prices, which will lead to reduced competitiveness.

- Inflation is a measure of the rate of increase of prices across an economy. If inflation increases the effect is to make goods and services more expensive. This can lead to these products being less competitive on international markets.

Benefits and problems of international competitiveness

👍 A country which is internationally competitive is likely to be able to enjoy export-led economic growth with positive implications for employment and its balance of payments on the current account. Higher demand for a country's exports will lead to increased AD with a rise in short-run economic growth and a positive multiplier effect.

👎 Exchange rates – a current account surplus can lead to a rise in exchange rates more expensive for foreign consumers and damaging to international competitiveness.

👎 Higher costs as the country becomes more developed – the cost of land, property and rent tends to increase as a country becomes more developed. Wages rates rise as a country engages more in international trade.

Now try this

1 Give two factors that can cause productivity to increase.

2 Describe how lower wage rates might improve international competitiveness.

Absolute poverty and relative poverty

Poverty can be classified as either **absolute poverty** or **relative poverty**.

Absolute poverty

Absolute poverty exists when a person's continued daily existence is threatened because they have insufficient resources to meet their basic needs. A person in absolute poverty will struggle to afford such things as food, clothing and shelter. By this definition, absolute poverty in the UK is very low, although it does exist.

> Over the past 10 years, world absolute poverty has fallen by more than 8%. Significant rates of economic growth in areas such as East Asia have seen a huge proportion of the population lifted out of absolute poverty.

Measuring absolute poverty

In 2015, the World Bank set the poverty line at $1.90 a day, measured at 2011 purchasing power parity (PPP). This is how absolute poverty is measured around the world.

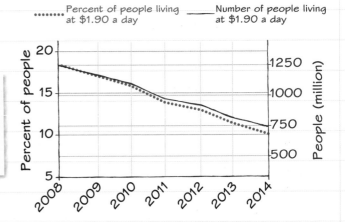

.... Percent of people living at $1.90 a day _____ Number of people living at $1.90 a day

Relative poverty

Relative poverty exists when a person is poor compared with others in their society. Most poverty in developed countries tends to be relative poverty.

In 2017 it was estimated that around 16% of the UK population lived in relative poverty. This figure has remained fairly stable over the past decade.

Measuring relative poverty

Relative poverty is measured in comparison with other people in the country and will vary between countries. People are considered to be in relative poverty if they are living below a certain income threshold in a particular country. For example, in the EU, people falling below 60% of median income are said to be 'at-risk-of poverty' and are classed as relatively poor.

Causes of changes in absolute and relative poverty

Economic growth – nations with high rates of GDP per capita have low rates of absolute poverty. In a free market economy, rising GDP leads to a rise in earnings for most households.

Government benefits policy – government policy linked to benefits, social housing and healthcare will influence how the most vulnerable groups in society are supported.

Causes of changes in poverty

Taxation and wage rates – any change in income tax, VAT or wage rates will influence the proportion of people who may fall below the 60% median income and the proportion of people living in relative poverty.

Trade and FDI – all policies that encourage international trade and FDI will lead to economic growth and the opportunity for employment and export of national goods and services.

Now try this

1 What is the difference between absolute poverty and relative poverty?

2 How is absolute poverty measured?

Inequality and its causes

Economic inequality refers to the difference in economic well-being between people within society. Both **wealth and income inequality** are important for most nations as income and wealth are not distributed equally in a market economy.

Wealth inequality

Wealth is the value in money of assets held by an individual. This might include property, land, money and shares. There are a number of reasons why wealth is not distributed equally. However, it is much easier to generate wealth (assets) when an individual already has some wealth. Wealth is distributed less equally than income in most nations.

Income inequality

Income is the amount of money an individual receives over a period of time, such as a week, month or year. A person's income can come from a number of sources including wages, salaries, interest on bank accounts, dividends from shares and rental income. Many factors can influence an individual's level of income.

Causes of income and wealth inequality

Government policy can lead to significant differences between income and wealth inequality within a nation and between nations. Over time, policies within a country will change (affecting inequality within that country) but political systems may vary hugely between nations, especially in different regions of the world (between nations).

Education and training – access to training and education is not equally accessible in different nations or even in different regions of a country.

Wage rates – certain skills are more in demand than others in an economy. Therefore, people with more desirable skills will command a higher wage or salary.

Tax system – tax systems can be used to redistribute income. More progressive tax systems will provide tax relief for the poorest in society and ensure the wealthiest contribute more.

Causes of income and wealth inequality

Ownership of assets – historically the wealthiest in society own more assets such as property, land and shares, and these are often passed down through inheritance. Owning these assets creates further wealth and income, which further increases inequality.

Trade union representation – the strength of trade unions and union membership can influence income inequality and the level of employment protection.

Social benefits – government policy will influence how the most vulnerable groups in society are protected from falling into poverty.

The negative impact of inequality

👎 Absolute and relative poverty remain high.

👎 It can restrict economic growth and waste people's talents. The poorest in society will find it difficult to generate enough capital to start their own businesses.

👎 As the rich become richer, they may tend to spend their income on imports. This money then leaves the circular flow of income and does not benefit the poorest in society.

👎 Crime and violence tend to rise because people do not have what they need.

Now try this

1 What is the difference between wealth and income?

2 How might a tax system help reduce income inequality?

Measuring inequality

The Lorenz curve

The Lorenz curve can be used to represent the distribution of income graphically. Along the horizontal axis is the cumulative percentage of the population, from poorest to richest. The vertical axis represents the cumulative percentage of income. The diagonal line intersecting the graph represents complete equality (as shown in the diagram on the right, 20% of population earn 20% of the income). The Lorenz curve is the curved line that sits below the diagonal complete equality line. The further away from the diagonal, the greater the level of inequality in the country.

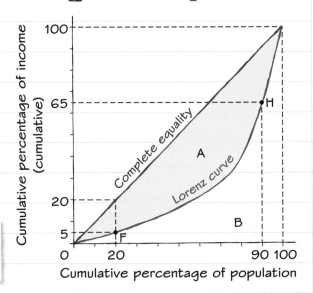

> At point F, 20% of the population only earn 5% of income.
> At point H The cumulative 90% earn 65% of the income. Therefore, the top 10% earn 35% of the income.

The Gini coefficient

The Gini coefficient is a measure of inequality that uses the Lorenz curve to find a numerical representation of inequality. Area A on the diagram above represents the area between the 45 degree horizontal line and the Lorenz curve. Area B represents the area beyond the Lorenz curve.

Real world **Iceland, UK and Mexico**

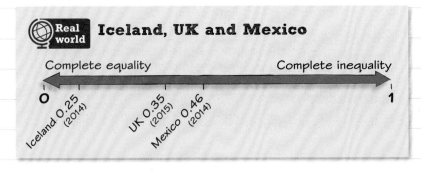

🖩 Maths skills   Calculating the Gini coefficient

$$\text{Gini coefficient} = \frac{\text{Area A}}{\text{Area A} + \text{Area B}}$$

The Gini coefficient can be represented as a decimal (0–1) or as an index number. The higher the Gini coefficient is, the more unequal the distribution of income.

The impact of economic development

As an economy grows, particularly developing economies, it is often true that inequality will initially increase. This is because workers will move from lower productivity jobs in sectors such as agriculture to the higher productivity manufacturing sector. Incomes will not increase at the same rate and inequality will grow. However, inequality will then start to decline as governments have greater means to redistribute income through benefits, progressive tax systems and the investment in education and training.

Inequality in free markets

In a capitalist free market economy inequality is inevitable as people with higher skills and abilities attract higher wages. Private ownership of resources means than some people can acquire considerably more assets than others. However, inequality in free market economies is not always bad. Inequality:

1 provides incentives for people to work harder to earn more

2 encourages enterprise, creating new businesses and opportunities for people to find work

3 encourages people to work instead of claiming benefits

4 may create a 'trickle-down effect' – as the rich become richer they will spend more on goods and services, creating income for the poor.

Now try this

What would a Gini coefficient of 0.63 indicate?

Measures of economic development

Measuring economic performance can be difficult. For this reason, economists also like to measure the general **economic development** of nations to gain a clearer picture of performance. A key measure of economic development is captured through the **Human Development Index** which gives an indication of a country's **social and human welfare**, also known as the **quality of life**.

The Human Development Index (HDI)

The Human Development Index was developed by the United Nations to measure and rank countries' levels of social and economic development. Social indicators are a way of gaining a fuller picture about the quality of life in a country. There are three components to the HDI:

1 Health – the health of a nation is measured by the life expectancy in that country (on average, how long are people expected to live).

2 Education – as measured by average and expected years in school.

3 Standard of living – as measured by real GNI per capita, using the principle of purchasing power parity (PPP).

 **Synoptic link** See pages 52–53 for more on GNI and PPP.

Real world — HDI rankings

The HDI ranks all nations and uses an index number (1–0) to score development in each nation: 0.8 and above indicates a very high level of human development; 0.7–0.79 high human development; 0.5–0.69 medium human development; and below 0.5 a low level of human development.

Country	Hdi	Life expectancy	Expected years of schooling
Norway	0.953	82.3	17.9
Switzerland	0.944	83.5	16.2
Australia	0.939	83.1	22.9
South Sudan	0.388	57.3	4.9
Central African Republic	0.367	52.9	7.2
Niger	0.354	60.4	5.4

HDI of top 3 nations and bottom 3 nations (2017).

Advantages and limitations of using HDI to compare levels of development between countries/over time

👍 The data is easy to collect and standardise across nations.

👍 An index can easily track levels of development over time.

👍 The HDI gains an insight into well-being, which is a growing concern for many nations.

👎 A long life expectancy is not the same as a high quality of life. Western societies live longer but may also have greater levels of stress and mental illness.

👎 Number of years in school is a poor indicator of the quality of that education.

👎 HDI does not measure the level of inequality in a nation.

👎 Two countries can achieve the same HDI but have very different profiles.

Now try this

1 What are the three factors that contribute to the HDI?

2 Why is the HDI easy to use?

3 Identify two other measures of development other than the HDI.

Growth and development 1

Economic factors can influence economic growth and development in different countries.

Primary product dependency

Many developing nations are dependent on primary products (commodities) that are extracted from the earth, such as wheat, rice or fruit, or minerals such as copper or zinc. The demand for most commodities is price inelastic, therefore any change in global demand will have a significant impact on price. Any economy reliant on these industries may find it more difficult to encourage economic development.

Volatility of commodity prices

The below factors create a disincentive for investment in primary industries:

- The value added on primary products is low – farmers and miners make little profit when exporting these commodities.
- Agricultural products can easily be damaged by natural disasters, such as drought.
- The volatility of commodity prices means incomes can fluctuate considerably in these industries, therefore earnings are very uncertain.

Savings gap and the Harrod–Domar model

In many low-income countries, high levels of poverty make it almost impossible to generate sufficient savings to fund investment projects. This increases reliance on high interest borrowing to finance capital investment. This problem is known as the **savings gap**.

The **Harrod–Domar model** states that the growth rate of an economy is directly linked to:

- the level of savings in an economy
- the efficiency with which capital in an economy can be deployed.

Increasing either of these factors will ultimately lead to faster rates of economic growth.

Foreign currency gap

The foreign currency gap occurs where capital outflows from a country are greater than capital inflows. It can be caused by:

- Dependency on exports of primary products (low value added) and import of manufactured goods (high value added).
- High proportion of income servicing debt (borrowing instead of saving for investment).

Overall, low income countries receive less for their exports and have to pay a premium for the goods they import.

 Synoptic link The level of investment in an economy is closely linked to the propensity to save. See pages 79–81.

 **Synoptic link** Foreign currency gap is an example of a 'leakage' or withdrawal from the circular flow of income – see page 75.

Capital flight and absence of property rights

Capital flight refers to the problem of people moving their savings abroad instead of holding them domestically.

Reasons for capital flight	Impact
• Lower tax rates and/or higher interest rates abroad. • Political instability. • Absence of property rights – without clear laws and legal controls, property rights (ownership of land and assets) may be uncertain.	• Governments don't receive taxes from savings abroad. • People less willing to risk investment. • Lower levels of development.

Now try this

1 What is the savings gap?

2 Why would absence of property rights deter people from investing?

Growth and development 2

There a number of international economic factors that will influence growth and development in different countries. Non-economic factors may have an impact too.

Education, demographics and skills

Demographic factors can have a significant impact on the rate of development in a country. For example, in countries with fast-growing populations there is typically a fall in GNI per capita and people's standard of living. These factors will result in lower skills and a less productive workforce.

- One result of a fast-growing population is an increase in the number of children. In turn, this puts pressure on a country's education system and fewer children may receive a good education.

- Poverty is one of the most important factors keeping children out of school. In cases of extreme poverty, children may need to work to earn an income instead of going to school.

An ageing population results in a greater proportion of dependents vs the working population, which places pressure on social benefits and healthcare.

International debt

In the 1980s many developing countries took out low interest loans in US dollars from developed countries. As interest rates and the value of the US dollar rose, many countries struggled to pay their debts. The problem caused an increasing flow of money out of these developing countries – the opposite of what was intended. It took until the 2000s for many developing countries to resolve their debt problems through faster rates of economic growth and growth in net exports.

Access to credit and banking

Developed countries tend to have sophisticated systems for banking and stock markets. People can buy equity in companies, and have access to saving and borrowing mechanisms. Overall, people in developed countries can save now and spend in the future, grow their investments and borrow money with favourable terms. In less developed countries these opportunities may not be available or may be harder to access, therefore restricting opportunities for savings, investment and growth.

Infrastructure

Countries with high levels of development tend to have extensive and well-developed infrastructures. Growth in physical capital is important if the pace of development is going to increase. Investment in the following aspects of infrastructure will support development:

Roads	Ports	Airports
Railways	Utilities (water, gas, etc.)	Broadband

Non-economic factors

There are several non-economic factors that may also restrict the level of development in a country. They are often beyond the influence of economic policy.

War – war and international conflicts will not only lead to the disruption of international trade and low business confidence, but also loss of human and physical capital.

Geographical – the location of mountain ranges, climate and access to coasts are key contributing factors that may benefit or disadvantage a country from development opportunities such as the ability to grow crops or access trade routes.

The impact of non-economic factors

Corruption – corrupt government regimes often mean economic policy is not applied in the interests of society. In such circumstances the few will benefit at the cost of economic development and equality.

Disease – diseases such as HIV/Aids and malaria continue to have a heavy impact on affected countries such as Uganda.

Now try this

1 What factors may prevent a child from accessing a good education?

2 Why is access to effective banking systems important for economic development?

Market-orientated strategies

There are a wide range of strategies used to encourage growth and development. They include market-orientated strategies which promote market forces and create incentives for investment.

 ❶ Trade liberalisation
 ❷ Promotion of foreign direct investment (FDI) – see page 144 and page 170
 ❸ Removal of government subsidies

Market-orientated strategies

❹ Floating exchange rate system
❺ Microfinance schemes
❻ Privatisation – see page 145

Removal of government subsidies

Government subsidies for producers and consumers can support domestic industries, reduce absolute poverty and correct market failure (see page 36).

However, allocating subsidies efficiently is difficult. Artificially low market equilibrium prices also encourage inefficiency and there is a huge opportunity cost for governments as often the money could be spent more effectively elsewhere in the economy. Therefore, removing subsidies is one way to support trade liberalisation. Removing subsidies is politically dangerous and very unpopular as many people have a vested interest. Perhaps the best time to remove a subsidy would be when market prices are falling.

The removal of a subsidy leads to a rise in the equilibrium price and a fall in the quantity demand and supplied

Trade liberalisation

Trade liberalisation involves opening an economy up to a free-market philosophy and the opportunities of open (non-protectionist) trade with other nations. Trade liberalisation is outward looking and the opposite approach to protectionism (see page 181.

> **Synoptic link**   See also pages 25-27 on taxation and subsidies and page 69 for more on protectionism and its impact on trade.

Benefits and drawbacks of trade liberalisation

👍 Creates the opportunity to exploit a country's comparative advantage through export-led growth.

👍 Firms are encouraged to invest and seek new export markets.

👍 Increased efficiency of industries and competitiveness.

👍 Only the most efficient industries will survive and there will inevitably be job losses in industries than cannot compete.

Floating exchange rate systems and microfinance schemes

- A **floating exchange rate** could be adopted. Although import and export prices will be subject to volatility, governments do not have to intervene.

> **Synoptic link**   See pages 170–171 for more on exchange rate systems.

- Microfinance refers to the availability of small scale loans be available to entrepreneurs and businesses. Developing countries tend to have weak financial sectors but improving the banking system can support entrepreneurialism. As there is a savings gap in developing countries, anyone looking to start a business or invest in growth will need access to loans. Access to microfinance goes hand-in-hand with the principles of private ownership and control of markets (privatisation).

Now try this

Why might a government choose to remove a producer subsidy in the farming industry?

Interventionist strategies

The opposite of market orientated approaches to growth and development is interventionist strategies where a government will seek to directly influence the economy through supply-side policies and market intervention (see pages 91–92).

1 Development of human capital

2 Protectionism

3 Managed exchange rates (see pages 170–172)

Interventionist strategies

4 Infrastructure development

5 Promotion of joint ventures with global companies

6 Buffer stock schemes

Human capital and infrastructure

The private sector is only likely to invest in the development of human capital and infrastructure (such as new schools and roads) if it is profitable. This is not always the case. Through an interventionist approach to growth, government will be the principal builder of infrastructure because there are significant economic and social benefits. The success of government funded investment in infrastructure may depend on the availability of resources and the efficiency of the project – both may be better delivered through the private sector.

Protectionism

Protectionism is a form of government intervention designed to support the development of domestic industries and protect them from international competition. Fuelling growth through a protectionist approach may involve import substitution by subsidising and investing in domestically made goods. It may also include imposing tariffs and quotas on foreign goods.

 Synoptic link For more on protectionism and government intervention, see pages 35–37, pages 143–145 and pages 167–168.

Joint ventures with global companies

Governments may seek to encourage foreign direct investment (FDI) and partnerships with international companies as this can support economic development through:

- capital inflows creating jobs and higher national output
- higher wages and better working conditions
- improved knowledge and expertise – transfer of human capital.

Capital inflows can improve the current account deficit (see page 74).

Buffer stock schemes

Developing countries are often reliant on the export of primary products (commodities). Through various factors, including global demand and weather conditions, commodity prices can fluctuate considerably, leading to uncertainty of income in many industries. A buffer stock scheme aims to protect buyers and sellers through maximum and minimum prices (see pages 35–37).

During periods of excess supply (such as during a bumper harvest) a government will buy up the excess supply and stockpile it. During a period where there is a shortage in supply, the government will then release the buffer stock to increase supply and maintain a stable price for consumers.

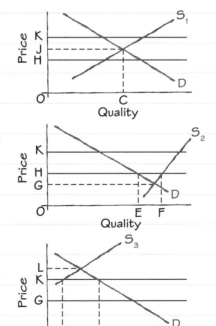

1 The minimum price is set at OH and a maximum price at OK. As the market equilibrium (OJ) is between these two prices, no intervention is required.

2 The market equilibrium price OG is lower than the minimum price. Therefore the buffer stock scheme will increase demand by purchasing EF in order to raise the price back to OH.

3 The market equilibrium price is OL above the maximum price of OK. The buffer stock scheme will release AB stock into the market in order to increase supply and lower the price to OK.

Now try this

When might a government apply a buffer stock scheme?

Other strategies

Industrialisation: the Lewis model

In developing countries, the majority of labour is deployed upon the land in the agricultural sector. The Lewis model assumes that there is excess labour in this sector (the same output could be achieved with fewer workers). Therefore, there is no opportunity cost of these workers transferring from agriculture to industry (manufacturing) to take advantage of higher paid jobs. Criticism of the Lewis model includes:

- transferring labour is not easy and requires investment in education and training
- industry can be capital intensive and not create many new jobs
- agriculture is seasonal and demand for labour is high during harvest so excess labour will be utilised at harvest time. As a result, the presumption of excess labour may not be true throughout the year.

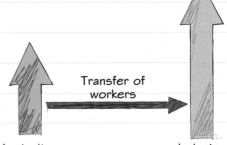

Transfer of workers

Agriculture   Industry

The transfer of workers from agriculture to industry means there is no fall in agricultural output, but a growth in industry where there is greater added value (through exporting goods) than agricultural produce.

Development of primary industries

Developing countries may choose to use the incomes generated from the export of commodities such as copper, wheat and coal in order to diversify their industries so they are less reliant on markets where added value is low and prices can fluctuate greatly. For example, Chile is a recently diversified economy, exporting more than 2,800 distinct products to more than 120 different countries.

Development of tourism

A considerable growth opportunity for developing countries is to grow their tourist industry which can create significant inflows of income (tourism is effectively an export). Growth in tourism also creates jobs and encourages FDI. However, limitations of tourism include it being extremely seasonal, and it can lead to an increase in imports (bad for balance of payments) and cause environmental damage.

Aid and debt relief

- Aid involves transferring resources from one country to another. Aid can reduce absolute poverty, the savings gap and foreign exchange gap, and create a multiplier effect directly increasing aggregate demand.
- The savings gap can lead to developing countries having high levels of debt. Large amounts of income are then spent on servicing those debts (paying off interest).
- Debt relief involves cancelling a country's debt – it does not have to be repaid. Debt relief can lead to money being freed up for public services, healthcare, education and investment in industries.

Fair trade

The principles of fair trade seek to ensure producers in developing countries receive a fair price for their goods and that production is sustainable, with spending to minimise resource depletion and negative externalities.

Downside of aid and debt relief

They could lead to a dependency culture where the developing country anticipates future debts will always be cancelled. There is also the danger of corrupt governments using aid inappropriately or the donor nation using aid to secure 'favours' in the future.

Consumers are becoming increasingly conscious of how and where their products come from and may only buy products that are fair trade.

Now try this

What does the Lewis model suggest developing countries should do to create economic growth?

International organisations and NGOs

There are a number of international organisations such as the World Bank and the International Monetary Fund (IMF), and non-government organisations like Water Aid and Unicef, that have been set up with the purpose of supporting economic development across the globe.

The World Bank

The World Bank was set up in 1944 to promote economic development. Some of its services include providing low-interest loans, interest free credit, and grants for developing countries to support industry development, healthcare and education. The World Bank also supports the development of infrastructure and capital investment to encourage international trade.

The World Bank is made up of five institutions including the International Bank for Reconstruction and Development (IBRD) and the International Development Association (IDA).

Global goals:

1. End extreme poverty by decreasing the percentage of people living on less than $1.90 a day to no more than 3%.

2. Promote shared prosperity by fostering the income growth of the bottom 40% for every country.

The World Bank Group has set two goals for the world to achieve by 2030.

International Monetary Fund (IMF)

The IMF was set up in 1945 to ensure the stability of the international monetary system. Each member country has a quota on the amount of financial resources they have to make available to the IMF. These resources are then used to offer loans to poor countries with the aim to support projects that fight poverty and improve living standards.

The IMF also provides support and guidance to developing countries on policies that maintain economic stability.

Non-government organisations (NGOs)

NGOs are private organisations and charities that support similar objectives of reducing poverty, protecting the environment, creating equality and supporting sustainable economic growth. NGOs generally operate on a small scale and support projects at a community level. Examples of NGOs include:

- Water Aid
- Cancer Research UK
- Tusk
- The Prince's Trust
- Christian Aid

World Trade Organization

The World Trade Organization (WTO) promotes the liberalisation of trade and fair trade across the globe (see opposite and page 180 on trade liberalisation). The WTO acts as a forum to support governments in negotiating trade deals and removing trade barriers. The WTO also acts as an arbitration court in issues of dispute. (For more on the WTO, see page 166.)

Views of international organisations

Most international organisations have their critics. For example, most organisations prescribe a set of economic policies and conditions for accessing their support. These policies may not always benefit the country involved and may lead to inequality. Some critics view them as westernised organisations that act in the interest of the developed world.

Now try this

1 What is one goal of the World Bank?

2 Identify three NGOs that may support economic growth in developing nations.

The role of financial markets

Financial markets provide finance to banks, other financial institutions, firms, governments and individuals.

Types of finance

> **Finance provided by financial markets**

Short-term finance is typically that provided for up to one year, such as Treasury Bills.

Long-term finance is that provided for more than one year, such as bonds, long-term loans to governments or mortgages.

Types of financial markets

1 **Money markets** – provide short-term finance, such as borrowing and lending. The government borrows short-term finance by issuing Treasury Bills, which are repayable in 91 days.

2 **Capital markets** – provide long-term finance, mainly by the trading of bonds and shares.

3 **Foreign exchange markets** – where different currencies are traded.

Different purposes of financial markets

Role	Explanation
Facilitate saving	Financial assets include money, shares, bonds and bank deposits. These can be used for saving money. Financial institutions provide the opportunity for firms and households to use these assets.
Lend to businesses and individuals	Households, firms and governments borrow money for a range of reasons. Households borrow to pay for goods and services, including mortgages. Firms might borrow money to invest in new facilities and equipment.
Facilitate the exchange of goods and services	Financial institutions create payment systems to ensure goods and services can be traded. The central bank, for example, prints notes and mints coins. Banks process cheques and debit/credit card transactions, including contactless payments.
Provide forward markets in currencies and commodities	Firms prefer to have certainty when making decisions. So they often choose to buy or sell forward. A potato farmer may choose to sell 10 tonnes at £1 500 for delivery in 3 months. Forward markets (see below) are made possible by financial institutions.
Provide a market for equities	Equities are the shares (or stocks) of companies. Issuing shares is an important way for firms to raise finance to fund investment. Stock markets trade shares.
Forward markets	A forward market is for transactions that will happen at an agreed time in the future. Contracts (which are called **futures**) are made at a price agreed today but which will be supplied later. Forward markets exist in markets for food commodities and other commodities such as gold, oil and copper, and also for foreign currencies. They are used by producers and buyers to even out price fluctuations. For example, an ice cream manufacturer may agree to buy 500 kg of sugar at an agreed price of 20 pence per kg, for delivery in 12 months. This gives the firm certainty over its costs in the future.

 Real world **Households and financial markets**

A household may typically use a range of financial institutions and financial markets. For example:

- a savings account to save for a new car
- a mortgage to pay for the house
- paying for weekly groceries using a credit card
- visiting a travel agent to buy foreign currency for a holiday abroad.

Now try this

1 Give three roles that financial markets play.

2 Describe how forward markets work.

Market failure in the financial sector 1

You need to know about market failure in the financial sector.

 **Synoptic link** Look back at page 29 to re-cap market failure.

Market failure

Market failure occurs when free markets fail to deliver an efficient or socially optimum allocation of resources. The financial crash of 2007–08 is one example of market failure in the financial sector, but this was an extreme example. Market failure can be said to exist with examples of banks defrauding customers, or where the price of an asset is driven well above what it should be.

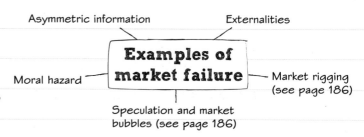

Asymmetric information   Externalities

Examples of market failure

Moral hazard   Market rigging (see page 186)

Speculation and market bubbles (see page 186)

Asymmetric information

This exists where one party in a transaction has more information than other parties. This can lead to a buyer or seller with more information being able to exploit the information gap and lead to an inefficient outcome. In the financial sector there are lots of complex products and systems, and this can lead to consumers making poor decisions.

 **Synoptic link** See page 34 for more on asymmetric information.

🌐 **Real world** **PPI**

In the 1990s and 2000s, banks sold millions of insurance contracts – payment protection insurance (PPI) – to customers who took out credit cards, mortgages or loans. Often, these contracts were not appropriate for customers' needs but the detail and information was often so complex that customers did not challenge the payment. This was an example of market failure as more PPI policies were sold than if customers had been fully aware of what they were paying for. An information gap – asymmetric information – caused this market failure.

Externalities

Externalities are costs paid by other individuals, firms or governments, but not the financial markets creating the costs. During the 2007–08 financial crisis, some banks and financial institutions had to be supported – bailed out – by the government, and therefore by the taxpayer.

For example, during the financial crisis the government spent £133 billion nationalising (taking into public ownership) several banks and building societies. One of the reasons this was necessary was the poor management of those banks and building societies.

Moral hazard

This occurs when someone is more willing to take risks because they understand that someone else will pay any costs if anything goes wrong. For example, banks might be more likely to provide loans to risky customers if they know that the government, taxpayers or central bank will bail them out. Moral hazard involves excessively risky behaviour.

Now try this

1 Give an example of a moral hazard an individual might take.

2 Explain why the government bailing put banks during the 2007–08 financial crisis is an example of externalities.

Market failure in the financial sector 2

Other examples of market failure in the financial sector are speculation and market bubbles and market rigging.

Speculation and market bubbles

- **Speculation** involves buying assets at a relatively low price and selling them at a later date at a higher price, with the aim of making a profit. Speculation involves risk. If the asset falls in price, then the speculator will lose money.
- **Market bubbles** occur when the price of an asset is forced excessively high – well beyond its true value – before then falling back. Speculators buy assets because others are doing so. This increases demand and pushes up the price. When the price is felt to have reached its maximum, investors sell the assets and the price falls.

Asset price bubbles

Market bubbles can also be known as 'asset price bubbles'.

Market rigging

This occurs when individuals or a group **collude** to fix prices or exchange information to help them make gains for themselves at the expense of others.

 Bitcoin

Bitcoin is a digital and global currency. Money can be exchanged without being linked to a real identity. Since it was first developed in 2008, bitcoin has been an asset that has been subject to speculation. In December 2017 the value of one bitcoin reached over £14000. Its value fell sharply in January 2018 (at one point falling by around £1400 in just one hour). It has proved to be a highly volatile currency. Many speculators who have purchased bitcoin have borrowed money to purchase the currency, and in a lot of cases have suffered big losses.

Collusion

Examples of market rigging have included banks fixing the prices of foreign exchange rates and fixing the interest rate (read about the LIBOR scandal below). Another example is insider trading, where an individual or institution has knowledge about something that will happen in the future and which is not available to other participants in the market.

 The LIBOR scandal

The LIBOR scandal unfolded from 2007 and involved a group of banks, including Barclays, Citigroup and the Royal Bank of Scotland, working together to fix the London Interbank Offered Rate (LIBOR). This is an average interest rate which is used globally to fix other interest rates.

The banks colluded to fix the rate in their favour

Now try this

1 Give three examples of market failure in the financial sector.

2 Why is speculation an example of market failure?

Role of central banks

A central bank is a financial institution in a country that is typically responsible for the printing and issuing of notes and coins. In the UK, the central bank is the Bank of England. The role of a central bank is very different from a high street bank. It plays a key part in the operation of economic policy in a country.

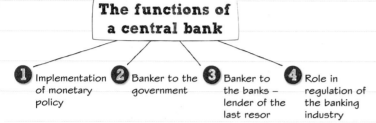

The functions of a central bank

1 Implementation of monetary policy
2 Banker to the government
3 Banker to the banks – lender of the last resor
4 Role in regulation of the banking industry

2 Banker to the government

The central bank manages the national debt of the government, for example, by issuing bonds. It also handles the accounts of different government departments and makes short-term loans to the government.

3 'Lender of the last resort'

The central bank supports commercial banks by acting as lender of the last resort, or in other words, 'banker to the banks'. This is a vital role for the stability of the banking system. Banks can sometimes run short of liquidity – having enough money to pay liabilities. The Bank of England lends money to banks on a regular basis to ensure they are solvent and can survive.

4 Regulation of the banking industry

Regulation of the financial sector is needed to prevent customers being adversely affected by risky behaviour of financial institutions. Regulation is in place to prevent **systemic risk**, where the financial system may collapse without such regulation. Regulation includes:

- reserve requirements – banks are required to have a certain percentage of their assets in the form of reserves, to ensure they have sufficient reserves to cover losses

- ensuring that competition exists in financial markets, to make sure consumers are not exploited

- ensuring that financial rules are adhered to by banks and financial institutions. Regulators have the ability to impose large fines and penalties on any firms that break rules.

1 Implementation of monetary policy

Monetary policy (see page 88) involves the government's manipulation of interest rates and the money supply to achieve its objectives.

The central bank can:

- manage the money supply by setting the availability of credit or its cost, mainly through the setting of interest rates

- influence the amount of lending banks provide by setting capital requirements that banks must keep

- affect the exchange rate through the buying and selling of currencies by changing interest rates. The table below shows a summary of how these tools can affect the economy.

	...increases	...decreases
Availability of credit	↑ AD ↑ Inflation	↓ AD
Amount of bank lending	↑ AD ↑ Inflation	↓ AD ↓ Investment
Exchange rate	↓ AD ↓ inflation	↑ AD ↑ Inflation

What you need to know

For the exam, you do not need to know details of regulations but may be expected to examine the possible consequences of those mentioned in, for example, a data response question.

Now try this

1 Describe what is meant by 'lender of the last resort'.

2 Describe two ways that a reduction in interest rates by the central bank might affect the economy.

Types of public expenditure

Public expenditure refers to government spending on behalf of the country's citizens – the public. Spending may be for a wide range of reasons, from the provision of education and healthcare, through to roads and railways and pensions and benefits. You need to know about the different types of public expenditure and the significance of the size of public expenditure as a percentage of GDP.

Types of public expenditure

Public expenditure is a broad term and covers three specific categories of government spending. The total amount that the government spends is also known as **total managed expenditure** (TME).

Types of public expenditure

1 **Capital expenditure** – long-term investment expenditure by the government on capital projects. For example, Crossrail or new hospitals.

2 **Current expenditure** – the government's day-to-day expenditure on goods and services. Examples include wages and salaries of civil servants, and drugs used by the NHS.

3 **Transfer payments** – payments made by the state to individuals without an exchange of goods or services. There is no production in return for these payments. Typically, transfer payments are used as a means of redistributing income. UK examples include Employment and Support Allowance for sick and disabled people and child benefit.

Real world **Size of UK's public expenditure**

The chart (right) shows a breakdown of UK public expenditure for the fiscal year 2018–19. Social protection is the largest component of government spending, and includes spending on welfare and pensions. Education and health are also major areas of public expenditure. In total, government (public) expenditure was planned to be £809 billion in 2018–19. It is more useful to view this figure as a percentage of GDP. For 2018–19 the £809 billion represents just below 40% of GDP (see below).

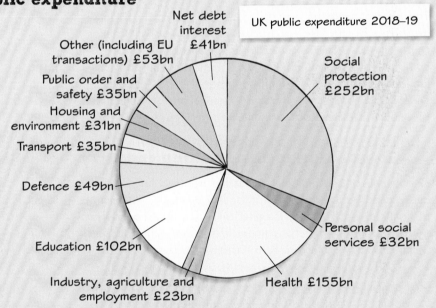

UK public expenditure 2018–19

- Net debt interest £41bn
- Other (including EU transactions) £53bn
- Public order and safety £35bn
- Housing and environment £31bn
- Transport £35bn
- Defence £49bn
- Education £102bn
- Industry, agriculture and employment £23bn
- Health £155bn
- Personal social services £32bn
- Social protection £252bn

Size of public expenditure as a percentage of GDP

The table (right) shows that UK public expenditure as a percentage of GDP is planned to fall. This is despite the actual money value of public expenditure rises between 2018–23. One reason for the fall in value as a percentage of GDP is that GDP increases by a greater proportion than public expenditure.

Planned TME of the government from 2018–23

	18–19	19–20	20–21	21–22	22–23
TME (£ billion)	809.3	826.7	849.9	871.7	896.8
TME as % GDP	38.5	38.3	38.2	37.9	37.7

Now try this

Describe the difference between capital expenditure and current expenditure.

Changes in public expenditure

You need to know about possible reasons for changes over time in the size and composition of public expenditure in a global context.

Reasons for the changes

1 **The economic cycle** – in periods of recession or slow economic growth, public expenditure in developed countries rises due to increased spending on welfare benefits.

2 **Changing age distribution** – ageing populations in developed countries place greater pressure on established healthcare systems.

3 **Changing expectations** – new technology in services such as health and education results in increased expectations.

4 **Financial crises** – the government may have to spend money bailing out financial institutions.

5 **Economic philosophy** – countries such as the USA are market orientated, relying less on public spending to provide services such as healthcare. Individuals must buy health insurance, unlike many European models where the state provides services through taxation.

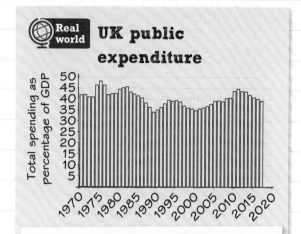

Real world UK public expenditure

Changes in UK public expenditure
In the mid-1970s the figure was almost 50% of GDP. This was mainly due to the economic cycle and performance of the economy. From 2007 onwards the figure increased again, this time due to the financial crisis and the need of the government to support the financial sector, plus the deterioration in economic growth as a result of the financial crisis.

Impact on the economy of changes in the size of public expenditure as a percentage of GDP

	Positive and negative impacts of changes
Productivity and growth	• Public spending on infrastructure (roads, healthcare, education) leads to improved supply-side performance of an economy. Private sector firms often cannot undertake investment that has very long-term gains. • Free market economists argue that cutting public expenditure will lead to spending being transferred to the private sector, resulting in more efficient and productive outcomes.
Living standards	• Public spending can have a big impact on living standards. • With zero public expenditure there would be market failure. Absolute poverty would exist, as individuals who could not earn an income would have no means of survival.
Crowding out	This involves public expenditure leading to lower private sector investment spending. **Resource crowding out** occurs when the economy is operating at full employment and the expansion of the public sector means that there is a shortage of resources in the private sector. **Financial crowding out** arises when the expansion of the state sector is financed by increased government borrowing. This causes an increased demand for loanable funds that drives up interest rates and crowds out private sector investment.
Level of taxation	• If public expenditure is high then levels of taxation must also be high to fund this. • Free market economists favour lower levels of public expenditure to allow free enterprise to grow and generate economic growth.
Equality	• Public spending on education can help to create more equal opportunities for citizens. • High levels of public expenditure can mean higher benefits and pensions, which improves living standards.

Now try this

Describe why strong economic growth will lead to lower public expenditure as a percentage of GDP.

Changes in tax rates 1

There are three categories of taxation. Changes in direct and indirect tax rates have an economic impact on a range of variables. On this page, you will revise two of these: incentives to work and tax revenues (the Laffer curve).

Synoptic link   This builds on work covered on aggregate demand and supply (pages 70–71), the multiplier (page 79), demand-side policies (pages 88–90) and different types of taxation (page 90).

Categories of taxation

Progressive – as income rises, a larger percentage of income is paid in tax (e.g. UK income tax).

Proportional – the percentage of income paid in tax is constant, no matter what the level of income.

Regressive – as income rises, a smaller percentage of income is paid in tax (for example, excise duties on tobacco, alcohol and petrol in the UK).

Adam Smith's 'canons of taxation'

Adam Smith, writing in the 18th century, suggested that a 'good' tax had four key characteristics. These became known as the canons of taxation and are:

1 the cost of collection should be low relative to the yield

2 the timing should be certain and clear

3 the means of collection should be convenient for the taxpayer

4 taxes should be levied based on the ability to pay of the taxpayer.

Incentives to work

Free market economists believe that lower tax rates increase incentives and improve the supply-side performance of an economy. Higher marginal tax rates are a disincentive to economic activity.

A tax on profits (corporation tax) can lead to less incentive for firms to invest. Higher rates of income tax can lead to reduced incentives for workers to work extra hours, preferring instead to substitute leisure time.

Marginal tax rates

Marginal tax rates are the rate of tax on an additional £1 of income.

Tax revenues: the Laffer curve

It would seem logical that higher tax rates lead to higher tax revenues for government. However, if workers view higher marginal tax rates as a disincentive to work, then potentially some workers may choose not to work, with the result that tax revenue falls. This idea was put forward by Arthur Laffer (see the Laffer curve, right). The effect of the change in tax rates on tax revenue may be explained by the following factors:

- increased disincentives to work
- an increase in tax avoidance and evasion
- a rise in the number of tax exiles (individuals who choose to leave the country to avoid paying tax).

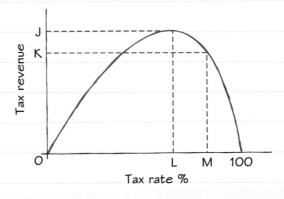

The Laffer curve shows that when the tax rate is increased to point L, tax revenues increase. However, a further increase in the tax rate from L to M causes a fall in tax revenue from J to K.

Now try this

1 Give two reasons why higher tax rates might lead to lower tax revenue for government.

2 A tax rises by 5% and this leads to an individual on lower income being worse off but a higher income earner being no worse off. What type of tax is this? Explain why this tax rise has this effect.

Changes in tax rates 2

On this page, you will revise the economic effects of changes in direct and indirect tax rates on income distribution, real output and employment, the price level, the trade balance and FDI.

VAT – a regressive tax

In 2011 the standard rate of VAT in the UK rose from 17.5% to 20%. Critics saw this as being unfair on low income households. The chart shows the effect of this increase on different income groups. The poorest 10% of households pay almost 20% of net household income as VAT, whereas the richest 10% were impacted much less (less than 10% of net income). This suggests that VAT is a regressive tax, but note: for all except the poorest 10%, the effect is broadly similar.

Income distribution

Income distribution refers to how total income is divided within a population. A progressive tax, such as income tax, will tend to redistribute income from those on higher incomes to those on lower incomes if the tax revenues raised are used for benefits to the poor.

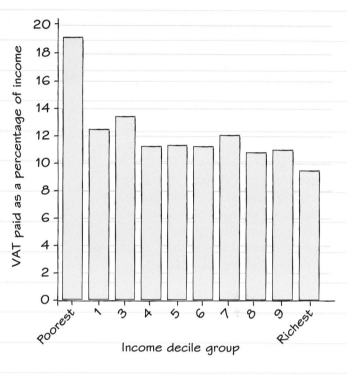

Real output and employment

- An increase in taxes will **reduce aggregate demand** because taxes are a leakage from the circular flow of income. In turn, this might reduce real output and cause an increase in unemployment (see diagram below).

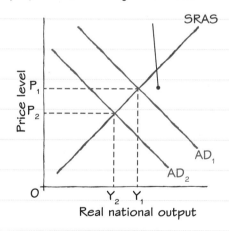

- In the long run, changes in tax rates can **impact on aggregate supply**. Lower direct tax rates can lead to higher incentives, which lead to increased investment by firms and increased participation in the labour market. The effect of this is an increase in economic growth and a rise in employment (see diagram below).

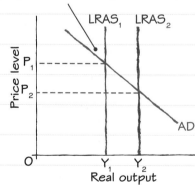

The price level

An increase in indirect taxes can be inflationary if it causes a wage–price spiral. For example, increased indirect tax causes a rise in prices, which, in turn, leads to increased wage demands by workers causing firms' costs to rise and a further rise in prices.

The trade balance and FDI

An increase in income tax would reduce disposable income and consumption. In turn, this would reduce demand for imports and so result in an improvement in the balance of trade. A higher rate of corporation tax might deter FDI if rates are lower in other countries.

Now try this

Describe how a rise in the income tax allowance might affect the distribution of income.

Public sector finances

This page builds on your understanding of fiscal policy and considers government spending and aspects of fiscal policy through the use of taxation.

 Synoptic link

To recap fiscal policy, see page 68 and page 79 on the multiplier.

Discretionary fiscal policy

Discretionary fiscal policy involves the government making decisions about its spending or taxes. Discretionary policy is different to automatic changes that occur (see automatic stabilisers right). In the budget of November 2017 the government announced that excise duty on cigarettes would rise by 2%. This was a discretionary decision taken by the government to help to reduce spending on a product that can cause serious negative externalities.

Automatic stabilisers

Some fiscal policy occurs **automatically** as the economy moves through the economic cycle. During a recession, government spending on non-means tested benefits will increase automatically when people become unemployed. This is not a decision the government has taken – it is **not discretionary**. Such automatic aspects of fiscal policy work to correct the effects of the economic cycle.

When spending on benefits increases as unemployment rises, this prevents AD from falling by as much as it would if there were no state benefits, thus offsetting the effects of the recession. In this sense the increased spending on benefits is helping to **stabilise** the economy – hence automatic stabilisers.

Fiscal deficit and the national debt

- A **fiscal deficit** occurs when government spending exceeds tax revenue in a financial (fiscal) year, necessitating the need for the government to borrow money.
- The **national debt** is the cumulative total of past government borrowing.

In the 2017 budget the government announced that UK government borrowing for 2017–18 would be £49.9 billion. The total national debt at this time was £1786 billion.

Cyclical and structural deficits

- A **cyclical fiscal deficit** occurs during a downturn in the economy because tax revenues will be falling and government expenditure (for example on social benefits) will be increasing. Such a deficit should disappear when the economy returns to its trend growth rate.
- A **structural fiscal deficit** remains even when the economy is operating at its full potential. It is, therefore, regarded as a more serious problem than a cyclical deficit.

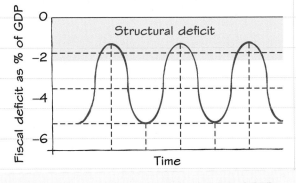

In this case, there is a structural deficit of 2.5% of GDP because the lowest level of cyclical deficit is 2.5% of GDP

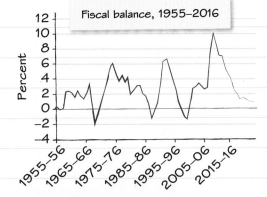

Fiscal balance pattern

It is clear from the diagram that the pattern of the fiscal balance follows the economic cycle. For example, during the late 1990s the economy enjoyed a period of strong growth. The result of this was that the government received higher tax revenue and had to pay out less in benefits (due, in part, to the effect of automatic stabilisers). As a result, the fiscal balance was positive. Contrast this to periods where the economy suffered slow growth or recession, such as the late 1980s/1990s and 2007–08.

Now try this

Give three examples of government decisions that are discretionary fiscal policy.

Factors affecting size of fiscal deficit and national debt

This page builds on your knowledge of public finances and explores the factors that influence the size of fiscal deficits and the national debt.

Factors affecting the size of fiscal deficits

The fiscal debt can be affected by a number of factors.

- **Economic cycle** – during periods of economic growth, fiscal deficits tend to be small or become surpluses.

- **Housing market** – during periods of growth in the housing market, tax revenues for the government increase due to a rise in the amount of stamp duty – a tax of house sales – received.

- **Political priorities and unplanned events** – occasionally, governments have to respond to unforeseen events that are not covered in budgets set aside. For example, the financial crisis of 2007–08 led to the government spending billions to bail out financial institutions.

Factors affecting the size of national debts

The size of national debt may be influenced by **government policy**. Where a government embarks on policies that require high levels of borrowing, this will translate into higher national debt. Where current borrowing is on aspects that improve the supply side of the economy, for example, investment in new transport infrastructure such as Crossrail and HS2, the longer-term effect should be increased productivity and therefore higher employment and higher tax revenues for government. These should lead to a reduction in the national debt in the future. If, on the other hand, current spending by government is on short run aspects, such as higher pensions or wages for public sector workers, the effect may to lead to a higher national debt.

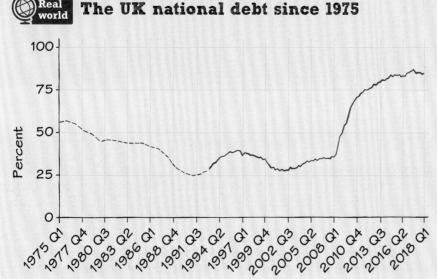

Real world The UK national debt since 1975

UK national debt since 1975 (% of GDP).

The chart (left) shows how the national debt in the UK fell from 40% of GDP to 30% between 1997 and 2000. This was due to the growth of the economy and the fact that government ran a budget surplus during this period, meaning the national debt was being paid off.

The national debt began to increase thereafter, most notably from 2008 and the financial crisis, when the government had to spend hundreds of billions of pounds – paid for by both borrowing money and through quantitative easing – to prevent the banking system from collapse.

Now try this

State two factors that affect the size of the national debt.

Significance of size of fiscal deficits and national debt

The size of the fiscal deficit (or surplus) and the national debt have some implications for other economic variables, such as interest rates and taxation.

Interest rates

A rise in government borrowing may lead to a rise in interest rates. This is because the demand for funds rises relative to their supply. The price of borrowed money is the rate of interest. So the rise in demand should lead to a rise in interest rates. Higher interest rates can have serious effects in the economy, such as leading to lower AD as consumers are deterred from spending. It may also lead to crowding out.

The rate of inflation

If a government needs more money as tax receipts do not cover expenditure, it has two options: borrow money or print money. Printing money should lead to higher inflation as more money would be in circulation. On the other hand, borrowing money – higher fiscal deficit and national debt – means that the government spends more as a percentage of GDP, and the private sector spends less. There is no increase in AD and therefore little impact on inflation.

Debt servicing

As the national debt grows the total amount of interest paid will increase. Debt interest features in current spending and therefore affects the fiscal balance. Higher interest payments therefore can lead to an increase in the fiscal deficit.

The amount of debt interest paid by the UK government

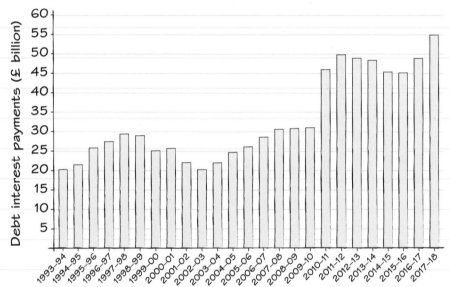

Inter-generational equity

It can be argued that by the government borrowing today, future generations have to pay this back. As a result, today's generation benefits from the spending at the expense of future generations. However, this argument can be questioned. If borrowing today leads to improved infrastructure, for example, then future generations will benefit in addition to current generations.

A country with a large debt is less attractive to foreign direct investment (FDI) as foreign investors will be less certain about the future prospects for the country. The investment may be deemed too risky.

Credit ratings

Countries are given credit ratings by private investment companies. These ratings estimate the likelihood that a country will default – not be able to pay – on its debts. The best rating is AAA and the worst is D. Credit ratings then affect the rate of interest at which governments, and companies, can borrow. Whilst the size of a national debt can influence the credit rating, other factors, such as a country's financial history, also affect credit ratings. For example, the UK and the USA governments have never defaulted on their debts.

Now try this

Describe why a growing national debt might be bad for future generations.

Macroeconomic policies in a global context

There is a range of policies that governments use to achieve their goals. The policies you need to understand are: fiscal policy, monetary policy, exchange rate policy, supply-side policies and direct controls. On this page, you will revise fiscal policy. Other macroeconomic policies will be covered on the following pages.

 **Synoptic link** Look back at page 89 to recap fiscal policy.

The use of fiscal policy

In the post-war period, Keynesian fiscal policy was popular with governments in trying to manage the economy. Taxes and government spending were used, as well other approaches such as monetary policy, to manage demand. This approach was known as **demand management** and it had implications for the fiscal balance and therefore the national debt.

Types of fiscal policy

- **Expansionary fiscal policy** – use of taxes, public spending and government borrowing to stimulate the economy and increase AD.
- **Deflationary fiscal policy** – use of taxation and reduced public expenditure to reduce the level of AD in the economy.

Impact of fiscal policies on fiscal balance

Expansionary fiscal policy	Deflationary fiscal policy
Reduce taxes to stimulate spending and investment Increase public expenditure ↓	Increase taxes to discourage consumer spending Reduce public expenditure ↓
Increased public sector borrowing – leads to higher fiscal debt ↓	Reduced public sector borrowing – leads to lower fiscal debt or fiscal surplus ↓
Increased AD	Reduced AD

Effects of fiscal policy on poverty and inequality

Governments in developed countries use fiscal policy to help reduce poverty.

1. **Welfare benefits** – provided when individuals are unemployed, on low incomes or in poor health and unable to work.
2. **Provision of certain goods and services** such as rent subsidies and educational courses – for individuals on low incomes.
3. **Progressive taxes** – these narrow the gap between people's disposable income and the revenue raised can be used to pay for benefits or the provision of goods and services.

Impact of fiscal policy on national debt

Any increase or decrease in the fiscal balance will impact on the national debt.

Expansionary fiscal policy	>	Increased fiscal deficit	>	Increased national debt
Deflationary fiscal policy	>	Reduced fiscal deficit	>	Reduced national debt

Now try this

1 Outline two features of expansionary fiscal policy.
2 What is meant by the term demand management?

Other government policies

Other policies that governments use to achieve their goals include **monetary** and **supply-side policies**. Monetary policy involves decisions on interest rates, the money supply and exchange rates.

Synoptic link Look back at pages 88–92 to remind yourself about these policies.

The use of monetary policy

Monetary policy can have a major impact on aggregate demand – it can be used as a **demand-side** policy.

The main instrument of this policy is the ability to set interest rates, typically set by the central bank of a country. Interest rates affect borrowing, saving – and therefore spending – and also investment. Consumption and investment are components of AD, so if these increase – due to lower interest rates – AD rises. Note, however, that investment can impact on the **supply side** of the economy, by leading to improved technology and infrastructure and therefore improved productivity.

Control of the money supply

Control of the money supply – an important aspect of monetary policy – is extremely difficult, as it is nearly impossible to actually measure the amount of money. Control of inflation is becoming more difficult as the influence of globalisation increases. For example, the growth of China has pushed up prices of commodities, including food, causing cost-push inflation.

This makes the decisions of policy makers all the more difficult, causing more uncertainty about the future.

The aims of monetary policy

The main aim of monetary policy is to set interest rates to control inflation. In the UK, the MPC has a target to hit 2% CPI inflation. This is a **symmetric target** meaning that it has to be within plus or minus 1% of the target. Some central banks have an **asymmetric inflation target**. For example, the European Central Bank aims to keep inflation close to but below 2%.

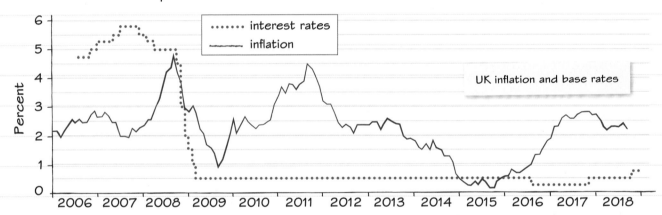

UK inflation and base rates

The use of supply-side policies

Supply-side policies are designed to increase the productive potential of the country and, therefore, increase its long-run aggregate supply. Such policies are often advocated as part of a strategy to increase economic development because they include:

- improving education so that people acquire appropriate skills required in a modern economy
- improving healthcare so that life expectancy increases
- advocating entrepreneurship to encourage the growth of small businesses
- encouraging increased labour force participation.

Effects of supply-side policies

Supply-side policies improve the productive capacity of the economy by shifting to the right the LRAS line (see chart on page 191). Successful supply-side policies can lead to improved international competitiveness due to improved productivity, which leads to lower average costs for firms.

Improved competitiveness should lead to increased exports and less reliance on imports, leading to higher economic growth and lower unemployment.

Now try this

Explain how the use of monetary policy can be used as a demand-management approach.

Direct controls and exchange rate policies

Other policies that governments use to achieve their goals include exchange rate policies and direct controls.

↩ Synoptic link

Look back at pages 171 and 181 to remind yourself about exchange rate policies.

Exchange rate policies

Central banks may use exchange rate policy to allow the exchange rate to deviate from its equilibrium rate. This may be achieved by either buying or selling reserves of currencies on foreign exchange markets. However, central banks and governments now rarely use policies involving setting exchange rates, relying on a policy of floating exchange rates. Instead, changes in exchange rates are what occur as a result of changes in monetary policy. For example, if the Bank of England raised the interest rate to cool inflationary pressures in the economy, there will be an impact on the exchange rate. In this case, higher interest rates are likely to attract global flows of 'hot money', thus increasing the demand for pounds and therefore raising the exchange rate.

Impact of exchange rate policies

Changes in exchange rates impact on the economy through their effect on prices. However, changes can affect international competitiveness of an economy. An exchange rate policy which seeks to keep the exchange rate below the equilibrium rate, will help to stimulate international competitiveness. A reduction in the exchange rate will, *ceteris paribus*, mean that the prices of exports for foreign consumers is reduced, leading to higher demand and an increase in AD. However, an impact of this is that imports become more expensive which can feed through in the form of cost-push inflation.

The use of direct controls

Direct controls are forms of control that work outside the market system. They are a government measure that is imposed on the price or quantity of a product or a factor of production. Examples include:

1 maximum price controls – for example, these might be used in developing countries to control the price of food

2 minimum guaranteed prices – for example, national minimum wages and wage controls

3 fixing quotas on imports

4 limiting the amount of foreign currency that a citizen can buy in a year

5 fixing maximum interest rates that payday lenders can charge their customers.

 Direct controls

Payday loan caps come into force

In 2015 the UK government introduced a direct control on the market for short-term ('payday') loans. Interest and fees on all high-cost short-term credit loans were capped at 0.8% per day of the amount borrowed. If borrowers do not repay their loans on time, default charges must not exceed £15. In addition, total fees charged by lenders are capped at 100% of the original loan.

 US government imposes steel quotas

In 2018 the US government took steps to limit imports of steel into the country, as a way of protecting the domestic steel industry. In addition to tariffs, the government is also introducing quotas to limit the physical amount of steel coming into the US.

Now try this

What effect would a significant reduction in commodity prices have on an economy?

External shocks

Macroeconomic policies may be used to respond to external shocks to the global economy and to control the operations of transglobal companies, and may cause issues for policymakers.

External shocks are unpredictable events such as sudden and significant price changes for key commodities like oil and foodstuffs, or financial crises, like the 2007–08 shock that hit the global financial system. The effect of a commodity price shock is detailed right.

Measures to control transnational companies

Measures to control the operations of global companies might include:

- requirement that local factors of production, such as labour and local component suppliers, are used

- requirement that the global company exports a certain proportion of its output

- requirement to set up joint ventures with technology transfer to the domestic firm (a joint venture involves two or more firms working together in a single venture)

- transfer pricing – see right.

🌐 Real world External shocks: rise in commodity prices

The price of crude oil increased by almost 50% between 2017 and 2018. This had major impacts for global economies. The effects of this can be shown using AD/AS analysis.

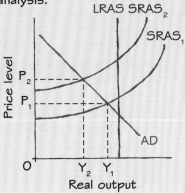

The rise in oil prices causes SRAS to shift to the left, shifting the economy to a position below the LRAS level of output (to Y_2), and also an increase in inflation (P_2). As a result of this the economy ends in a position of below average growth.

Transfer pricing

Transfer pricing refers to the pricing policies adopted by groups of companies for transactions between companies in the group, such as the sale of goods or the provision of services. With corporate tax rates varying considerably from country to country, there is the potential for global companies to reduce their global tax charge by manipulating the prices charged on intra-group transactions. Measures to regulate transfer pricing are more difficult for less powerful countries. One limit to a government's ability to control global companies is that many are 'footloose'. This means they may be able to move to another country easily and with little cost. However, international agreements such as TRIMS (Trade Related Investment Measures) introduced by the WTO have, for example, banned the use of local content requirements.

Problems facing policymakers

Inaccurate (or out-of-date) information	May include GDP, unemployment or the balance of payments on current account when setting interest rates. Information can sometimes be inaccurate because it is difficult to collect. For example, GDP figures are revised many times after their first release.
Risks and uncertainties	It may be difficult for the authorities to predict the impact of some policies, such as quantitative easing, or the impact of a country leaving the Eurozone. For example, car manufacturers such as Honda and Toyota have yet to fully decide what will happen with their UK factories once the UK leaves the EU. Further uncertainties relate to the future behaviour of consumers or businesses in their spending and investment plans.
Inability to control external shocks	In an increasingly globalised world in which countries are more closely integrated economically, it becomes more and more difficult for an individual country to isolate itself from external shocks.

Now try this

State two problems that policymakers face when applying macroeconomic policies.

Exam skills 1: Section A

Section A of **A level Paper 2** consists of multiple-choice and short-answer questions. Each question starts with some stimulus material, such as tables, charts, statistics and case studies.

Worked example   AL

1 The chart below shows UK inflation between 2008 and 2018.

(a) With reference to the chart, explain **one** possible cause of the change in inflation between September 2015 and September 2017.   **(2 marks)**

One possible cause is an increase in consumption, which is a component of AD and therefore AD would increase, which would lead to shift of the AD curve along the SRAS line. <u>As a result,</u> this would cause inflation in the short term, such as the rise in CPI from 0%–3% shown in the chart.

Explain

'Explain' questions require you to make a point to demonstrate knowledge (AO1), before offering some development of this point (AO3 analysis). Where a question is based on a particular context, you may also need to demonstrate application (AO2). For more tips on how to answer 'explain' questions, see page 201.

A level Paper 2 covers **Theme 2** and **Theme 4**. Make sure you know which paper you are taking and which themes they cover.

One cause has been identified. The 'increase in consumption' has then been developed to show how it might lead to inflation by explaining the impact on AD/AS. The answer also makes reference to the chart as required in the question.

Using 'As a result…' helps to show development/explanation, which is vital in 'explain' questions.

Worked example   AL

(b) Explain how monetary policy can be used to impact on the rate of inflation. Use an AD/AS diagram in your answer.   **(4 marks)**

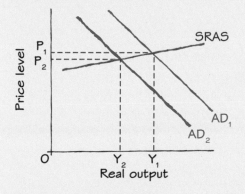

🔗 **Links** This question refers to Theme 4 page 196 and Theme 2, page 88.

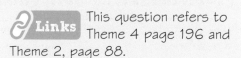

Increasing interest rates is an example of monetary policy and this can be used to reduce the rate of inflation. As can be seen in the diagram, higher interest rates lead, *ceteris paribus*, to lower AD. This is because consumption is a component of AD and consumption is affected by interest rates. The leftward shift in AD causes a movement along the SRAS line. <u>As a result</u> of this, inflation falls from P_1 to P_2.

This is a good response with a well-labelled diagram drawn using a ruler. The diagram is then referred to in the written answer, for example, '… leftward shift of AD'. There's also good use of technical language (e.g. *ceteris paribus*, consumption).

The answer is clearly developed and answers the question directly.

Exam skills 2: Section A

Section A of **A level Paper 2** may also include 'calculate' questions. These require you to use your knowledge of formulae and economics and apply this using the statistics provided (AO2 application). 'Calculate' questions may involve completing information in a table, or working out from a chart or diagram. Below are some exam-style 'calculate' questions with exemplar answers.

Worked example

AL

2 The table below shows information about a government's finance, borrowing and national debt.

	£ billion			
	2015	2016	2017	2018
Government spending	400	450	500	550
Government revenue	360	400	460	570
Government borrowing	40	50	40	−20
Annual fiscal balance	40	50	40	−20
National debt	40	90	130	110

Calculate the total national debt for 2018. Use the last two rows for your working. **(4 marks)**

National debt (2018) = £110 billion
This is found by 40 + 50 + 40 − 20

The student has approached this in a two-step way. First of all, the table has been completed accurately. This then allows the student to identify the correct answer, which they have written in the available space.

Worked example

AL

3 A government decides to increase the top rate of income tax from 40% to 80% as a way of raising more revenue. The result is a fall in tax revenue. This is shown in the Laffer curve below.

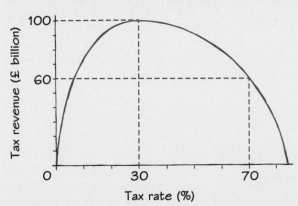

Calculate the percentage fall in tax revenue as a result of this increase in the tax rate. You are advised to show your working. **(2 marks)**

$\frac{20}{70} \times 100 = 28.57\%$

Some questions may require you to calculate answers based on an economics diagram, using the figures from the diagram.
Read the information on the diagram carefully.

Exam skills 3: Section A

Below are some more exam-style 'explain' questions with exemplar answers.

 Links For tips on the techniques used to answer 'explain' questions, see page 199.

Worked example

4 Explain **one** cause of a current account deficit in a country.

(2 marks)

One cause of a deficit on the balance of payments is a rise in incomes where a country has a high marginal propensity to import. Rising incomes will lead to increased demand for foreign imports which, providing the demand for exports remains constant, will lead to a current account deficit.

You are asked to 'Explain **one** cause' so you just need to make one point and then develop it.

Important – it is not necessary to provide a definition of the term in the question (current account). Try to be aware of the time you have and don't write too much for questions with 2 marks.

This is a good answer because it identifies a clear cause – a rise in incomes. This is knowledge (AO1) – the student *knows* what can cause a deficit on the current account. They then go on to develop the point by showing how this will lead to a deficit. This linked strand is the analysis (AO3).

Worked example

5 Explain **one** effect in a country of a system of progressive taxation.

(4 marks)

The main effect will be <u>a more equal distribution of income</u>. <u>This is because</u> progressive taxes lead to higher earners paying proportionally more tax than lower earners, which therefore leads to a transfer of income from richer citizens to government. <u>As a result</u>, this money can then be used by government on public services which benefit lower income families.

The question is worth 4 marks because it requires 3 strands of development. Don't fall into the trap of writing about 'effects' (plural).

This is a good answer because it identifies one effect (AO1 knowledge) and then develops this with three **linked** strands of development (AO3 analysis). The strands of development have been made with phrases such as 'This is because...' and 'As a result...'.

Exam skills 4: Section B

Section B of **A level Paper 2** contains a range of economic data and information based on a real-world topic. Read this stimulus material carefully before looking at the worked examples on pages 203–205.

The falling value of sterling (£)

Extract A: The decline of sterling

Figure 1 Sterling against dollar ($ per £), 1967–2017.

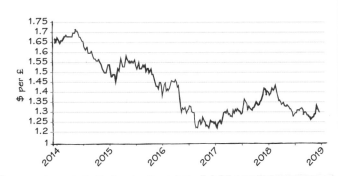

Figure 2 Sterling against dollar ($ per £), 2013–2018.

Reference: The Financial Times

> Note that over the period, the value of sterling has fallen against the dollar.

Extract B: What's behind the decline of the pound?

Figure 1 shows the decline of the pound over the past 50 years. A pound would buy $2.50 in 1967. What has followed is a pattern of declining value, a pattern hastened by the Brexit vote in June 2016, which saw the pound fall to close to $1.20.

> This paragraph provides some of the reasons for the decline.

There are a number of reasons for the decline. Firstly, in 1967 the UK government carried out a 14% devaluation of sterling.   5

Secondly, over the period the UK has tended to import more than it exported. Foreigners pay for UK goods and services using pounds they purchase. If the UK is selling them fewer goods and services, then the demand for pounds falls and so does the value. Thirdly, the Brexit vote pushed the value of the pound from $1.48 to $1.23. This was caused as investors   10 saw the uncertainty around Brexit and this made sterling less attractive as an investment.

> Devaluation is a deliberate downward adjustment of a currency by a government or central bank.

Reference: The Financial Times

Extract C: Economy picks up despite worries over global trade

The Office for National Statistics (ONS) released data in August 2018 to show that economic growth in the UK was picking up, growing by 0.4% in the 3 months to June 2018 (see chart below). Economic growth appears to be accelerating. The data supports the belief that the UK economy is now recovering after years of below-trend growth.

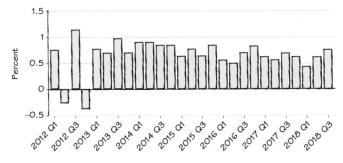

Figure 3: UK Economic Growth, 2012–2018.

Source: ONS

Exam skills 5: Section B

Section B consists of one case study, divided into several part questions. The question will enable you to demonstrate all the assessment objectives – knowledge (AO1), application (AO2), analysis (AO3) and evaluation (AO4). The exam-style 'examine' question and exemplar response below are based on the information on the falling value of sterling recently and over the past 50 years on page 202. Read the stimulus material carefully before looking at the worked example.

> **⮾ Links** In the exam, the data-response question may cover a range of economic concepts and topics. For the exam-style question below, you may find it helpful to revise AD/AS, causes of economic growth and the multiplier effect.

Worked example   (AL)

6 (a) With reference to the evidence, examine **two** possible effects on the UK economy of a rise in the rate of economic growth.
(8 marks)

One effect on the UK of the increase in economic growth could be that this leads to inflation. An increase in AD will cause a shift of the AD line to the right, a movement along the SRAS line. This is shown in the diagram below:

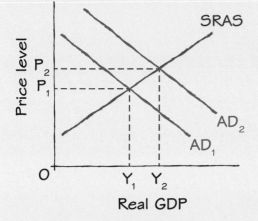

As a result of this increase in AD, price inflation increases from P_1 to P_2. This may result in inflation increasing beyond the Bank of England target of 2%, which might ultimately lead to higher interest rates. <u>However</u>, economic growth is only increasing modestly. Figure 3 shows that the quarter to June had growth of 0.4%, with the previous quarter being 0.2%. Yearly growth is therefore well below the trend rate of growth of around 2.5%, so therefore the effects on inflation are likely to be low.

A second effect is that economic growth can lead to rising incomes. This occurs through more people being employed, wages rising and consumption increasing. <u>However</u>, one impact of rising incomes is that demand for imports tends to increase due to UK consumers' high propensity to import. The effect of this can be a deterioration of the exchange rate, as demand for German cars, French wine, etc. increases. Figure 2 suggests that the exchange rate of the pound has weakened recently, at the same time as economic growth is accelerating.

Examine

For 'examine' questions you need to identify at least one different reason or factor, then explain it before offering some evaluation. To demonstrate application (AO2) your response must be in the context of the question and should not be generic. To evaluate the factors, you could consider the drawbacks of each.

 An AD/AS diagram has been used appropriately and then explained effectively.

 Remember to structure your answer using paragraphs. Here, three paragraphs have been used.

 The student has approached their response in a logical manner. They have identified two effects and explained them. The response is very clearly in the context of the UK economy and uses evidence from the stimulus material, for example, reference to data from Figure 3.

 Each effect is evaluated, with the student considering the drawbacks of each benefit. In both cases, the Evaluation begins with, 'However…'. Note that each effect is also in context – they refer to the UK and the effect of a change in the rate of economic growth.

Exam skills 6: Section B

Read the stimulus material on page 202 carefully before looking at the worked example and the exemplar answer.

Worked example (AL)

(b) Assess the possible effects on the UK of the changes in the exchange rate of the pound. **(10 marks)**

The exchange rate of the pound has weakened over recent years, and over a longer timescale. The effects of this can be positive and negative. A weakening of the exchange rate makes UK goods and services cheaper to foreign consumers, which can lead to higher exports. As net exports – imports less exports – are a component of AD, an increase in exports should lead to an increase in AD. As a result of this there is an increase in economic growth in the short run. This can be shown using an AD/AS diagram:

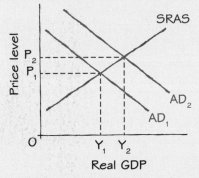

The evidence from Figures 1 and 2 seem to support this. As the exchange rate has weakened, economic growth appears to be increasing and this must be at least contributed to by an increase in net exports.

However, cheaper exports on the one hand <u>must mean more expensive imports, and this can have serious implications for UK consumers and businesses that import materials and commodities.</u> Higher import costs can lead to higher prices. An effect of this may be to shift the SRAS line to the left, as shown in this diagram:

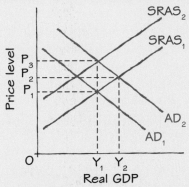

The effect of this is an increase in cost-push inflation to P_3, and a reduction in economic growth back to Y_1, thus reducing the positive effects of the cheaper exports.

A second effect...

Assess

'Assess' questions test all four assessment objectives and require you to weigh up a scenario before offering some evaluation. To demonstrate application (AO2), your response must be in the context of the question. There are no right or wrong answers – it is up to you to present your arguments.

You must also provide an evaluative comment. For example, you might indicate how, as a large importer and exporter, any change to the exchange rate will have a significant impact for the UK.

 You don't need an introduction or definitions. Get straight to the point.

 Clearly drawn and labelled AD/AS diagrams are explained effectively.

 The answer is in the context of the UK economy. You need to show that you can link your knowledge to the context and use relevant examples.

 Here the student considers the negative effects of the weakening exchange rate. This shows evaluation by balancing the original point and is in the context of the UK economy. An alternative route to evaluation could be through considering the J-curve or Marshall–Lerner condition.

 The student goes on to consider the negative aspects of a weakening exchange rate. This shows analysis (AO3), providing linked strands of development.

 The question refers to 'effects', so a second effect is required. You might consider the impact on employment.

Exam skills 7: Section B

'Discuss' questions enable you to demonstrate all the assessment objectives – knowledge (AO1), application (AO2), analysis (AO3) and evaluation (AO4). The exam-style 'discuss' question below is based on the information on the falling value of sterling recently and over the past 50 years on page 202. Read the extracts carefully before looking at the worked example.

> **Links** In the exam, the data-response question may cover a range of economic concepts and topics. Here you may find it helpful to revise exchange rates and competitive devaluations.

Worked example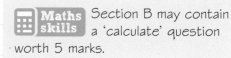

7 (a) With reference to Figure 1, calculate the percentage fall in the value of the pound against the dollar as a result of the referendum in 2016. **(5 marks)**

Value of the pound fell from $1.48 to $1.23

Fall is 1.48 – 1.23 = 25

$\frac{0.25}{1.48}$ = 0.1689

0.1689 × 100 – 16.89%

> **Maths skills** Section B may contain a 'calculate' question worth 5 marks.
> To calculate a percentage change, remember:
> $\frac{change}{original} \times 100$

Worked example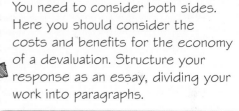

(b) Discuss the likely impact on the UK of a devaluation of its currency, such as that in 1967. **(15 marks)**

A <u>devaluation</u> occurs when a government or a central bank causes a downward adjustment of a country's currency. In 1967 the UK government was forced to devalue the pound by 14%. There are a range of effects of such a move.

One positive effect of such a devaluation is that the UK's exports will be cheaper for foreign consumers. This is because goods are priced in the local currency, and this currency can now buy more pounds per unit. As a result of this the demand for UK goods and services will increase, which will lead to an increase in AD. On the face of it this is really positive for the UK economy. This is what the government in the 1960s hoped to achieve.

However, a problem with such an approach is that the effects of the devaluation will take time to feed through into the economy. Indeed, in the short run, due to the existence of contracts and supply chains, the devaluation may not lead to an increase in exports.

A further impact on the UK of a devaluation is...

> You need to consider both sides. Here you should consider the costs and benefits for the economy of a devaluation. Structure your response as an essay, dividing your work into paragraphs.

> You need to know what is meant by 'devaluation'.

> A developed explanation showing knowledge (AO1) and analysis (AO3).

> Here the student offers some evaluation (AO4) by considering the downsides of the benefit.

> You could suggest a negative impact of devaluation, such as the fact that imports will become more expensive, before balancing this point. For example, you might suggest that, as contracts for supplies exist which fix prices in the short run, the impact on prices might not emerge for some time.

Exam skills 8: Section C

Section C of **A level Paper 2** consists of two extended open-response ('evaluate') questions. The questions are stand-alone and are not based on the case study in Section B. You are required to answer **one** question only. You need to write your response in essay style, using paragraphs, before arriving at a conclusion. An exam-style 'evaluate' worked example is given below.

Worked example

AL

8 In the UK, the top 1% of earners pay 28% of total income tax, a figure which is rising. The percentage of adults that pay no income tax is rising.

Evaluate the likely macroeconomic consequences of a tax system which taxes the rich proportionally more than lower income earners.

(25 marks)

A tax system which taxes the better off more than lower income earners is called a progressive tax system. One positive effect of such a tax system is that this creates a fairer system for workers who do not earn high incomes. This is an example of a system which creates more equity, which is an important economic goal for governments.

Another consequence is that this tax system creates an incentive for workers to enter the labour market. This is because relatively lower marginal tax rates must be paid by lower income earners, if the top 1% are paying such a high proportion. If the effect is to increase labour supply, then this is a benefit to firms who will be able to take advantage of a wider stock of available labour, which could increase productivity.

However, there are some negative consequences of higher earners paying the largest proportion of income tax. One consequence is that high marginal rates of tax for higher earners can affect incentives...

'Evaluate' questions require you to consider both sides. Here you need to consider the costs and benefits for the economy of a tax system which takes a high proportion of tax from higher income earners. Structure your response as an essay, dividing your work into paragraphs.

To complete the response, you would need to consider the negative consequences before arriving at a conclusion. You might consider:

- effect on incentives for higher earners
- impact on government tax revenues – Laffer curve
- a conclusion – on balance, what is the effect of such a tax system.

Use of the 'it depends' rule can help.

Exam-style practice: Section A

On this page, you will find exam-style multiple-choice and short-answer practice questions for Section A of **A level Paper 2**. There are answers on page 218.

AL

1 Which of the following is a definition of a tariff?   **(1 mark)**

A A ban on a particular type of import.   ☐

B A physical limit imposed on the volume of imports.   ☐

C A tax on imported goods   ☐

D A subsidy on an imported product.   ☐

Links You will need to use your knowledge of trade restrictions to answer this question (see pages 167–168).

AL

2 The average cost of the EU tariff on each imported motorcycle is $2200 and the value of that tariff is 31%.   **(2 marks)**

(a) Calculate the average price (in dollars) in the EU of an imported Harley-Davidson motorcycle. You are advised to show your working.

Maths skills This question requires you to demonstrate your ability to 'calculate, use and understand percentages…' (Specification, Appendix 3). $2200 is 31% of how much?
$$\frac{2200}{0.31} = \$7096.77$$
Also, make sure you show your answer in dollars – use the $ sign!

AL

(b) Explain the effect in a country of an imposition of a tariff on imports. Use an AD/AS diagram in your answer.   **(4 marks)**

Links Recap tariffs on pages 167–168.

There are two parts to this question – the diagram and the answer. Make sure your diagram is clear – use a ruler and label axes, price, quantity and curves.

Exam-style practice: Section B extracts

On this page, you will find exam-style stimulus material for Section B of **A level Paper 2** data response. Before you answer the exam-style questions that follow on page 209, make sure you read the extracts carefully, highlighting any key terms and annotating useful points.

Tariffs

Extract A: American firms hit hard by EU tariffs

American firms will be hit hard by retaliatory tariffs

In June 2018 the European Union (EU) introduced a range of tariffs of products from the USA. The duties apply to over $2 billion worth of US goods that are exported to the EU each year. The tariffs were introduced because the US itself imposed tariffs of 10% on steel and 25% on aluminium produced in the EU.

5

Reference: The Economist

> Take a few minutes to read through all the extracts carefully, highlighting any key points and economic themes.

Extract B: Harley-Davidson, US tariffs and EU response

One company affected by the US tariffs on steel and aluminium – and the EU retaliation – is the US motorcycle manufacturer, Harley-Davidson. The company is affected in two ways:

1. Higher costs due to tariffs on steel and aluminium from the EU. Although it uses some domestically-sourced materials, it also imports from the EU.

5

2. Higher prices in the EU for its motorcycles – the tariff imposed is 31%, which raises the price significantly for EU customers.

Harley-Davidson reported the following effects of the EU tariffs:

Number of motorcycles sold in Europe in 2017	39,773
New level of EU tariff (from 6%)	31%
Average cost of EU tariff on each motorcycle exported from US	$2200
Additional expenses for Harley-Davidson in 2018 due to tariffs	$45 million

10

Harley-Davidson has responded to the trade war by announcing that it plans to move production of motorcycles for the EU destinations outside the US.

Exam-style practice: Sections B and C

On this page, you will find exam-style practice for **A level Paper 2** Section B data response and Section C extended open response. Before you answer questions 3 (a) and (b) below, make sure you read the extracts on page 208 carefully. There are answers on page 218.

AL

3 (a) It is claimed that by the US government protecting domestic industries through the use of tariffs, the US economy will benefit. Assess the impact on US consumers of imports being subject to import tariffs. **(10 marks)**

 Links Recap the impact of protectionist policies on pages 167–168.

Provide a balanced argument. Remember that impacts might be positive or negative – it depends on individual consumers and households.

AL

(b) Discuss the likely costs and benefits of globalisation for producers such as Harley-Davidson. **(15 marks)**

 Links Recap the impacts of globalisation on page 160.

There is no right or wrong answer for these questions. It is all about presenting your arguments and showing your knowledge.

Aim to spend 15 minutes on writing your response and use evidence from the extracts in your answer.

AL

4 Evaluate different measures the government could use to reduce poverty and inequality. **(25 marks)**

Structure your answer using paragraphs. Provide different methods and consider advantages and disadvantages of each.

You must provide a conclusion. You might suggest what the best methods are for the government.

You could consider discretionary government policies, such as increasing the minimum wage, and also the effects of strong and sustained economic growth as something which will reduce poverty and inequality.

Exam skills 1: Paper 3

Paper 3 is synoptic, which means that it covers all four themes. The paper is divided into two sections: A and B. Each section starts with a case study, including a range of evidence such as charts, tables and extracts, which is followed by one question, divided into parts (see page 214). The case study below is referred to in the worked examples and exemplar answers on pages 211 and 212.

The falling value of sterling (£)

Extract A:

Royal Mail – a natural monopoly

The origins of the Royal Mail date back to the 16th century. Until 2015 Royal Mail was a <u>nationalised</u> industry and was seen to have a <u>natural monopoly</u> position. In 2015 the business was <u>privatised</u> and became Royal Mail plc.

Despite having a natural monopoly, the UK still has one of the lowest price systems in the EU for domestic postage.   5

In the exam, before answering the question, make sure you read the stimulus material carefully, highlighting or underlining any key words and annotating with useful points. For example, you could annotate the key terms, 'nationalised', 'privatised' and 'natural monopoly': 'Prices are low due to government regulation'.

Extract B:

Royal Mail fined £50 million for breaking competition law

In August 2018 Ofcom, the communications regulator, fined Royal Mail £50 million for breaking competition law. The fine is for Royal Mail's actions in 2014 when one of its rivals, Whistl, was trying to become the first competitor for Royal Mail in the wholesale business mail delivery market. This involves collecting and delivering bulk mail from businesses to deliver to customers. Royal Mail retained the monopoly   5
position of collecting and delivering domestic (household) postage.

Ofcom found that Royal Mail had abused its dominant market position. In January 2014, Royal Mail issued contractual notices to change its wholesale prices for other postal operators to access its delivery network. These services, known as 'access mail', are worth £1.5bn to Royal Mail each year. They involve access operators such   10
as Whistl collecting and sorting bulk mail from large organisations – such as bank statements, utility bills and information from councils – before handing mail over to Royal Mail to complete delivery.

Any company wishing to collect bulk mail has no choice but to use Royal Mail's access mail services to deliver a large proportion of those letters. Royal Mail's   15
2014 price changes involved different price plans for wholesale customers, depending on whether they were able to hit mail volume targets for areas covering the whole of the UK. In practice, if a company wished to start delivering bulk mail in some parts of the country, as Whistl did, it would have to pay Royal Mail around 0.25p (1.2%) more per letter than companies that used Royal Mail to deliver across the whole   20
UK. In this way, Royal Mail sought to charge higher prices for the same services.

Whistl complained to Ofcom that Royal Mail's price changes were unlawful, and in February 2014 Ofcom opened an investigation under the Competition Act 1998.

Source: Ofcom.org

Exam skills 2: Paper 3

In each of Sections A and B, you must answer questions (a), (b) and (c), and then choose **either** question (d) or (e). The command words in Paper 3 are the same as you have encountered in Papers 1 and 2. The approach to answering the questions is also the same.

The exam-style questions below relate to the case study on page 210.

> **Links** You may find it helpful to revise government intervention on page 143.

'Discuss' questions

Questions (a)–(c) in Paper 3 may also include a 'discuss' question. For a reminder of the skills required to answer 'discuss' questions, see page 153. There is an exam-style 'discuss' question on page 153.

Worked example   (AL)

(a) With reference to Extracts A and B, explain one way in which Royal Mail did not act in the public interest. **(5 marks)**

Royal Mail was in a monopoly position and therefore had control over customers and other firms. Royal Mail increased the price that other firms, such as Whistl, had to pay. This was against the public interest as it had the effect of preventing competition. <u>As a result</u> prices were higher than they would be under conditions of <u>perfect competition</u>. This led to <u>consumers</u> spending more on postal services than might have been the case.

 The key here is your knowledge that a monopoly is a single supplier in a market.

 Some technical language is used appropriately, such as perfect competition and consumers.

 The response is clearly developed using phrases such as 'As a result…' and directly addresses the case study and Royal Mail's dominant position.

Worked example   (AL)

(b) With reference to Extracts A and B, examine the impact on the UK of the Royal Mail having a natural monopoly in domestic postal services. **(8 marks)**

Royal Mail has a natural monopoly as it is the only firm with responsibility for collecting domestic post. One positive impact of this position is the efficiency gains. Natural monopoly is characterised by increasing returns to scale at all levels of output – so the LRAC curve falls as production expands. Extract A points out that the UK has some of the lowest costs for postage. [This can be shown using a diagram showing the downward sloping section of an LRAC line.]

The diagram demonstrates that operating on a large scale leads to efficiency gains, which leads to lower prices for consumers. As a result, UK consumers benefit from these low costs.

However, one negative impact of Royal Mail's natural monopoly is …

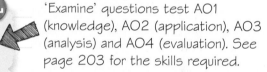 'Examine' questions test AO1 (knowledge), AO2 (application), AO3 (analysis) and AO4 (evaluation). See page 203 for the skills required.

 A good logically approached response which starts by showing knowledge of natural monopoly. Evidence is used from the source and then one positive impact – efficiency gains from natural monopoly – is identified. This is well analysed using clear chains of reasoning. An LRAC diagram (not shown here but see pages 116-117 for one to use) supports the analysis.

The response is in the context of the Royal Mail and uses evidence from the stimulus material.

Finally, consider what the main impact might be. Consider using the 'it depends' rule (see page 154). For example, if Royal Mail does not abuse its monopoly position, the impact of such a natural monopoly is positive.

Evaluation can occur throughout a response.

Now the student needs to identify a negative impact to show balance. For example, they might consider the ability of monopoly to charge higher prices, the inefficiency that can occur with monopoly and the fact that regulation will be required.

Exam skills 3: Paper 3

Questions (d) and (e) in Paper 3 Sections A and B are 'evaluate' questions each worth 25 marks.
You must answer **one**. This exam-style question and answer relates to the data on page 210.

 Links Revise monopolies on page 133.

Worked example

(d) With reference to information provided and your own knowledge, evaluate the microeconomic and macroeconomic effects on the UK economy of greater regulation of large firms.   **(25 marks)**

A monopoly exists when a single supplier exists in a market. Pure monopoly is rare. In a legal sense, a monopoly is said to exist when a firm has a 25% market share or more, such as Royal Mail and the delivery of business and domestic mail. To ensure that such firms operate in a way that is not harmful for consumers, the government uses a number of methods to control their behaviour. One method is through the use of regulators. In the case of Royal Mail, Ofcom is the regulator which controls the actions of the firm.

At a microeconomic level, monopolies lead to prices higher than would exist under perfect competition. In the diagram below the monopolist produces at the profit maximising level of output – where MC = MR. At this level price is P_1. Under perfect competition price would be lower at P_2, and output higher at Q_2. Also, the firm is not operating at a point of allocative efficiency (where P = MC), as P > MC.

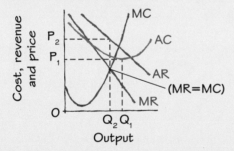

In this case the role of Ofcom is to ensure Royal Mail is not able to charge excessively high prices. So, price is closer to P_2 than P_1. In this way consumers benefit as the market is encouraged to operate more as if it were competitive rather than as a monopoly.

However, a problem with greater regulation is that the profits of the firm can be restricted, which leads to lower funds available for the firm to invest. This might lead to fewer innovations for the future and a lack of dynamic efficiency. Royal Mail has improved efficiencies over recent years, through digital sorting and delivery systems. This is beneficial for consumers as mail is delivered more quickly and accurately. Regulation, through bodies such as Ofcom, does not lead to greater efficiencies as such, but serves to limit price rises and the profitability of firms. Regulation in itself does not contribute to greater productive or allocative efficiency. ...

You need to write in essay style, using paragraphs. For a reminder of the skills required to answer 'evaluate' questions, see page 154.

Remember, in 'evaluate' questions you need to identify one or two microeconomic effects and one or two macroeconomic effects, before evaluating (for and against) each.

The student has outlined what is meant by monopoly and regulation, and refers to the case study. This is good contextualisation.

Positive microeconomic impacts are considered and a diagram is used. You should have a full range of economics 'tools' so as to be able to tackle questions like this.

The positive microeconomic impacts are evaluated – the student considers why greater regulation might not be effective. Weighing up different options is a route to evaluation.

The student now needs to consider macroeconomic impacts – for and against – before arriving at a conclusion. Your plan might be:

- Positive macroeconomic impacts of greater regulation.
- Evaluation of the macroeconomic impacts
- Conclusion – on balance, what is the effect of greater regulation?

Exam-style practice: data

On this page, you will find an exam-style case study for Paper 3. Before you answer the exam-style practice questions that follow on page 214, make sure you read the evidence carefully, highlighting any key terms and annotating useful points.

Changing habits: the use of indirect taxation

Extract A:

Do 'sin taxes' work?

Indirect taxes are used to persuade individuals not to consume products such as alcohol, tobacco, sugar, fatty food and so on. In the USA, 40% of people are now obese, up from 15% in 1980. Some US cities, along with other countries, have introduced a so-called 'sugar tax' on sugary drinks in recent years.

Policymakers are correct to believe that sin taxes lead to lower consumption. One   5
study suggested that a 1% increase in tobacco tax led to a 0.5% fall in sales. So, such taxes can be effective. One criticism of sin taxes, however, is that they are inefficient. A person who has an occasional alcoholic drink is treated in the same way – having to pay a higher price – than serious alcoholics. A similar logic applies to sugar taxes.

It is easiest to justify taxes on particular goods when they present what economists   10
call 'negative externalities'. When a driver buys fuel for his car, both he and the petrol station benefit. Yet cars emit carbon dioxide in their wake, which suggests that it would be only fair for drivers to pay taxes to offset the environmental damage they cause. Some policymakers argue that people who engage in unhealthy habits also impose negative externalities, since they tend to present taxpayers with bigger medical   15
bills. In practice, however, these costs tend to be overstated. While obese people probably do present net costs to governments, smokers tend to die earlier, meaning that they probably save governments money since they draw less from state pensions. Policymakers should still consider implementing sin taxes if they intend to intervene to change individuals' behaviour. But they should be aware that the bulk of the   20
damage that smokers, drinkers and the obese do is to themselves, and not to others.

Source: The Economist

> The case study and evidence will not necessarily be based on the UK. The qualification is set in a global context. The case study on this page is based on the USA.

Figure 1: The effect of sin taxes

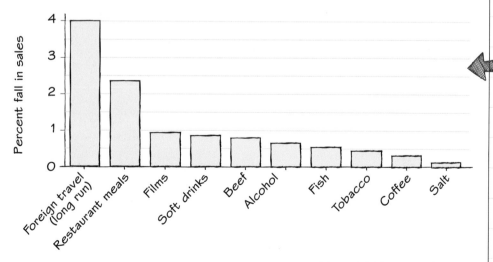

The effect in the US of a 1% increase in indirect taxes on different products.

Source: The Economist

> In the actual exam, you may have at least three pieces of evidence in total.

Exam-style practice: Paper 3

On this page, you will find exam-style practice questions for the case study on page 213.

There are answers on page 225 and page 226.

 Links For the exam-style questions below, you may find it helpful to revise demand (page 11), price determination (page 20) and government intervention (pages 35–37).

1 (a) With reference to Extract A, explain **one** possible cause of a rise in demand for goods such as alcohol and sugary drinks.   **(5 marks)**

 Make sure you refer to the evidence in your answer. Remember, when asked about a change in demand, there is an opportunity to use a demand/supply diagram.

(b) With reference to the evidence, examine the likely impact on an economy of increased rates of obesity.   **(8 marks)**

 As this is an 'examine' question, you will need to consider different impacts before considering the likely extent of this impact. Extract A gives you some clues here – make sure you read the evidence carefully.

(c) Discuss the likely impact of government intervention in the market to reduce levels of obesity.   **(12 marks)**

 Aim to spend 12–15 minutes on this question. Remember to use evidence from the sources in your answer.

You need to present your arguments and knowledge, and consider both the positive and negative impacts of government intervention to reduce obesity. Remember that a drawback of government intervention might be that government failure occurs.

You should write your response as an essay, dividing your work into paragraphs.

 Aim to spend 20 minutes on this question.

(d) With reference to the information provided and your own knowledge, evaluate the possible microeconomic and macroeconomic effects on an economy of increased use of indirect taxation.   **(25 marks)**

OR

(e) With reference to the information provided and your own knowledge, evaluate the possible microeconomic and macroeconomic effects of a reduction in government intervention in an economy.   **(25 marks)**

You could consider discretionary government policies, such as increasing the minimum wage, and also the effects of strong and sustained economic growth as something which will reduce poverty and inequality.

You need to present your arguments and knowledge, and consider both microeconomic and macroeconomic effects of reduced government intervention.

You should write your response as an essay, dividing your work into paragraphs.

Answers

1 Economics as a social science
1 An economic model is a simplification of how an economy or individual market works. Economic models can be used to forecast and explain the interactions between economic agents.
2 It is difficult to apply the scientific method in economics because individual variables cannot be isolated. Nor can control groups be used.

2 Positive and normative economic statements
1 Positive economics involves economic statements and theories that can be proven or rejected.
2 Normative economic statements are subjective and carry value judgements. They are difficult to prove.
3 Political decisions involve value judgements because there are multiple economic factors that influence the outcomes of political policy. For example, most political decisions involve trade-offs in society.

3 The economic problem
1 The factors of production are land, labour, capital and enterprise.
2 Scarcity is a problem because it means that all economic wants and needs cannot be satisfied for all people.
3 One opportunity cost for a car manufacturer is the decision to invest in a new car model. The opportunity cost of this decision might be the investment in promoting its existing range.

4 Production possibility frontiers: 1
1 A PPF shows the potential combinations of economic goods an economy can produce assuming all resources are fully and efficiently employed.
2 The margin involves a comparison of the additional (or marginal) benefits and costs of an activity.

5 Production possibility frontiers: 2
1 A capital good is a good that is used in the production of other goods, for example, a factory.
2 Productive efficiency is any point along the PPF. It is the lowest cost of production.
3 Allocative efficiency is the combination of economic goods that will lead to maximum social welfare.

6 Specialisation and division of labour
The benefits of division of labour are that it allows economies, firms and individuals to specialise, allowing for a greater range and quantity of goods to be produced and traded.

7 The functions of money
1 Money acts as a measure of value as it allows for the value of similar goods to be standardised against a monetary value. Without money, goods would have to be valued against other goods (e.g. 4 chickens = 1 goat).
2 Three forms of money that can be found in an economy are cash, near monies and money substitutes.

8 Types of economy
1 The market mechanism refers to a system where resources are allocated through the interactions of buyers and sellers.
2 Adam Smith was a proponent of free markets whereas Karl Marx believed that the greatest benefits to the population would be achieved through a planned economy.
3 In a command economy resources are allocated through central planning by the government through state-controlled industries.

9 Economic systems
1 In a free market economy, wealth is not distributed equally. Those who own resources are likely to have higher incomes than those that do not own resources.
2 Free market economies are the more efficient due to the existence of competition and the incentive to maximise profits.

10 Rational decision making
1 A consumer may choose to spend more money on one good instead of another if they believe the extra money spent will maximise their utility and outweigh the benefits of buying a cheaper good.
2 One factor an individual may consider when intending to maximise their economic welfare is how long it takes them to get to their place of work each day.

11 Demand
1 A movement along the demand curve will result from a change in price. For example, an increase in price will result in a contraction in demand.
2 A shift to the left in the demand curve means that demand has fallen. Demand will be lower at all given price points.

12 The conditions of demand
1 Real income affects demand because as incomes rise consumers will purchase more of all normal goods at any given price point.
2 A fall in the price of train fares will have the result of reducing demand for petrol as some people will switch from using their cars to commuting via train.
3 The law of diminishing utility is where consumers place less value on the last unit bought.

13 Price elasticity of demand
1 Elasticity is a measure of how much the quantity demanded will be affected by a change in price, income or another factor.
2 The formula for PED is $\dfrac{\Delta QD}{\Delta P}$
3 A good has inelastic demand when a percentage change in price will bring about a smaller percentage change in demand.

14 Graphical representations of PED
1 An inelastic good has a steep demand curve, therefore a change in price will have a proportionately lower impact on a change in the quantity demanded.
2 For a good that has perfectly inelastic demand (represented as a numerical value of zero), any change in price will have no impact on the quantity demanded.
3 A fall in the number of substitutes for a good will reduce its elasticity of demand – demand will become more inelastic.

15 Income and cross elasticities
1 An example of a complementary good for a smartphone would be headphones as these are typically bought with smartphones in order to listen to music.
2 Necessities have an income elasticity of demand between 0 and +1 because a change in price will lead to a relatively smaller change in the quantity demanded.

16 Elasticities of demand and revenue
1 A firm's revenue would be maximised when its price is equal to PED of 1 (plus/minus).
2 A government might use information on CED in order to understand the relationship between two goods, for example, the extent that Pepsi might be a substitute for Coca-Cola based on the relative change in sales of Pepsi as a result of a change in price of Coca-Cola (and vice versa).

17 Supply
1 A contraction in supply is where there is a fall in supply as prices fall – a movement along the supply curve.
2 Three conditions of supply are the cost of production, the price of substitutes and the impact of new technology.

18 Price elasticity of supply
1 The formula for price elasticity of supply is:

$$\dfrac{\text{percentage change in quantity supplied}}{\text{percentage change in price}}$$

2 A price elasticity of supply of 1.2 means that supply is price elastic, that is there is a more than proportionate response in the quantity supplied to a change in price.

19 Determinants of elasticity of supply
1 The production capacity of suppliers will influence PES because if suppliers can quickly increase (or decrease) supply then they will be better equipped to respond to a change in price. Where capacity of production is fixed, supply is price inelastic.
2 The long run refers to a period where all factors of production are variable – sellers and buyers can adapt.

20 Price determination
1 Demand and supply diagram:

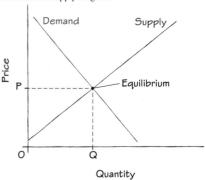

2 The market clearing price is the price where supply meets demand. All goods will be sold at this price.
3 Excess supply is where there is a greater quantity supplied than there are buyers in the market.

21 Changes in supply and demand
1 A shift to the right in the demand curve would create an expansion along the supply curve and result in prices rising.
2 A shift to the left in the supply curve would create a contraction along the demand curve and result in prices rising.
3 In theory, a market should always tend towards equilibrium due to the price mechanism. Excess supply will create a downward pressure on prices until equilibrium is reached through an increase in demand. Similarly, excess demand will put upward pressure on prices until supply rises in response and equilibrium is achieved.

22 The price mechanism
1 The price mechanism may ration a scarce resource by limiting the number of consumers or firms that are able to afford its purchase.
2 Excess demand will cause prices to rise. This creates an incentive for suppliers to produce more due to the profit potential. The market always tends towards equilibrium.

23 Price mechanism in real markets
1 One factor that may influence the supply of oil is the political conditions in an oil producing nation.
2 One factor that may affect the demand for housing is income levels in an economy. As incomes fall, consumers cut back on purchasing big ticket items such as houses.

24 Consumer and producer surplus
1 Consumer surplus will fall as a result of the demand curve shifting to the left.
2 Producer surplus will rise as a result of the supply curve shifting to the right.

25 Indirect taxes
1 An *ad valorem* tax is one where the cost of the tax levied increases with the price of the goods or service. For example, 20% VAT on goods priced £10 will be £2, while the VAT on goods priced £100 would be £20.
2 The incidence of tax is how the burden of a tax is distributed between consumers and producers.

26 The impact of subsidies
1 A subsidy is a grant given by the government to incentivise the production and consumption of a particular good or service.
2 A government might offer a subsidy to the fishing industry to make firms operating in the fishing industry more competitive in international markets.
3 The impact of the introduction of a subsidy will shift the supply curve downwards and to the right.

27 The effect of elasticities
One situation where a tax would wholly be paid for by a producer is where supply is perfectly inelastic – where supply does not change, no matter what the price.

28 Alternative views of consumer behaviour
1 A consumer may buy a product even though they know they can buy it cheaper elsewhere if they believe the effort required (time and energy) to purchase the other product is not worth the difference in the price.

2 Social norms can lead to consumers making decisions on the goods and services they buy that are based on social acceptance rather than the actual benefits, such as satisfaction, from the good or service itself.

29 Market failure

1 Externalities are an example of market failure because prices and profits do not fully take into account the costs and benefits of economic transactions. Where externalities are unaccounted for, things like the environment and social welfare can be eroded.

2 An example of an information gap might involve a consumer purchasing a washing machine, but not knowing what features they should be looking for or not knowing the average price of a washing machine they wish to purchase.

30 Externalities

Social cost = private cost + external cost
The social cost is greater than external cost because it also takes into account private costs.

31 Externality diagrams

1 The socially optimal level of output is the point where MSC meets MSB. It is the point where negative externalities are minimised or positive externalities are maximised.

2 The welfare loss area represents the cost to society of production or consumption between the free market equilibrium and the socially optimal level of output.

32 Impact of externalities and government intervention

1 Over-consumption of alcohol can cause negative externalities and lead to social problems because excessive consumption of alcohol can lead to such problems as domestic abuse, depression and family breakdown.

2 A government might increase the regulation of a market to ensure resources are allocated efficiently and minimise the risk of market failure through externalities.

33 Public goods

1 Two characteristics that distinguish public goods are non-rivalry and non-excludability.

2 Public goods are underprovided by free markets because the free rider problem means that there is no incentive for people to pay for the good.

34 Information gaps

1 Where there is asymmetric information, a seller may exploit a buyer by over presenting the benefits of a product, for example, over-selling the potential return on investment from shares and stocks.

2 A young person may not pay into a pension scheme, even though it will have considerable benefits for them in the future, because they are unaware of the long-term benefits for them at retirement age and instead choose to spend the money now to maximise their economic welfare, e.g. paying for a loan on a new car.

35 Government intervention 1

1 A government might introduce an indirect tax in order to reduce output to minimise the impact of a negative externality or to raise revenue to support the market/industry or contribute towards other government policies.

2 A limitation of increasing the rate of an indirect tax is an increase in the cost of production for producers. Producers will try to pass on the incidence of the tax but are likely to pay a proportion, which will depend on the elasticities of demand. An indirect tax could lead to a loss of jobs and lower competitiveness of some firms.

36 Government intervention 2

Introduction of a subsidy might correct market failure by encouraging consumers to consume more of a good that has positive externalities that might be otherwise under-consumed.

37 Government intervention 3

The government might choose to launch a campaign to inform the public of the dangers of excessive sugar consumption by children in order to educate the nation and influence buying habits in order to lower the demand and consumption of sugar, therefore reducing the negative externalities caused.

38 Government failure

1 A government might not always act in the best interests of society when it is influenced by an upcoming general election. In this case, political parties might make decisions that favour their supporters in the hope that they will get re-elected.

2 One example of an information gap that may lead to government failure is inaccurate scientific research into the causes of heart disease, leading to the government spending millions of pounds on treatments that have little impact on reducing heart-related illnesses.

39 Government failure in various markets

1 A quota might fail to reduce consumption or market failure if the level of the quota is set too high or too low.

2 A policy of setting a maximum price may fail as it could lead to under supply of a good because the profit incentive has been limited by the set price, which will be below the market equilibrium.

47 Exam-style practice: Section A

1　B

2
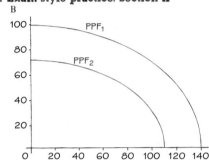

3　The government could have used a quota to manage fish stocks. This would involve the government setting a limit on the number of fish that could be caught each year, making sure that it was set at a sustainable level. This would prevent overfishing and would allow fish stocks to continue to grow.

4　C

5　One impact of the rise in value of white fish is that some customers may be reluctant to pay this higher price and may look to purchase relatively cheaper types of fish instead. Demand for these substitutes may rise which could lead to an increase in their price and increase in the quantity traded.

6　D

7　$22\% \div \dfrac{7.50 \div 6.00}{6.0} \times 100 = 25\%$

50 Exam-style practice: Section B

8　When drivers make decisions on whether or not to undertake a journey, they will balance the marginal benefit gained from the journey against its marginal cost so in a free market Q_1 journeys will be undertaken. However, as congestion creates negative externalities such as pollution this means that the marginal social cost is higher than the marginal private cost. Society would be better off with less congestion with the number journeys falling to Q_2. A congestion tax works like a tax as it increases the marginal private cost of travel, shifting it left. This will eliminate the deadweight welfare loss area of ABC.

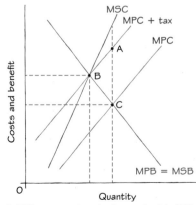

9　In 2017 government received approximately £160m of income from the London Congestion Charge, which was approximately £10m less than in 2015. Falling income means that there is less money available to pay for the costs of running the service or for investing in other areas of the transport network. For example, government may use some of the funds generated by the congestion charge to subsidise bus travel. With less income available, this subsidy may fall which would mean that bus travel may become more expensive and could deter some commuters from using the bus.

However, the fall in income is relatively small (approximately £10m between 2015 and 2017). The congestion charge is also still generating a surplus of income over expenditure of approximately £90m so the scheme is still self-funding and still generates a sizable surplus to invest in other areas of the transport network. The government will also benefit as the fall in income may have been caused by a fall in the number of motorists driving in central London. This will reduce negative externalities such as pollution which would have caused respiratory illness for local residents. The government will therefore benefit from less pressure on NHS services in London, allowing hospitals more time to treat other patients.

Overall, the impact on government from a fall in income from the congestion charge is likely to be minimal as income has only fallen by roughly 6% and the scheme still generates a surplus. However, the primary purpose of the congestion charge is to reduce traffic in central London. As the fall in income is a consequence of falling traffic levels then government will be pleased that the scheme is achieving its objectives.

10 (a) $\dfrac{£160m - £125m}{£125m} \times 100 = 28\%$

(b) $\dfrac{£12.5m}{£250m} \times 100 = 5\%$

11　One factor that could influence demand for bus journeys is the relative price of rail fares. Rail journeys are a substitute to travel via bus. This means that there is a cross-elasticity of demand between these two services. Cross-elasticity of demand measures the proportionate response of the quantity demanded of one good/service to the proportionate change in the price of another. Therefore, if the price of rail fares falls (perhaps through a subsidy by the government) it is likely that the demand for bus journeys will fall. However, this will depend on the bus route and there may not be a suitable alternative rail route.

Another factor that may determine demand for bus journeys is incomes. As incomes rise, many people will switch from inferior goods to luxury goods. Some people may consider travelling by car to be preferable to travelling by bus and as incomes rise they may be able to afford to travel by car instead. This will reduce demand for bus journeys. However, if a rise in incomes is also met with a rise in the price of petrol, then fewer people are likely to switch from buses to cars as fuel prices may counteract the benefit experienced from a rise in incomes.

12　A subsidy is money given to businesses or consumers in order to influence behaviour and correct market failure. There are social benefits of individuals using rail travel as a rise in the proportion of journeys taken by rail in comparison to car will help reduce congestion and CO_2 emissions. Another positive impact of rail travel is that it increases the mobility of labour, making jobs more accessible. The impact of a subsidy paid to Network Rail (EG) could result in ticket prices falling. This would increase the number of people (output) in rail journeys from A to B at the optimal level of output where welfare is maximised.

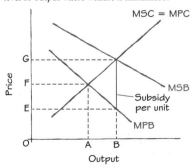

A negative impact of the increase in subsidy paid to Network Rail is the fact that rail ticket prices are already high and have been rising since 1995.

Between 1995 and 2017, prices have increased by an average of 121.3%. An increase in subsidy may have little impact on how customers perceive prices, if they already consider rail travel to be too expensive. Also, an increased subsidy may not bring down ticket prices. Network Rail may choose to use the subsidy to upgrade infrastructure instead. Although this may improve the service, it may also support a case for ticket prices to rise, which would adversely affect customers.

Overall, a subsidy should certainly help lower rail ticket prices as there will be an expectation that the subsidy will be passed on to consumers. Nevertheless, governments will only subsidise industries that need supporting and there may be many areas of spending that Network Rail need to focus on before they can lower ticket prices. In the long term, increasing the subsidy to Network Rail will benefit customers, but it is unlikely that they will see an immediate fall in the price of rail tickets.

13 Many visitors to London are likely to arrive by train or aeroplane and are therefore unlikely to have access to a car. While there are several options for travel around London, some of these visitors are likely to want to use taxis and private hire vehicles to visit major attractions. As such, it could be argued that taxis and attractions are complementary goods for some visitors. Therefore, an increase in demand for taxis would also lead to an increase in demand for tourist attractions. As a result of increased demand, attractions may be able to increase the prices they charge in order to ration access. This may lead to increased profitability which could mean that there is greater investment in improving the attractions over time, making them more dynamically efficient by, for example, investing in more interactive exhibits.

However, there is insufficient data to make a judgement on the impact on tourism as it isn't clear what the cause of increased taxi journeys is. It may be that people are increasingly using this method of travel to commute to work, especially given the cost of substitute travel, such as driving your own vehicle, has been rising. The benefit to particular tourist attractions may also depend on how accessible they are by other methods of transport. It is more likely that visitors will use taxis when it is difficult or time consuming to make the journey by bus or by the underground.

Overall the impact on tourism of an increase in taxi use and private hire vehicles is likely to be positive as a proportion of these journeys is likely to have been taken for leisure purposes. However, to make a more accurate judgement it would be useful to know the proportion of these journeys taken for leisure compared with commuting or other purposes.

51. Exam-style practice: Section C

14 A maximum price is when the government sets a limit on the price of a good or service which is below the market equilibrium price. By imposing a maximum price on rail tickets, this will reduce the cost of rail travel which means it becomes relatively cheaper compared with other methods of travel. Consequently, there would be an extension in demand for rail travel with demand rising from Q_2 to Q_3. At the same time some rail operators will find their profitability has fallen so there will be a contraction in supply from Q_2 to Q_1. As a result, there will be excess demand between Q_1–Q_3.

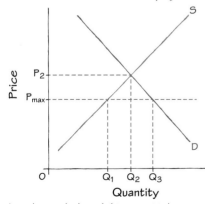

A maximum price is needed to prevent train operators abusing their dominant position in the market. As train operators are given franchises to run lines, this effectively gives them a monopoly

on that line for a period of time. During peak times the demand from consumers is likely to be quite inelastic. Many consumers use the train to commute to work, particularly those who find the cost of living in cities too high so have moved out of the city. Train operators have an incentive to increase prices for these consumers as there would be a less than proportionate fall in demand, therefore increasing revenues. With few alternative methods of transport available, many consumers would have no alternative but to pay these higher fares. A maximum price for rail tickets will help to keep train tickets affordable.

Another benefit of keeping train tickets affordable is that it helps to improve the geographic mobility of labour. If the price of rail tickets was too high, it would deter people from looking for work outside their local area and may make it more difficult for firms to recruit employees. This may be a particular problem for businesses in London where the high price of property means many can't afford to live and must commute in every day. Without these workers the London economy would not be as productive and labour costs would be much higher.

However, a problem of using maximum prices is the excess demand it creates. As more people wish to travel by train, and with firms looking to supply fewer train journeys, there is likely to be severe overcrowding, particularly at peak times. This is regularly the case in the UK with commuters often having to stand in cramped carriages for the entirety of their journey. It may also lead to individuals spending more time queuing to give themselves the best possible chance of boarding a train. This represents a severe cost to individuals in terms of the time wasted while doing this.

Another problem is that with lower profits train operators may begin to reduce levels of investment. With less certainty that they can make a return, they will spend less on improving the quality of train carriages. If supernormal profits fall there is less chance of dynamic efficiency being achieved which may mean that the quality of service provide to rail travellers begins to deteriorate further.

In conclusion, maximum prices can be a very effective way of preventing monopolies from abusing their dominant position. In situations where it is difficult to weaken the power monopolies have, then maximum prices are likely to be the best possible solution. However, there is a potential trade off as protecting consumers from higher prices in the short term may lead to worse outcomes in the long term if there is less finance available for firms to invest in their rolling stock.

15 Many believe that healthcare should be provided by government as it is a merit good which generates significant positive externalities. Many individuals may undervalue the benefits of consuming healthcare, possibly because they only consider the short term. A healthy population also has significant benefits for third parties. For example, if people are healthier they are less likely to be absent from work. Businesses will benefit from an increase in productivity which will allow them to reduce their average costs of production and increase profit margins if prices remain constant. The diagram below shows that in a completely free market the consumption of healthcare would occur where marginal private benefits equal marginal private costs, as individuals do not consider the benefits their consumption has on third parties. However, this means that healthcare would be under consumed as the socially optimal level of consumption occurs where marginal social benefits equal marginal social costs. This means that if consumption increased from Q_1 to Q_2 there would be a gain in welfare equal to the area ABC. There would be an improvement in allocative efficiency as more resources are directed towards healthcare.

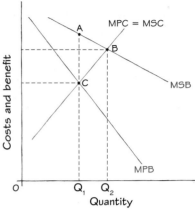

It could also be argued that healthcare should be provided free of change on equity grounds. In a free market healthcare would be unaffordable for many, particularly those on low incomes such as students, the unemployed and those in low-paid jobs. Many would argue that healthcare is a basic human right in a developed country and that it is not acceptable for some individuals to potentially die because they are denied access to healthcare they cannot afford.

However, it could be argued that providing healthcare free of charge has resulted in an overconsumption of healthcare. This has resulted in people making appointments with doctors which they fail to attend or people going to accident and emergency wards for trivial reasons. This is a highly ineffective use of scarce resources as too many resources are being allocated to the provision of healthcare. If consumers were forced to pay for their healthcare this would put less pressure on the system and would mean consumers would be less likely to make appointments for minor illnesses such as coughs and colds. Wastage and abuse of the system would be reduced as people will now only consume healthcare if the marginal private benefit is at least equal to the marginal private cost.

It could also be argued that as a state run monopoly the NHS is highly inefficient. The lack of competition may lead to inefficiency as there is little incentive to minimise costs and use resources efficiently. The lack of competition and profit motive also means there is less incentive to provide a high-quality service.

Finally, as the largest government run organisation in the UK and fifth largest employer in the world, the NHS is likely to suffer from significant diseconomies of scale. These occur when an increase in output leads to an increase in average costs of production. The complexity of running such a large organisation, difficulties of coordinating work and communication problems which are likely to arise mean that the costs of providing the service are likely to be high. This is witnessed regularly in the NHS with major cost overruns on IT projects which regularly fail to be implemented effectively.

In conclusion, it is difficult to argue that in the 21st century as a developed nation that we should not be able to provide universal healthcare for all. While there is some inefficiency and abuse of the system this is preferable to some individuals missing out as they cannot afford it. However, the current system of providing this free at the point of use is unlikely to remain sustainable with an aging population and continued strain on public finances. The government may need to consider implementing some minimal charges for services such as doctors' appointments to try and ration this scarce resource and ensure that consumers carefully consider whether treatment is necessary. However, it is important that these charges are not set at a level which would be unaffordable for those on low incomes.

52 Economic growth

1 GDP per capita is the national output of an economy divided by the estimated population.

2 The difference between GDP and GNI is that GNI takes into account net property income from abroad and not simply income generated within the economy. Examples include interest from foreign investments and remittance income.

53 Comparing economic growth

1 A basket of goods is a theoretical collection of goods that are used to represent the average prices across nations. The theoretical basket of goods can be used to calculate PPP and inflation.
2 To be part of the G7, the UK will have a high level of economic output as measured by GDP. It will also have advanced infrastructure and developed industries.

54 Limitations of measuring economic growth

1 When comparing GDP across nations, the actual quality of goods (in terms of utility) is not accurately measured. Furthermore, there are many goods and services that are not measured by national GDP and the proportion of these goods against those that are measured will differ across nations.
2 Income is not always a good indicator of economic well-being because the influence of real incomes on people's happiness diminishes past a certain level. For example, in a rich nation an increase of 10% real incomes for a poor family will have a greater impact on well-being than the same increase for a wealthy family. Real incomes are not a comprehensive indicator of the standard of living.

55 Inflation and its measurement

1 Disinflation is the reduction in the rate of inflation, e.g. from 4% to 2.5%.
2 An index number is an economic data figure that reflects prices compared with a standard or base value. The base year is set at 100. Therefore, an index of 102 will show a 2% increase in price from the base year.
3 One difference between CPI and RPI is that RPI takes into account council tax and other taxes.

56 Causes of inflation

1 Two factors that contribute to cost-push inflation are increasing wage rates and a rise in commodity prices.
2 Two causes of demand-pull inflation include a rise in consumer spending and a sharp rise in UK exports.

57 Impact of inflation

An inflation rate of 6% is undesirable because wages are unlikely to rise at the same rate and this lowers the buying power of consumers.

58 Employment and unemployment

1 The difference between unemployment and the inactive population is that those people included in the unemployment statistic are actively seeking employment.
2 In the UK, the unemployment rate is measured by the claimant count and the Labour Force Survey.

59 Causes and types of unemployment

1 Frictional unemployment is unemployment caused as people move between jobs as the labour market changes. However, structural unemployment is more serious and is where the supply of labour is persistently greater than demand.
2 Cyclical unemployment is caused by changes in the business cycle as the economy moves between periods of boom and recession.

60 The impact of unemployment

1 Two social problems that can be caused by high rates of unemployment are a rise in crime rates and family break-ups.
2 Migration helps the UK by increasing the size of the labour force and providing important skills that are in shortage. However, increased migration can also reduce wage rates through an influx of cheap labour.

61 Balance of payments

1 The balance of payments account is made up of the current account (trade in goods and trade in services), the capital account and the financial account.
2 A trade deficit means that the value of goods and services imported is greater than the value of goods and services exported. This means that there is a net deficit flow of money out of the economy.

62 The current account imbalances

1 A large, long-term trade deficit is bad for the UK because it could lead to a rise in unemployment caused by a lack of foreign demand for UK exports.

2 The current account is linked to the government's objective to maximise economic growth because a rise in imports leads to a flow of money out of the economy, which subsequently reduces aggregate demand.

63 Aggregate demand

1 If interest rates fall, households will be able to borrow money at a lower rate. This will result in an increase in consumption.
2 An increase in UK imports will result in a fall in aggregate demand.

64 Movements along and shifts of the AD curve

1 Inflation is an increase in average prices. Inflation of 3% represents an increase in average prices. Therefore, an increase in the average price level would cause a contraction along the AD curve because consumers' purchasing power would have been reduced.
2 If a government cuts spending and increases taxation, this will lead to a shift to the left of the AD curve. This is because government spending (G) is a factor in aggregate demand. If the government spends less, AD at any given price level will be lower.

65 Consumption

1 Disposable income is the income available for spending or saving after deduction of taxes and the addition of welfare benefits.
2 A rise in unemployment figures could lead to some people worrying about their job security of their own jobs. This will reduce consumer confidence and more people will cut back on spending due to the uncertainty of their future potential earnings.

66 Investment

1 Over time, capital stocks depreciate. If firms are to maintain the value and effectiveness of their capital stocks, such as factories and machinery, they must invest in order to replace them. The difference between new investment for growth and the replacement level of investment is known as net investment.
2 As the world economy grows and experiences a boom, investment in the UK will rise. This is because firms will invest in new capital stocks in order to meet the growing demand for UK exports.

67 Further influences on investment

1 A government might encourage firms to invest by reducing corporation tax. This would mean firms' profits rise and more profit can be retained to finance investment.
2 Animal spirits refers to the attitudes of business owners and their optimism and willingness to take a risk and invest for future growth.
3 If the base rate of interest falls, then new investments will be more profitable. This is because the repayments on loans used to finance investment will be less.

68 Government expenditure

1 Fiscal policy refers to government decisions around the level of government spending and the level of taxation.
2 A government might set a budget deficit in order to boost spending in order to stimulate demand in the economy and encourage economic growth without raising taxes, which could cut consumption and investment.
3 A government might cut back on spending in order to reduce a budget deficit and reduce inflation rates.

69 Net trade

A government may impose a tariff on a good in order to increase the price for domestic buyers. This will cut demand and reduce imports of that good into the country. This will help the net trade balance and protect domestic producers of that good.

70 Aggregate supply

1 SRAS is the short-run aggregate supply in an economy. SRAS is linked to changes in the average price level in the economy and responds in a similar way to the microeconomic supply curve.
2 The classical long-run aggregate supply curve is vertical because in the long run real GDP does not depend on the average price level. Changes in aggregate demand can only cause a temporary change in an economy's total output. The LRAS curve can be shifted when the factors of production change.

71 Factors affecting SRAS

1 If the government cuts corporation tax, the impact on SRAS will be for it to shift to the right. Aggregate supply will increase as firms' costs (taxation) will fall.
2 If world oil prices rise, SRAS will shift to the left. Oil is a key factor in the production and transportation of goods and will result in prices rising for firms.

72 Classical and Keynesian AS curve

1 The Keynesian AS curve is horizontal at low levels of output because an increase in real output will have minimal pressure on prices as excess resources are utilised.
2 In the Keynesian model of AS, costs will start to rise as the economy reaches full capacity because underutilised resources are being used, bottlenecks in production start to occur and there is a shortage of workers, forcing wage rates up.

73 Factors influencing LRAS

One way that government policy can increase the productive capacity of an economy is focusing on supply-side economics and investing in capital goods that will eventually lead to a shift to the right in LRAS.

74 National income

1 National output equals national income because the money spent by firms to create goods and services (national output as measured by GDP) is transferred to households who own the factors of production used to create the goods and services. This money then becomes the national income for households.
2 National income equals national expenditure because the money used by households to purchase goods and services (the national expenditure) comes from the national income of households generated through selling the factors of production (land, labour and capital) to firms.

75 Injections and withdrawals

Exports lead to an injection into the circular flow of income because exports lead to goods and services leaving the economy, but additional flows of expenditure from abroad enter the system. This expenditure then becomes income, which leads to greater output.

76 Changes in AD and AS

1 The axes on an AD/AS diagram represent the average price level in the economy (Y) and real output as measured by GDP (X).
2 The point where AD meets AS is known as the equilibrium level of real national output.

77 Perspectives on changes in AD

1 If the economy is at full employment, then output cannot be increased. An increase in AD will only have the impact of raising prices because there will be demand-pull inflation.
2 If there is excess capacity in the economy, then an increase in AD will only use up spare capacity, therefore there will be minimal pressure on the price level.

78 Changes in LRAS

1 A rise in LRAS will reduce the price level in an economy.
2 The classical model of AS suggests that in the long run AS is fixed. Any economy has a productive capacity. Real output may fall below this level, but it cannot exceed it. The Keynesian model suggests that where an economy is operating at less than full employment, such as in a recession, AS is horizontal and any increase in real output will not affect the average price level until the employment level starts to reach full capacity, where the average price level will start to rise.

79 The multiplier

1 Formula for the marginal propensity to consume: $\dfrac{\Delta C}{\Delta Y}$
2 $\dfrac{1}{1 - MPC}$

So $\dfrac{1}{1 - 0.6} = \dfrac{1}{0.4} = 2.5$

Therefore £50m × 2.5 = £125m

80 Marginal propensity to withdraw

1 MPW = MPS + MPT + MPM
2 The marginal propensity to import (MPM) is the proportion of a change in income that is spent on imports. The MPM is a withdrawal from the circular flow of income. The greater the MPM, the smaller the effect of the multiplier.

81 The impact of the multiplier on the economy

1 If interest rates rise this will encourage people to save rather than spend. This will ultimately increase the marginal propensity to save. A fall in interest rates will have the opposite effect.

2 The multiplier can be calculated without using MPC or MPW by calculating:

$$\frac{\text{change in real GDP}}{\text{initial change in spending}}$$

82 Causes of growth

1 Actual growth is measured by GDP and is an increase in economic activity fuelled mainly through an increase in aggregate demand.

2 Potential growth refers to an increase in LRAS – an increase in the long-run potential capacity of the economy.

3 An increase in net exports can lead to real growth as an increase in exports leads to an injection (flow of income) into an economy that will lead to a more proportionate increase in GDP.

83 Output gaps

1 A characteristic of a positive output gap is 'overheating' over-utilisation of resources, such as employees working overtime.
Other characteristics could include upward pressure on inflation, low rates of unemployment and higher business/consumer confidence.

2 A characteristic of a negative output gap is downward pressure on inflation due to falling AD.

84 The trade (business) cycle

1 Three characteristics of a recession are high rates of unemployment, business failures and easing pressure on inflation (possibly leading to deflation).

2 Two possible drawbacks of a boom period are rising levels of imports, leading to a balance of trade deficit on current account.

85 The impact of economic growth

1 Three possible benefits of economic growth are increased tax revenue for governments, improved incomes for households and increased investment in firms.

2 Three possible drawbacks of economic growth are an upwards pressure on inflation, damage to natural habitats, and inequalities between the wealthiest and poorest in society.

3 During periods of economic growth not everyone benefits. Often the wealthiest in society benefit from wealth creation, whilst the poorest may not see a short-term improvement in their incomes. In the long-term, economic growth leads to improved living standards, especially for developing economies.

86 Possible macroeconomic objectives 1

1 Lowering unemployment would help raise government revenue through income tax and lower the cost of benefits paid to those seeking employment. Lowering unemployment also reduces poverty and increases aggregate demand as consumption rises.

2 Inflation is linked to economic growth as a rise in aggregate demand will put upward pressure on prices unless the economy is operating below its productive potential.

87 Possible macroeconomic objectives 2

1 The government might set environmental targets linked to the destruction of natural wildlife habitats and targets around carbon emissions linked to global warming.

2 A government might set a deficit fiscal budget, therefore increasing the net borrowing, as an expansionary policy to boost economic growth and increase aggregate demand in the economy.

88 Monetary policy

Higher interest rates make saving more appealing as a higher rate is earnt on the balance of savings and borrowing becomes more expensive.

89 Fiscal policy

An example of a direct tax is income tax.

90 Historical examples

At the start of the Great Depression, the US government had a relaxed approach to economic policy, relying on free markets with minimal government intervention.

91 Supply-side policies 1

1 Free market supply-side policies aim to remove factors that may get in the way of a market growing successfully.

2 Two examples of supply-side policies used to incentivise investment are off-setting tax on investments in research and development and lowering the tax on company profits, in order to attract investment from firms.

3 Supply-side incentives may fail if they fail to get people into employment and increase poverty.

92 Supply-side policies 2

A government could increase competition in a market by privatising industries and removing 'red tape'.

93 Macroeconomic conflicts and trade-offs

1 Possible conflicts involved in policies used to raise AD are the consequences of upward pressure on inflation and the potential for increased demand to be spent on UK imports.

2 Two conflicts associated with improving the environment are the trade-off of capital investment in new factories and infrastructure on 'greenfield sites' and the trade-off of spending on other areas of the economy, such as education or healthcare.

94 Conflicts in economic policy

The limitation of using interest rates to control inflation is that high rates of interest may cut consumption and lower inflationary pressure, but it also has the impact of curbing investment (therefore limiting the productive potential of the economy) and appreciating the value of the currency (negatively impacting on UK exports).

102 Exam-style practice: Section A

1 A

2 A

3

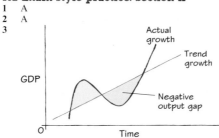

4 Drones may lead to lower costs of production and could improve the efficiency of firms in the economy. This may occur because of less congestion on UK motorways as distribution firms would not have as many lorries on the roads. In the short term the SRAS curve may shift to the right, reflecting the lower production costs which would come directly from more efficient distribution of goods and raw materials within the economy. This would reduce inflationary pressure and lead to an increase in economic growth. The rise in productivity due to reduced delivery times may also shift the LRAS curve to the right. The consequence for the UK economy would be an increase in productive capacity and ultimately long-run economic growth. Rising efficiency would also result in lower pressure on cost of production which may place downward pressure on inflation, allowing future increases in aggregate demand without the consequence of demand-pull inflation. The UK economy would also be likely to gain in terms of international price competitiveness due to improved efficiency which would lead to a rise in the demand for exports from the UK. This would result in the current account position moving from deficit to surplus in the long term.

5 $\frac{1}{1 - \text{MPC}} = 4$

X \$28BN = £112bn

104. Exam-style practice: Sections B and C

6 An increase in the quantity of wind turbines will increase the ability of the UK to produce energy which is required to produce goods and services. This would have the effect of increasing the productive capacity of the economy as more capital and consumer goods can now be made. This would lead to a shift outwards of the PPF curve or a shift to the right in LRAS.

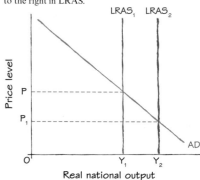

7 One consequence to the UK economy of a reduction in the consumption of coal is that structural unemployment may occur as workers in the coal energy sector may not have the transferable skills to work in other 'renewable' energy sectors. This would lead to a rise in the number of long-term unemployed which may increase government spending on welfare payments. This loss of employment may lead to a negative multiplier effect in certain areas of the UK which may result in further job losses and an increase in poverty levels.

Secondly, although the provision of renewable energy is increasing, it may take time to fully replace the supply which coal accounted for. There may be a short-term decrease in the supply of energy which may lead to an increase in market prices for homeowners and firms. If prices rise, this will increase cost of the production for firms which may lead to SRAS shifting to the left. This would potentially cause cost-push inflation and reduce economic growth.

8 The balance of payments account is a record of all financial dealings over time between countries. A key component of this is the current account which includes the trade in goods. Palm oil is a major export for both Malaysia and Indonesia. Therefore, as countries look for alternative sources of plant oil, it could reduce the demand for palm oil in these countries. This will reduce the balance of trade in goods and lead to net exports falling. As palm oil is a significant component of the economy in these countries it could lead to a trade deficit in goods.

On the other hand, trade in palm oil is only one industry and both countries will export many other popular goods around the world. If there is a growth in other exports such as wheat or minerals, then the impact of a fall in demand for palm oil might be limited. Similarly, Malaysia and Indonesia have very developed industries that specialise in the production of plant oils. It is likely that any alternative fuel will be developed and produced by these nations also.

Overall, the impact of growth in alternative oil-based crops will have a limited impact on the balance of payments on the current account for Malaysia and Indonesia. This is because palm oil remains the highest yielding crop. The growth of any alternative will not be as efficient and probably more expensive to produce. In the short term, palm oil will still dominate and be the main form of crop-based oil, but in the long term technologies will develop, and other crops may come to replace it as a more efficient alternative. Both Malaysia and Indonesia will have to develop their industries to ensure there is not a significant impact on this very important export industry.

9 The growth in palm oil as a component of food products and as a substitute fuel can significantly support countries like Malaysia in achieving its macroeconomic objectives. One important macroeconomic objective is economic growth. This is measured by an increase in GDP and will lead to greater employment opportunities in this industry and improved living standards due to rising incomes and wealth. As palm oil is a major export of Malaysia, growing international demand will increase net exports and support a surplus on the balance of payments on the current account.

However, increasing the production of palm oil in Malaysia has led to the destruction of rainforest in order to make room for palm oil crops. The preservation of natural habitats and the protection of the environment is another key macroeconomic objective. Malaysia will also face international pressure from NGOs such as Greenpeace and the World Trade Organization to limit the impact on the global environment of increased palm oil production. The growth of palm oil will create jobs, but it may also cause job losses in other farming industries such as grain and livestock. In turn, this could lead to national shortages in some types of food and the need to import from abroad.

There is a clear trade-off between the macroeconomic objective of protecting the environment and economic growth fuelled by the development of the palm oil industry in countries like Malaysia. However, this trade-off could be minimised by an effective environmental policy that helps sustain other industries and limits the impact of palm oil growth on areas of the rainforest. This might include the regeneration of land for farming or the development of oil-based crops that have a higher yield than palm trees. Subsidising other farming industries may also help protect jobs and incomes.

10 The growth of the renewable energy sector is likely to create new jobs and reduce unemployment levels. These jobs may be directly related to the industry itself or indirectly down the supply chain. This growth in employment will likely lead to a rise in incomes for households and stimulate more consumption in the economy as people are more willing and able to spend. Consumption is the largest component of AD so it is highly likely that AD will increase.

However, the growth of the renewable energy sector may not result in that many new jobs. In reality, many workers may be able to switch from the non-renewable sector as that declines. This would therefore not result in any additional income for households or corresponding increase in AD.

As the renewable energy sector expands, it is likely to require a significant amount of investment by both government and private sector firms in capital. As investment and government spending are both components of AD, it is likely to increase total levels of expenditure in the economy.

However, we need to consider the impact of depreciation of capital in the economy as a whole, in particular in the non-renewable sector. Although gross capital investment may rise, when taking into account depreciation, net capital investment spending may not increase as substantially.

It may also be argued that as the renewable energy sector expands it is likely to result in higher prices of electricity, particularly as, in the short term, economies of scale may not be exploited fully by the energy companies, leading to average costs being higher than what would otherwise have been the case with non-renewables. This may actually lead to rising costs of production for firms and less retained profits. As a consequence, firms in the economy may reduce investment spending in the short term, leading to a fall in AD. Households may be in the same position as energy prices rise, which would also lead to fall in consumption and therefore a further decrease in AD. It therefore depends on the market price of renewable energy as to whether or not AD will increase.

11 Ultra-low interest rates have resulted in a lowering of the cost of borrowing and a reduction in the incentive to save. Consumers and firms should therefore increase borrowing and spend more on both household goods and capital goods. C and I are both components of aggregate demand which should lead to the AD curve shifting to the right. This causes an expansion along the AS curve and an increase in the output of goods/services in the economy, ultimately leading to economic growth.

An increase in the demand for goods and services also results in a rise in the demand for labour. As a consequence, there has been a decline in the unemployment rate to record low levels of around 4%. This has a positive impact on the budget position of the government. Lower spending on benefits and increased tax revenues from income tax will most likely lower the budget deficit. This means that the government is more able to afford to increase spending on supply-side policies for the future benefit of economic performance.

The increased affordability of borrowing for firms has also led to a rise in spending on capital goods. The increased quantity of capital goods

in the economy has shifted the LRAS curve to the right. The represents a rise in the productive capacity of the economy and long-run economic growth. AD is now able to rise in the future to exploit this additional capacity without the risk of demand-pull inflation occurring.

However, as the bank rate has been reduced to such a low level, commercial banks may not pass on the reduction to firms and consumers. This is known as a liquidity trap. Given that the bank rate is already at historically low levels, this is less likely to happen and the real cost of borrowing would actually remain constant and would not lead to increases in AD or AS and any of the subsequent employment and growth benefits.

Given the time period that rates have been so low, there is now a risk that households and firms have borrowed too much and are therefore more highly indebted than ever before. They are therefore very exposed to any future rises in interest rates as the economy recovers and the central bank decides it is time to raise rates. The long-term effect of this is that disposable income may be reduced as rates increase which would lower consumer spending, leading to a fall in AD, a contraction along the AS curve and a reduction in national output. Lower national output of goods and services would ultimately reduce economic growth along with the demand for labour and increase unemployment levels.

Overall the decade long period of low interest rates has been effective at bringing the UK economy out of the financial crisis and back to recovery, almost certainly improving economic performance in the short term. However, the difficulty for policy makers today is in how to increase rates back to any kind of 'normal' level without causing an economic shock. The longer term consequences of low rates may therefore be more harmful than expected.

105 Why some firms grow

1 As a firm grows in size it can benefit from economies of scale, which means lower average costs. This helps to reduce risk as it allows the firm to reduce price and therefore maintain or enhance competitiveness.

2 Reasons why a firm may not want to grow in size (any two): A. To maintain close relationships with customers. B. Lack of finance. C. Operates in a niche market.

3 The principal–agent problem is a situation that can occur in larger firms where the shareholders ('principal') have different objectives to managers ('agent') leading to conflict which can impede the performance of the firm.

106 Public and private sector organisations

1 Private sector organisations are assumed to have profit maximisation as an objective, whereas public sector organisations have social goals such as providing a high quality service.

2 Not-for-profit organisations are those which conduct business without the purpose of gaining a profit for the owners or managers. With private organisations, profits are distributed to shareholders. With not-for-profit organisations, surpluses are instead used to fulfil the objectives of the organisation.

107 How firms grow

1 Examples of forward vertical integration include:
A. dairy farm merges with a cheese producer
B. double-glazing manufacturer merging with a retailer of doors and windows.
Examples of backward vertical integration include:
A. steel manufacturer buying iron ore mines
B. car manufacturer merges with a tyre manufacturer.

2 A merger is where two or more firms join together by mutual agreement to become one single entity. On the other hand, a takeover is where one firm buys another firm. This might not be by agreement, such as a 'hostile takeover'.

3 An aerospace company merging with an airline would be an example of forward vertical integration as it involves an aeroplane manufacturer merging with a business which uses these aeroplanes to provide a service.

108 Advantages and disadvantages of growth

1 Possible advantages of growth using vertical integration (any two):
  • The firm has more control over its supply chain.
  • Economies of scale.
  • Speed – quicker growth than by organic means.

2 One advantage is that the firm will control a stage earlier in the supply chain, which will guarantee supplies of the standard and quality that the firm requires.

109 Constraints on business growth

1 Business owners may have high profits, high dividends or market share as their business objective.

2 Regulation places a limit on the actions of firms. For example, a business may believe that it can increase its sales by selling alcohol to under-age customers. If it could do this, sales would increase and the business would grow. However, regulation prevents this by placing age restrictions on such sales.

110 Demergers

1 Synergy exists when two or more activities are combined and result in increased output or productivity. For example, a web developer joining with a photography company might result in attracting a greater number of customers across both services.

2 Three possible reasons for demergers include:
  • cultural differences
  • larger companies can find it more difficult to manage the larger workforce
  • due to competition authorities requiring a split.

111 Revenue 1

1 Marginal revenue is the addition to revenue as a result one extra unit of output.

2 Marginal revenue = £15
$\left(\dfrac{\text{change in revenue}}{\text{change in quantity}} = £\dfrac{15}{1} = £15 \right)$

3 If a business sells 10 units for £7 each, total revenue = £70.
The average revenue per unit is $\dfrac{70}{10} = £7$. This is the same as price.

112 Revenue 2

1 When demand increases due to falling prices, marginal revenue (MR) falls by proportionately more than the fall in price. This is because the lower price is paid by all consumers and not only the marginal consumers.

2 If demand is price inelastic, a rise in price will result in a smaller proportionate change in quantity demanded. As a result of this revenue will increase. Alternatively, if demand is price elastic, a rise in price will result in a larger fall in quantity demanded. Consequently, revenue will fall.

11 3 Costs

1 Examples of fixed costs may include rent, salaries, insurance.

2 Variable costs are those directly linked to the level of output. As output changes, these costs also change. For example, a bakery will use more flour if it increases its production of bread.

3 As variable costs increase as output rises, so the TVC curve – which shows variable costs – slopes upwards to reflect the impact of variable costs.

114 Short-run cost curves

1 Additional workers are initially able to increase the level of marginal output. However, adding more of a variable factor – workers – to a fixed stock of capital means that eventually workers are unable to access machinery. The effect is that additional workers add less marginal output than the previous worker. Diminishing marginal productivity is said to exist.

2 If AC is £10 and the MC of an additional unit of output is £9, then AC must fall. The MC of £9 has the effect of reducing overall AC.

3 If the marginal cost of an additional unit of output is higher than the average cost, then it follows that the average cost must increase.

115 Economies of scale

1 Larger firms are able to borrow money more cheaply because they are seen as less risky by lenders such as banks. They are more able to repay any loan they receive due to their higher levels of cash flow and profitability. They also have more assets, such as land and capital, which can be used as collateral should the firm be unable to repay a loan. Hence, banks are more likely to offer a lower rate of interest.

2 Buying in bulk can lead to suppliers offering lower unit prices, as they are selling on a larger scale with a smaller profit margin per item.

116 Diseconomies of scale

1 Two disadvantages of a firm growing in size are co-ordination problems and lack of control.

2 If a firm cannot communicate quickly and clearly with its large workforce, messages and instructions may be misunderstood. This can lead to higher average costs as incorrect actions following unclear communication might lead to resources and materials being wasted and thus leading to higher variable costs which then impact on average costs.

117 Profit

1 Examples may include: rent, wages, raw materials, advertising (any three).

2 Normal profit is the amount of profit a firm needs to make in the long run in order to remain in the market.

3 At this level of output MR is greater than MC. This means that by increasing output the total amount of revenue received will be higher than TC for the same increase in output. Therefore, profit will increase.

118 Supernormal profit and losses

1 Examples may include:
   • The objectives are not profit maximisation, but rather survival in the short-run.
   • Alternatively, if a business can pay its variable costs in the short-run and make some contribution to fixed costs, then it may be prepared to continue in operation.

2 Normal profit occurs where AC = AR. Supernormal profit is a short-run possibility for firms in perfect competition, and occurs where AR>AC.

3 Supernormal profit can occur when a lack of competition exists which would otherwise compete away the profits made by existing firms. A lack of competition might exist because of high barriers to entry in an industry. As a result of this, if a firm is making very high – supernormal – profits, these cannot be competed away as rival firms cannot easily enter the market.

119 Business objectives

1 Objectives of firms may include profit maximisation, revenue maximisation or sales maximisation.

2 If workers belong to a trade union, they can negotiate collectively on matters such as pay and conditions. A trade union can represent workers in meetings with the management to agree pay levels, for example.

120 Profit maximisation

1 In the long run all factors of production are variable, whereas in the short run some are fixed.

2 If a firm can cover variable costs in the short run, such as costs for labour and raw materials, and make some contribution towards fixed costs, then production can continue in the prospect of higher future sales and revenue.

121 Profit maximisation: diagrams

1 If a firm increases output then it will have incurred costs in producing the product, and also gained revenue from its sale.

2 If MR is greater than MC as a result of producing an additional unit of output, then profit will increase (or loss will be minimised). As such this is not the point of profit maximisation. Higher profits can be gained by increasing output, to the point where MC = MR.

122 Revenue maximisation

1 A business may have an objective of revenue maximisation due to the divorce of ownership from controls. Managers may have the objective of maximising revenue due to a link to their pay. Providing this does not compromise the ability of the firm to generate profit, this can be an objective.

2 If MR is higher than 0, then more revenue can be generated by increasing output.

123 Sales maximisation

1 Sales maximisation is achieved where:
   average revenue (AR) = average cost (AC).

2 A business may have an objective of sales maximisation due to the divorce of ownership from controls. Managers may have the objective of maximising sales due to a link to their pay. Providing this does not compromise the ability of the firm to generate profit, this can be an objective.

124 Satisficing

1 A firm may decide not to pursue profit maximisation as a business objective because managers may have other objectives and priorities. This can be explained by the divorce of ownership and control.

2 Satisficing may be described as 'aiming for the easy life' because the aim of managers is not to strive, at all costs, to achieve the highest level of revenue at the lowest level of costs (profit maximisation). This can lead to conflict within firms, for example, if workers are required to accept lower wages. Satisficing involves working to achieve acceptable levels of profit and sales.

125 Productive efficiency

1 Point C lies outside the PPF and is therefore unattainable.

2 In the long run all factors of production are variable. This means that it is the period of time in which a firm might invest in new machinery, equipment or skills. This results in a lower AC curve, showing lower average costs for different levels of output.

126 Other types of efficiency

1 Two possible reasons:
   • Size – larger firms can be more difficult to control and co-ordinate.
   • Costs – if costs are not carefully managed, this can lead to higher average costs.

2 At P = MC, the price that consumers are willing and prepared to pay for a product is equal to marginal costs of producing the product. If P > MC then consumers place a higher value on the last unit of output than it cost to make.

127 Perfect competition

1 Perfectly competitive firms are 'price takers'. They can supply as much as they can to the market without influencing the market price.

2 If a firm sells one more unit of output at the prevailing market price, then its AR will increase by the same amount. As P will not change, this will be the same as MR.

3 A homogeneous product is one that is identical to the products produced by other firms. For example, commodities such as coal and wheat are effectively the same wherever they are produced.

128 Perfect competition in diagrams

1 Possible reasons include:
   • To take advantage of the high (supernormal) profits earned by existing firms in the market.
   • To expand into different markets.

2 A perfectively competitive firm produces at the point where profits are maximised. This is always where MC = MR.

129 Monopolistic competition

1 A non-homogeneous product is one which can be differentiated from other products.

2

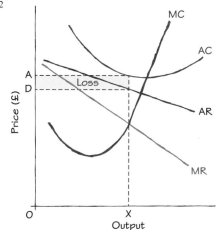

3

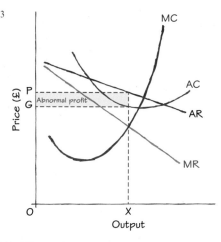

130 Oligopoly 1

1 Examples include: banking, brewing, car manufacturing, steel manufacturing (any three).

2 3-firm concentration ratio: 72.4% (add the market share of the three largest firms, then divide by the total value of the market:
$$\frac{40 + 35 + 30}{145} \times 100$$
5-firm concentration ratio: 96.5% (add the market share of the five largest firms, then divide by the total value of the market:
$$\frac{40 + 35 + 30 + 20 + 15}{145} \times 100$$

131 Oligopoly 2

1 With a small number of firms operating in a certain market, there will exist some uncertainty as to what actions competitors will take. If one firm decides to increase prices, will other follow, or will they retain their relatively lower prices and therefore secure a competitive advantage? Firms do not know with certainty how competitors will respond and so uncertainty is said to exist.

2 Collusion involves collective agreements between firms that help to ensure that they do not need to compete based on price competition.

132 Competition in oligopolistic markets

Examples of non-price competition include: branding, loyalty cards, product differentiation, advertising, celebrity endorsement.

133 Monopoly

1 If the firm reduces price, from £10 to £9, then all customers enjoy this lower price. This means that the MR from this level of output is lower than for the previous (higher) level of output.

2 Examples of barriers to entry: legal barriers, sunk costs, anti-competitive practices, natural cost advantages (any two).

3 If rival firms cannot enter an industry – tempted by the high levels of profit that are possible – then there is no incentive for the incumbent firm to reduce prices or to generally operate in a more competitive manner.

134 Price discrimination

1 Third degree price discrimination involves a firm charging different prices to different customers for the same product. This is achieved as the customers must have different PEDs. For example, with air tickets the demand of business travellers is much less price elastic than that of customers using air travel for leisure purposes. Business travellers need to be in a certain place at a certain time. Their firm is likely to be paying for their travel. Therefore, their demand is inelastic. Leisure travellers have much more flexibility in when, and what time, they travel. Their demand is therefore more price elastic. The monopolist is therefore able to treat the two markets separately and thus maximise profits.

2 Possible conditions for third degree price discrimination include (any two):
   • market power
   • information
   • limited ability to resell.

135 Monopsony
1 The NHS is an employer. It employs many doctors and nurses and is the main employer of these groups – it buys their services. The NHS therefore plays a key role in setting the wages levels of these groups – it has market power as a buyer and is therefore a monopsonist.
2 As a monopsonist pays a lower price for its supplies than it would under competitive conditions, it can pass on these lower costs to consumers in the form of lower prices.

136 Contestability
1 Contestability refers to how open a market is to competition. If new firms can easily enter and exit a market and compete with incumbent firms, then the market is said to be contestable.
2 If sunk costs are high, a new entrant risks losing lots of money in setting up a business in this market if it is unsuccessful and is forced to leave the industry. High sunk costs thus reduce the incentive to enter a market. This can have the effect of reducing the likelihood of new firms entering the market.

137 Demand for labour
1 Marginal revenue product (MRP) is the value of the physical addition to output from an extra unit of variable factor.
2 If the demand for ice cream falls, the demand for workers that produce ice cream will consequently fall. This is because the demand for ice-cream workers is derived from the demand for ice-cream itself.

138 Supply of labour 1
1 Opportunity cost is what is given up when a choice is made. A worker may give up increased time to spend on things other than work, such as leisure.
2 There is a large volume of low-skilled workers. A small increase in wages will see a greater than proportionate increase in supply of labour to this occupation. Many low-skilled workers may be unemployed, and they will be attracted to apply to an industry where wage rates are increasing.

139 Supply of labour 2
Possible examples include:
Education – improve general skills and qualifications.
Improve job centre guidance.

140 Wage determination 1
1 The productivity of workers may increase through (any three):
- Improved technology.
- More flexible working practices or
- Improved motivation of workers.
- Fringe benefits, such as company car, private health insurance.
- Opportunities for career progression.
2 A fall in the demand for labour means that fewer workers are required at the existing wage rate. As a result, excess supply is created which leads to wages being forced down.

141 Wage determination 2
Increased automation will lead to lower demand for workers in the particular industry, which will lead to higher unemployment of workers with these skills.

142 Government intervention 1
If a minimum wage were set below the equilibrium wage rate, workers would choose jobs where employers were paying the market (equilibrium) rate, which would be above the minimum rate.

143 Government intervention 2
1 For the purpose of regulation in the UK, a firm is considered to have monopoly power if it supplies 25% or more of the market.
2 A monopoly does not have the pressure of market forces to influence its decisions. In a perfectly competitive market, if a firm were to produce poor quality products it would lead to customers shifting to other suppliers which offer higher quality and, as a result, the firm would have to improve quality or leave the market. Under conditions of monopoly there are no such pressures. The government therefore has a role to play in controlling the behaviour of businesses with monopoly power which might otherwise exploit consumers.

144 Competition and contestability 1
1 Possible ways in which the government can promote contestability (any three):
- enhancing competition,
- deregulation and
- competitive tendering.
- privatisation.
2 By reducing the amount of regulation associated with starting a business, new entrants will be encouraged to enter different markets. The costs of starting a new business are sunk costs which cannot be recovered if the firm leaves an industry. Reducing the costs of starting a business will reduce sunk costs and therefore encourage new entrants.

145 Competition and contestability 2
1 Possible disadvantage of competitive tendering: Firms which are trying to win contracts to supply the public sector may exploit workers to win the contract, for example, by paying lower wages to keep costs down.
2 Large service providers have a range of expertise to supply different parts of the state sector. As a private sector firm it benefits from economies of scale which means it can provide the same service that the state might provide but for a lower average cost.
3 Possible ways in which the government can promote the creation of small businesses (any three):
- lower taxes for small business start-ups,
- business start-up grants and
- government policies promoting enterprise.
- national enterprise competitions
- education – raising awareness and knowledge of business and enterprise.

146 The impact and limits of government intervention
1 Possible methods the government could use to reduce prices to consumers (any two):
- lower taxes on spending – e.g. VAT
- subsidies for producers
- introduction of maximum prices (through regulators).
2 Asymmetric information is where imperfect information exists in a market. This may involve one party, such as the buyer, having more information than the seller.

155 Exam-style practice: Section A
1 B. A and D will affect the supply curve. B and C affect demand, but it is B which will cause the increase in demand.
2 $\dfrac{\% \text{ change in QD (+18\%)}}{\% \text{ change in price (−12\%)}} \times 100 = 1.5$
3 B Where MC = MR

157 Exam-style practice: Section B
4 An increase in the supply of vegetables will result in the supply line shifting to the right, as shown in the diagram.

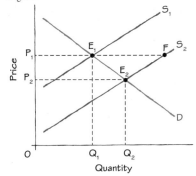

As a result of this increase, excess supply is created. This is shown by the difference between EF. As a result of this excess supply of vegetables, price is forced downwards to P_2 from P_1.
5 A monopsony is a single buyer within a market. This position can have significant impacts on consumers. A first impact is that monopsonists can ensure that they secure favourable prices from suppliers and that this can then lead to better value for money for consumers. By supermarkets having close relationships with farmers who produce the wonky vegetables, they can agree prices that are beneficial for the farmer, consumers and the owners of the supermarket. Extract C states that sales of the wonky vegetables is 'booming', with extra sales worth £500 million. This suggests that consumers are happy with the product and the price.

However, monopsony power can be abused and can increase the pressure on farmers. As the sole buyer, supermarkets can effectively dictate the price they are prepared to pay for the wonky fruit and vegetables. As these products are marketed by the supermarkets and are not as easily sold through other markets, farmers are left with little option but to sell at the stated prices. Whilst in the short run this might help consumers, if this results in farmers going out of business, this may lead to future potential supply problems and might leave the UK reliant on foreign suppliers and volatile global prices.
6 One impact on the farming industry is an increase in productivity when producing fruit and vegetables. As much of the produce which was previously not suitable for sale – Extract A suggests that up to 15% is wasted – is now popular (Extract C), farmers are selling more of what they produce. This leads to a reduction in average costs and a rise in profitability. As the farming industry can be viewed, in some ways, to be perfectly competitive, this can lead to a situation of supernormal profits, as shown in the diagram below:

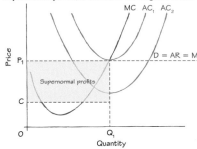

However, in the longer run this might lead to a reduction on the barriers to entry in the industry, as the potential for profitable activity is raised. This may potentially lead to an increase of supply in the industry as new entrants are tempted in. This can be shown using a diagram:

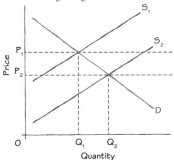

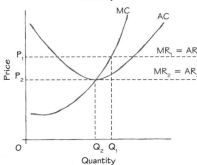

As a result of the increased profitability, supply shifts to the right and therefore causes a reduction in price to P_2, which results in the supernormal profits being 'competed away' by new entrant farmers,
In conclusion, the growth of sales of 'wonky vegetables' by supermarkets has some potentially significant consequences for the farming industry, most notably through the impact this has on efficiency. The theory above suggests that whilst this might lead to higher profits in the short run, in the long run the dynamic effects of the market may well lead to lower prices and lower profitability.

158 Exam-style practice: Section C
7 Suggested essay plan:
   1. Begin by explaining some of the problems with monopoly. Some of the issues include the ability to charge higher prices than firms in competitive markets, lower incentives to be efficient or to

innovate, allocatively and productively inefficient. Use a diagram in this part of your response.

2. Next, balance your response by considering the extent to which monopolies might be a good thing. You could consider:
   - high (abnormal) profits can be used for R&D – for example, pharmaceutical companies use their monopoly power and profits to develop new medicines
   - monopoly power means powers to match global companies – important in an age when globalisation is a reality
   - cross-subsidisation may lead to an increased range of goods or services available to the consumer.

3. In your conclusion, you could suggest how the answer to the question depends on which stakeholder group is involved. For example, consumers typically face higher prices as a consequence. However, high profits allow key investment to take place, for example, in pharmaceuticals and electric cars.

8   Zero hours contracts involve individual workers not having a contract of employment providing a set number of hours. Workers can be used by firms for any number of hours each week, according to the needs of the firm.

One effect of this for firms is to reduce average costs (AC), as they do not have to pay workers when demand is low and there is little work to do. The effect is to increase productivity. The effect on AC can be shown using the following diagram:

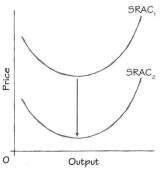

Lower average costs should lead to increased profits for firms, and therefore the effect of zero hours contracts can be regarded as a positive development for firms. However, a problem with zero hours contracts is the impact they can have on the motivation of employees, which itself can impact on productivity. If workers do not feel valued by their employer, and possibly believe they are being treated unfairly, this may well lead to them feeling less committed and becoming less productive. In this case the reverse of the first argument is true; such contracts may well lead to increased AC, from $SRAC_2$ to $SRAC_1$.

Another impact of such contracts is the flexibility they can offer to workers. Many people today – from students to older workers – actually prefer the flexibility offered by such contracts, which are offered by an increasing number of firms. As society moves to a more 'on demand' model – from takeaways, to home delivery, to peer-to-peer services (such as Uber) – so there is an increased demand for workers that this flexible approach appeals to. Zero hours contracts fit into the way the micro economy operates today.

However, one problem with this flexibility is the fact that it leads to increased in-work poverty, with many people not able to earn enough each week to avoid being reliant on benefits. This then has knock-on effects in the housing market, with fewer people able to buy their first home. The effect of this is to increase the gaps that exists between high-income and low-income families, and the distribution of income and wealth. Zero hours contracts actually contribute to the greater inequalities that exist in society.

In conclusion, the microeconomic impact of banning zero hours contracts depends on the individual firm and individual workers. There is no doubt that the rise of the so-called 'gig economy' is regarded as a positive thing for some workers. Those who prefer flexible working patterns can take advantage of not being tied to a particular contract and a particular number of hours. Students, for example, have found they can fit work into their studies and avoid times when less convenient. For

firms this can lead to lower labour costs as they are not fixed to contracts, which might not be beneficial for the firm. Lower unit costs leads to improved productive efficiency. In these cases, the ban would clearly be seen as a negative development. However, some economists argue that such a ban is necessary to avoid a 'race to the bottom' in terms of employment practices. As firms shift to a greater reliance on zero hours contracts, so workers are increasingly finding it difficult to earn enough money for things such as rent or mortgages. There is an equity argument against such contracts. A final decision on the effectiveness of the ban depends on the point of view being considered. For firms such as Uber, zero hours contracts are an essential part of the business model. Consumers who use Uber benefit directly from lower costs of taxi rides. For workers, however, who may prefer to have more job and income security, banning the zero hours and the 'gig economy' contract might be music to their ears.

159 Globalisation

1   Possible examples of firms operating on a global scale (any three): Apple, McDonald's, Rolls Royce, Samsung, VW.

2   A tariff is a tax paid on imports into a country. This has the effect of increasing the price of these goods and services.

160 The impacts of globalisation

1   Two possible environmental impacts of globalisation may include:
   - increased carbon emissions due to transportation and
   - deforestation, as more forests are cleared for factories or to create space for farmland.

2   One possible benefit of globalisation is that, as firms begin to operate on global scale, so they are able to increase profits and this may feed through to higher wages for workers.

161 Specialisation and trade 1

Possible reasons why a country may have an absolute advantage when producing a certain good (either one):
   - The country might have a plentiful and ready supply of the resources to produce the product. Russia, for example, has large reserves of natural gas and has an absolute advantage in its production when compared to countries such as France.
   - The country has the skills and expertise in its workforce to give the absolute advantage. For example, the UK has expertise in financial services and can deliver such services more efficiently than other countries.

162 Specialisation and trade 2

1   International trade s occurs where different countries sell goods and services to each other, as opposed to only domestic trade. A UK consumer buying a German car is an example of international trade.

2   The theory of comparative advantage makes the assumption that transport costs do not exist. In reality, transport costs are a key aspect of international trade, and can be a significant cost for producers.

163 Pattern of trade

1   1955: $\frac{3.4 + 1}{17.6} \times 100 = 25\%$

2014: $\frac{412.1 + 122.6}{1593.4} \times 100 = 33.56\%$

The value of imports has increased since the 1950s.

2   One explanation for the UK's changing pattern of trade is the changing comparative advantage that exists in the production of manufacturers. Foreign countries with low labour costs have gained an advantage in manufacturing, whereas in more developed countries the comparative advantage is with the services sector.

164 Terms of trade

1   Country's terms of trade index $= \frac{108}{120} \times 100 = 90$

2   A fall in the exchange rate will have the effect of increasing the price of imports which will, *ceteris paribus*, lead to a deterioration in the terms of trade.

165 Trading blocs

1   A common market has the same features as a free trade area, such as the removal of trade barriers between member states, but also includes the free movement of factors of production, such as labour and capital.

2   One possible benefit arising from a regional trade agreement is that trade between member states increases, which will lead, all other things being equal, to increased economic growth and falling unemployment.

166 World Trade Organization (WTO)

1   The World Trade Organization (WTO) is an international organisation which sets rules for trade between nations.

2   The WTO acts as an 'international regulator' in making sure that countries stick to WTO rules and agreements. Where countries do not do this, the WTO will investigate and ultimately make a judgement. This ensures that no countries are able to avoid the internationally agreed rules and that businesses are able to compete on a level playing field.

167 Restrictions on free trade

1   Possible reasons why countries might choose to restrict free trade (any three):
   - protection of domestic industry,
   - protect against dumping
   - correct imbalances in the balance of payments.
   - to protect jobs,
   - to ban certain goods.

2   A tariff is a tax on an imported product and has the effect of increasing the price of this good. This causes demand to be lower than would be the case if the market was perfectly competitive.

168 Impact of restrictions on free trade

Quotas will limit the physical quantity of a product and may result in less supply being available for consumers. The effect of the lower supply can be to increase price.

169 Balance of payments

The current account covers the country's trade in goods and services, whereas the capital and financial accounts cover the transfer of non-monetary and fixed assets.

170 Exchange rate systems

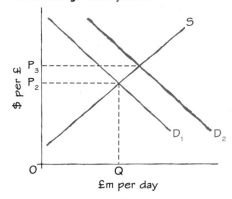

171 Exchange rate systems and competitive devaluation

Possible effects of changes in the exchange rate in an economy (any two):
   - Impact on the balance of payments position – if the exchange rate falls the current account position should improve.
   - Economic growth can occur if the exchange rate falls as exports become cheaper for foreign consumers.
   - Inflation – an increase in the exchange rate makes imports cheaper and puts downward pressure on inflation.

172 Changes in exchange rates

1   The effect on economic growth of a rise in the exchange rate will be that imports will become less expensive and exports more expensive for foreign consumers. Net exports will therefore decrease, causing a fall in the rate of economic growth.

2   The J-curve effect shows that imports will become cheaper and therefore demand will increase. At the same time, exports to foreign consumers will become more expensive. As a result, the current account position will deteriorate. However, in the short term there might be an improvement in the current account. This is because, according to the theory of the J-curve, the demand for exports and imports in the short run are price inelastic.

173 International competitiveness

1 Possible factors that can cause productivity to increase (any two):
- Investment in new technology.
- Training and education.
- Improved communication.
- Improved motivation – through fringe benefits and pay.

2 Lower wages lead to lower unit costs, which allow firms to reduce prices of their products. As a result, p roducts from the particular country will become cheaper than similar products from other countries. As a consequence these firms – and, by extension, the country – become more competitive.

174 Absolute poverty and relative poverty

1 Absolute poverty is when a person's income means they struggle to find the basic needs for life: food, clothing and shelter. People in relative poverty may be able to buy these things, but are poor in comparison to most other people in that society.

2 Absolute poverty is measured by the World Bank as anyone earning less than $1.90 a day.

175 Inequality and its causes

1 Wealth is the stock of assets owned by an individual, for example, land, property and shares. Income is the accumulation of money over time through sources such as wages and interest.

2 A tax system can help reduce income inequality by redistributing income. The richest in society can be taxed at a higher rate and this government revenue can then be distributed to the poorest in society through social benefits.

176 Measuring inequality

A Gini coefficient of 0.63 is very high. This would represent a country with very high levels of income inequality.

177 Measures of economic development

1 The three factors considered by the HDI are health, education and standard of living.

2 The HDI is easy to use because the information is easier to collect than other economic data such as unemployment figures. It is also easier to standardise the data across nations.

3 Two other measures of development are the percentage of a population with a mobile phone and the Genuine Progress Indicator (GPI).

178 Growth and development 1

1 The savings gap refers to the problem faced by less economically developed countries where a greater proportion of their income is spent and not saved. This reduces the money available for investment and creates a reliance on borrowing.

2 Absence of property rights creates uncertainty in an economy. If it is unclear/uncertain that a person owns land, property or some other asset, they are less likely to invest.

179 Growth and development 2

1 In developing countries, a fast rate of population growth may put pressure on an education system, resulting in many children being unable to access a good school. Another factor impacting on access to education is the pressure for children of a young age to work and bring in an income for their family instead of going to school.

2 Access to effective banking systems is important for economic development because most people do not have the wealth required to set up and invest in enterprise. For this reason, people require access to credit and financial support in order to become entrepreneurs.

180 Market-orientated strategies

A government might choose to remove a producer subsidy in the farming industry because the country's farming industry might be operating inefficiently and the subsidy could be spent to greater effect in other areas of the economy, such as social care.

181 Interventionist strategies

A government might choose to supply a buffer stock scheme to manipulate the price of commodities and protect domestic industries that are reliant on them.

182 Other strategies

The Lewis model suggests that developing countries should transfer labour (retrain) from agricultural jobs to industrial manufacturing.

183 International organisations and NGOs

1 One goal of the World Bank is to promote economic development through grants to developing countries.

2 Three examples of NGOs include The Prince's Trust, UNICEF and Cancer Research UK.

184 The role of financial markets

1 Possible roles that financial markets might play (any three):
- facilitate saving,
- lend to businesses and individuals, and
- facilitate the exchange of goods and services.
- provide forward markets in currencies and commodities,
- provide a market for equities.

2 A forward market is for transactions that will happen at an agreed time in the future. Contracts are made at a price agreed today but will be supplied later. Such markets are used by producers and buyers to even out price fluctuations. For example, a manufacturer may agree to buy 5000 tonnes of wheat at an agreed price of $1000 per tonne, for delivery in 9 months. This gives the firm certainty over its costs in the future.

185 Market failure in the financial sector 1

1 An individual might not be very careful with the security at their own home – such as locking doors and windows – because they know they have home insurance and that, if there was a break-in, they would not have to personally pay for the damages and losses.

2 Government spending is funded by taxpayers. Any government expenditure ultimately comes from the taxes that workers, firms and households pay. When the UK government bailed out the UK banks in 2008, the money used came from taxpayers, therefore something that had not been caused or been created by UK workers and households was being paid for by them. It was a cost imposed on them by the actions of others.

186 Market failure in the financial sector 2

1 Possible examples of market failure in the financial sector (any three):
- asymmetric information,
- externalities and
- moral hazard.
- speculation and market bubbles,
- market rigging.

2 Speculation affects the demand for assets and can cause an artificial rise – and fall – in the price of these assets. The result is that the price does not reflect the fundamentals of the market conditions. In fact, it gives an artificial picture of the asset.

187 Role of central banks

1 'Lender of the last resort' describes the important function of a central bank to lend money to financial institutions that run short of liquidity. This function provides certainty to the financial system and to customers that banks are secure and are not able to collapse.

2 Firstly, a reduction in interest rates will reduce the cost of borrowing and will lead to an increase in the amount of spending using loans and credit cards. This will lead to an increase in AD, which may be inflationary in the short run.
A second effect is that the level of investment may increase as the cost of borrowing is lower and this is a vital source of finance for investment by firms. The increase in investment will lead to a shift in the LRAS line to the right and to an increase in AD.

188 Types of public expenditure

Capital expenditure involves spending on investment goods that will be consumed over a long period, typically more than one year, and which will help to create economic growth in the future. Current spending is short term and has to be renewed each year and includes spending on wages and raw materials.

189 Changes in public expenditure

When economic growth increases, the government will receive more tax revenue as more people are employed. At the same time, spending on benefits will decrease as fewer people are unemployed. The result is that public expenditure will decrease.

190 Changes in tax rates 1

1 Possible reasons why higher tax rates might lead to lower tax revenue for government (any two):
- less incentive for workers to work,
- increase in tax avoidance.
- increase in tax evasion.
- rise in number of tax exiles.

2 This is a regressive tax. These taxes are felt more by people on low incomes. For example, a rise in fuel duty of 5% may cost two households £40 per month. For a lower income household this will represent a higher proportion of income than for the higher income household.

191 Changes in tax rates 2

Income tax allowance is how much can be earned before income tax is paid. Raising the allowance will benefit workers who earn lower incomes. As such this should help to create a more equal distribution of income.

192 Public sector finances

Possible examples of government decisions that are discretionary fiscal policy:
- an increase in the higher rate of income tax to 55% to improve the redistribution of income
- subsidising the purchase electric cars to help reduce CO_2 emissions
- increasing excise duty of alcohol to reduce consumption.

193 Factors affecting size of fiscal deficit and national debt

Two possible factors that affect the size of the national debt.
- The size of fiscal deficits.
- Government policies.

194 Significance of size of fiscal deficits and national debt

When a government borrows – and spends – money today, current generations benefit from this spending. For example, an increase in public sector borrowing in Year 1 to pay for improved health services will benefit the current generation by the improved health service they receive. However, this debt will take years to pay off. Taxes that future generations pay will go, in part, to debt repayments or on interest payments on the national debt, rather than on current spending priorities. In this sense, future generations are disadvantaged.

195 Macroeconomic policies in a global context

1 Possible features of expansionary fiscal policy include:
- Lower income taxes – this strategy will lead to consumers having more disposable income which they will then spend and therefore lead to higher AD.
- Increased government spending – as 'G' is a component of AD, higher government spending, for example, on healthcare or new infrastructure, will lead to increased AD.

2 Demand management is a Keynesian approach to managing the economy where the government plays a key role in influencing the level of AD. By reducing taxes, for example, households will have more money and will increase their spending, leading to higher AD. However, if inflationary pressures in the economy are increasing, the government might choose to curb the level of AD, for example, by raising taxes or reducing its own spending. This will lead to lower AD.

196 Other policies

By reducing interest rates, households have more disposable income. This is because loan and mortgage repayments are lower. As credit is also cheaper, consumption is encouraged. As consumption is the largest component of AD, so this leads to an increase in AD which can lead to economic growth. In this way the government can manage the level of AD in an economy.

197 Direct controls and exchange rate policies

The impact of a significant reduction in commodity prices would be to reduce input costs which would shift the SRAS line to the right and thus reduce inflation in the short run. This would be beneficial for firms and households and will, *ceteris paribus*, lead to increased output in the short run.

198 External shocks

Two from: inaccurate information; risks and uncertainties; inability to control external shocks.

207 Exam-style practice: Section A

1 C

2 (a) Price of a motorcycle imported into the EU:
$0.31 \times X = \$2200$
$\frac{2200}{0.31} = X$
$\$7097$

(b) The imposition of a tariff makes imports more expensive. For manufacturers this can lead to an increase in costs. As a result of this the SRAS line will shift to the left, leading to an increase in inflation to P_2.

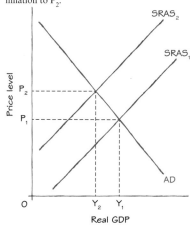

Furthermore, output falls from Y_1 to Y_2, which may lead to increased unemployment.

209 Exam-style practice: Sections B and C

3 (a) US consumers are likely to suffer as a result of tariffs being imposed on imports. On the one hand, tariffs on commodities like steel and aluminium will make these products more expensive for the firms that use them, such as manufacturers of cars and machinery, and house builders. As a result of this, these firms are likely to increase prices that will be passed onto consumers. Therefore, consumers will be affected indirectly, and negatively, by the imposition of tariffs. They will also be affected directly if imported products they buy are specifically hit by tariffs.

However, consumers may be less affected if they work in industries that are benefited by the tariffs. For example, President Trump has imposed the tariffs on EU steel to protect the US steel industry and domestic producers. If consumers work in these industries they are likely to benefit, in the short run, from the higher import prices. This may lead to increased employment, job security and higher wages.

Further, whether firms decide to pass on the higher costs depends on the price elasticity of demand for the product. If demand is price elastic, firms will be less likely to pass the cost on in the form of higher prices. Therefore, the effects of the tariffs might not be extensive.

In conclusion, the extent of the impact on consumers depends on their particular situation. Consumers that buy imported goods that are subject to tariffs will feel the effects more than those that tend not to buy such goods.

(b) Suggested essay plan:
Paragraph 1 – define globalisation, making clear that it involves the ever-increasing integration of the world's local, regional and national economies into a single international market. Globalisation has a range of effects on firms, workers and countries.
Paragraph 2 – benefits for Harley-Davidson – a transnational business that operates in and sells its products to a wide range of countries. Consider some of the positive effects of being a TNC: wider (global) markets leads to increased sales; economies of scale; increased economic growth (globally) leads to rising incomes and greater demand for luxury goods such as Harley-Davidson motorcycles.
Paragraph 3 – possible costs for Harley-Davidson – increased competition from foreign motorcycle producers (for example, Japanese producers can sell into the US market); diseconomies of scale; risk of trade wars between countries/trading blocs, such as the EU tariffs.
Evaluation – as a global brand the process of globalisation is likely to benefit Harley-Davidson. However, firms can become very dependent on other countries and other firms, e.g. Harley-Davidson and imported steel and aluminium. This can leave the firm vulnerable to changes in prices and can impact on costs.

4 Suggested essay plan:
Paragraph 1 – define poverty – relative and absolute – and inequality.
Paragraph 2 – outline one measure the government could use to reduce poverty and inequality. Examples include: higher benefits; increased minimum wage/adoption of 'living wage'; greater spending on education; lower benefits – to give incentive to work; improved job search systems; measures to improve occupational and/or geographical mobility. Within this paragraph – discussion of the possible weaknesses/drawbacks of this measures. For example, increased spending on education might only work in the longer term.
Paragraph 3 – outline a second measure. Then as paragraph 2.
Paragraph 4 – outline a third measure. Then as paragraph 3.
Paragraph 5 – conclusion. Use the 'it depends' rule. Arrive at a judgement on each of the methods used. Say which are likely to be most and least effective in different situations.

214. Exam-style practice: Paper 3

1 (a) Introducing an indirect tax causes the price of a product to rise. This is because it has the effect of shifting the supply curve to the left, as shown in the diagram below.

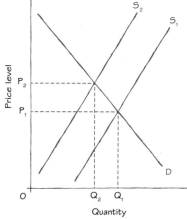

The shift acts like an increase in costs, part of which is passed on to consumers. As a result of this tax the quantity falls from Q_1 to Q_2.

(b) Increased rates of obesity are likely to have a damaging effect on the economy.

People who are obese tend to have more health issues and impose costs on the health service. These are negative externalities and might be due to the treatment they require, for example, for diabetes, which obese people suffer from more than people who are not obese. As the health service is paid for, in part, from taxation, this means that taxes are being used to pay for the poor health of some people. The taxes could have been used elsewhere, so there is an opportunity cost of the increased

spending on the health service.

However, Extract A states that the people who are affected most by obesity are the individuals themselves. Therefore the greater effect might be the reduced levels of productivity of workers through absence from work due to illness.

(c) Government intervention to reduce obesity can take a range of forms. The introduction of indirect taxes – so-called 'fat taxes' – work to increase the prices of takeaway and other unhealthy food. This can be shown in the diagram that shows that quantity falls following the introduction of the tax, as a result of higher price.

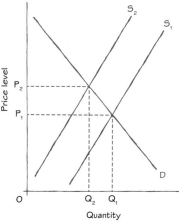

However, a drawback of this approach is that if the demand for a product is price inelastic, then the effect of the fat tax will be to increase price but to have limited impact on quantity sold. This can also be illustrated using a demand and supply diagram:

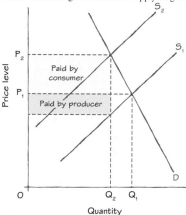

In this case, price increases by a greater proportion than the fall in quantity from Q_1 to Q_2. Further, it can also be seen that most of the burden of the taxation falls on the consumer, which raises equity questions. This burden falls on consumers irrespective of their income level and will therefore be felt more severely by lower-income groups. There are therefore equity arguments against such regressive taxes.

In conclusion, the effectiveness of indirect taxes depends on the price elasticity of demand for the goods and services being targeted. Extract B suggests that sales at restaurants/takeaways fall by over 2% as a result of a 1% increase in price, suggesting that the demand for these products is price elastic. This type of government intervention would appear to be effective in these circumstances.

(d) Suggested essay plan:
Paragraph 1 – define indirect taxation and how it might be used by a government. Give examples of indirect taxes – VAT, excise duty, etc.
Paragraph 2 – microeconomic effects of indirect taxes: impact on prices of individual products; to correct market failure, for example, by increasing the price of goods which cause negative externalities; use of demand and supply diagrams.
Paragraph 3 – evaluating microeconomic effects: impact of elasticity of goods/services; equity arguments – for example, lower income groups might be affected most by higher indirect taxes (regressive); other policies might be more effective – regulation, education, subsidising alternatives, encouraging competition, 'nudge' approaches.

Paragraph 4 – macroeconomic effects – raising tax revenue to spend on public services; reduced fiscal deficit/national debt; can be used to manage aggregate demand (use of AD/AS diagram); allow income taxes to be reduced to increase incentives to work.

Paragraph 5 – evaluating macroeconomic effects – results might be regressive and therefore lead to issues with equity; governments should allow markets to operate freely without intervention – capitalism/free market approach; markets self-correct.

Conclusion – make sure you draw a balanced conclusion. Use some evidence from the case study. You might use the 'it depends' rule. Indirect taxation has an important role to play in both the micro economy – through correcting market failure – and the macroeconomy – through raising taxes. There is not a right or wrong answer.

(e) Suggested essay plan:

Paragraph 1 – define government intervention and give examples of how governments intervene in an economy – laws, health, education, taxes, roads, etc.

Paragraph 2 – microeconomic effects of government intervention: left to their own devices, some markets may fail, therefore government intervention is essential. For example, street lighting, education – these would be under-provided by the market. Governments help to redistribute income through taxes and benefit – fairer society.

Paragraph 3 – evaluating microeconomic effects: possibility of government failure; markets will correct themselves; public sector can crowd out private sector investment – possibly leads to allocative inefficiency.

Paragraph 4 – macroeconomic effects – managing demand within the economy – central bank controlling interest rates; AD/AS; government role was essential in the 2007–08 financial crisis in preventing economic collapse.

Paragraph 5 – evaluating macroeconomic effects – government sector very expensive – 40% of GDP in the UK; government failure can occur.

Conclusion – make sure you draw a balanced conclusion. Use some evidence from the case study. You might use the 'it depends' rule. Some role for government is essential. The debate exists around how great the intervention should be. In the USA, model is for less government.

Notes

Notes